The South That Wasn't There

Southern Literary Studies

FRED HOBSON, SERIES EDITOR

THE SOUTH
THAT WASN'T
THERE

Postsouthern Memory and History

MICHAEL KREYLING

LOUISIANA STATE UNIVERSITY PRESS)|(BATON ROUGE

PUBLISHED BY LOUISIANA STATE UNIVERSITY PRESS
Copyright © 2010 by Louisiana State University Press
Manufactured in the United States of America
First printing

DESIGNER: Michelle A. Neustrom
TYPEFACES: Minion Pro, text; Gotham, display
PRINTER: McNaughton & Gunn, Inc.
BINDER: John H. Dekker & Sons

An earlier version of chapter 1 first appeared as "'Slave life; freed life—everyday was a test and trial': Identity and Memory in *Beloved*," *Arizona Quarterly* 63.1 (2007), and is reprinted by permission of the Regents of The University of Arizona. Chapter 2 was first published, in slightly different form but under the same title, "Robert Penn Warren: The Real Southerner and the 'Hypothetical Negro,'" in *American Literary History* 21.2 (2009): 268–95, with permission of Oxford University Press.

LIBRARY OF CONGRESS CATALOGING-IN-PUBLICATION DATA

Kreyling, Michael, 1948–
The South that wasn't there : postsouthern memory and history / Michael Kreyling.
    p. cm. — (Southern literary studies)
Includes bibliographical references and index.
ISBN 978-0-8071-3648-5 (cloth : alk. paper) 1. American literature—Southern States—History and criticism. 2. Southern States—Intellectual life. 3. Southern States—In literature. 4. Group identity in literature. 5. Regionalism in literature. I. Title.
PS261.K75 2011
810.9'975—dc22
                                                                                                    2009053709

For C. M. K. and F. T. K., and
in memory of R. T. K. (1994–2007)

CONTENTS

ACKNOWLEDGMENTS

The South That Wasn't There started in a lot of places, and knowing the saga of its germination might help readers understand what they have before them. The first chapter in the book is the first part I wrote, a questioning of Toni Morrison's *Beloved* as to its claims to be a recovery of the memory of slavery. There has never been much doubt about where Morrison wants to take her readers in *Beloved*—into that incomplete or perhaps unrecoverable territory where slavery had been suffered by innumerable bodies but not passed on. *Beloved* was aimed to overcome that loss or erasure of memory and identity. But I always wondered how Denver, Sethe's surviving daughter, embodied slavery's memory; Morrison gave her literacy, a job with a wage, a surrogate mother to vie with Sethe's traumatic memory, and facets of the "New Woman" of the late nineteenth-century United States. It seemed to me that Morrison realized that the memory of slavery needed a brokering term or phase, and that Denver was the clue to it. I first tried out this approach in the yearlong Robert Penn Warren Center for the Humanities Faculty Seminar in 2001–02. The theme of that seminar was "Memory, Identity, and Political Action," and I guess that seven-year-old presentation has seen its final revision here. Seven years later I hail my colleagues at Vanderbilt, some of whom have moved on to other universities: they directed me on the first long leg of the route of memory studies. I'm also thankful for the help of Laura Patterson, then a doctoral student at Vanderbilt, who helped me research the truly voluminous published record on *Beloved*. Grateful acknowledgment is extended also to the editors of *Arizona Quarterly*, in which a shorter, earlier version of the chapter on *Beloved* was published as "'Slave life; freed life—everyday was a test and trial': Identity and Memory in *Beloved*" (*Arizona Quarterly*, 63.1, 109–36). If it had not been for their early encouragement, I might not have continued.

Chapter 2 was originally published in a slightly different form but under the same title it bears in this book: "Robert Penn Warren: The Real Southerner and the 'Hypothetical Negro,'" *American Literary History* (21.2, 268–95). I thank the editor, Gordon Hutner, and the *ALH* referees for their faith in it. An invitation from Kristina Morris Baumli and Anthony Szczesiul to act as respondent to their papers on Warren at the 2005 American Literature Association meeting helped me to focus some questions about Warren upon the axis of memory. Anthony's work on Warren's poetry and Kristina's on Warren's editing of his own tape recordings for the published text of *Who Speaks for the Negro?* sent me back to Warren's essay in *I'll Take My Stand,* "The Briar Patch," and the question I'd always asked since the first time I read it: Why did Warren decline to mention the name of W. E. B. Du Bois, the obvious (to me, at least) "hypothetical negro" in the essay? I scented a kind of self-imposed, if scarcely admitted, amnesia that suggested a powerful triad of race, identity, and memory.

The other chapters have less defined origins, but they have had no less help along the way. A colleague from Tulane days, John Schafer, veteran of four years in Vietnam with International Voluntary Services and, with his wife Quynh, translator of Vietnamese writers on the war, helped me with the chapter on southern honor and its collision with the Vietnam War. For help with thinking my way through Michael Shaara's *The Killer Angels,* I thank the students of American Studies 100w at Vanderbilt in the spring semester of 2007. They helped me, a nonscientist, work on adapting the language of memory studies in psychology and neuroscience for use in discussing literature.

I thank students from another generation for help with the chapter on *Gone With the Wind* and its various sequels and parodies. Those who attended the Osher Lifelong Learning Institute at Vanderbilt, winter 2009, braved cold mornings and the occasional ice storm to puzzle out the meaning of sequels and the value of parody, to sort out which Rhett and which Scarlett do what to whom in which incarnation of the *GWTW* saga, and to give of their own life experiences to realize the world of *Gone With the Wind* at publication in 1936—and later in the memory-life of its sequels.

And a shout out to the graduate students of ENGL 321, spring 2009, who helped me map the weird triangular commerce involving Haiti, *Absalom, Absalom!* and Madison Smartt Bell's trilogy. Just repeat after me: *I dont hate it, I dont hate it. I dont hate it.* Sincere thanks as well to Donika Ross, who made the index to the book, taking time from her own graduate work.

Although the twin subjects of the South and memory are dusty commonplaces in the history of southern literary studies, I want to thank colleagues building the New Southern Studies, many of whom are acknowledged in the text that follows, for re-energizing the field, and for challenging me to translate for the next generation thinking formed among species of scholars and landmark texts now almost memories themselves.

Public thanks to Catherine Kadair, who edited this book, and to John Easterly and the rest of the staff of LSU Press, who stayed on deck with this manuscript and all the others during stormy times.

As always, deep thanks to Chris, who read this straight through in one long day, and said I could exhale, it was good. She knows; she is a writer.

The South That Wasn't There

INTRODUCTION
Memory, Culture, Identity

∞

Much as shared memory enriches our lives as individuals, loss of memory destroys our sense of self. It severs the connection with the past and with other people.

—ERIC R. KANDEL

I n the spring of 2008, the Max Planck Society, in partnership with the Alexander von Humboldt Institute—both internationally known for sponsoring laboratory and theoretical research in the "hard" sciences—announced the theme for the 2009 Max Planck Research Award: History and Memory. The award brings 750,000 euros over a three-year period to the winner and her/his associates in the successful international research team. A closer-than-usual reading of the society's brief invitation for proposals reveals much of the foundation for *The South That Wasn't There:*

> History and Memory has in the past two decades become an internationally
> visible research direction stimulating theory and empirical research equally.
> In its broader sense, it approaches culture in terms of social memory, i.e. the
> memory of social groups and communities. In its narrowest sense, it is con-
> cerned with the history of individual and collective memory, with particular
> reference to its production and distribution through media. (*New York Review
> of Books* 14 August 2008: 23)

The singular verb "has" in the first sentence, and the singular pronouns thereafter, seem to indicate that the scholars and researchers of the two prestigious German bodies consider history-and-memory to be the Moebius strip of cultural studies, a single continuous surface that paradoxically has two "sides."

History-and-memory is, visualized as a figure in space, a continuous paradox, at one extreme broad ("collective" and "social"), at the other narrow ("individual"). Memories that seem to begin as individual, mental acts of recovering one's historical past flow so seamlessly into the collective that, at any point along the strip, it is difficult to say which memories are individual and which collective. Perhaps the winning project in the Planck Society competition, if it comes from a literary studies group, will begin by deconstructing the announcement.

That deconstruction would be serious rather than idly semantic: How does history-and-memory differ from history and memory? When we talk about history, when does our subject become memory? If memory has a history (certainly memory studies does), the silent assumption of the final sentence of the Planck Society's call for proposals, does history also have a memory? Historian Tony Judt, we shall shortly see, devoutly believes so—he would purge memory from history in the name of dispassionate clarity about real events and real consequences. What is the relationship between the "broader sense . . . of social memory" and the "narrowest sense . . . of individual and collective memory"? In the chapters that follow, I argue that the relationship between history and memory is one of organic necessity; that southern "media" (novels, memoir, film, a collection of legal documents) spread before us as one of the most promising fields for extending the exploration of history-and-memory; that southern "media" deserve this study because the forms and structures of those media present us with a Moebius-like strip of collective, social self-narration, self-revision.

One reach of memory this book is *not* about (but a kind that is nevertheless vital to understanding what it *is* about) is the narrow or inward or individual memory to which the Max Planck Society announcement alludes: the intimate and personal memory that anchors individual consciousness in a self. I am not in a hunt for scenes of personal memory in southern texts—the beholding of long-lost heirlooms that trigger flashbacks, for example. Yet what I have to say here can't be fully grasped without due diligence to the thematics of memory narratives. The carved figures, pocketwatch, and other objects that Scout Finch remembers finding in the cleft of a tree are stunningly empirical yet talismanic; they function in *To Kill a Mockingbird* to *seem* to endow Scout's memory with the authority of the incontrovertible thing. The Moebius strip of memory-and-history in *To Kill a Mockingbird* inevitably encroaches on the Scottsboro case, and Atticus's closing address to the jury in the case of Tom Robinson flows through *Brown v. Board of Education*. In fact, Atticus seems to flirt with both sides of the issue of school desegregation in his speech to the Maycomb jury: "Thomas Jefferson once said that all men are created equal, a phrase that the Yankees and the distaff side of the Executive branch in Washington are fond of hurling at us. There is a tendency in this year of grace, 1935, for certain people to use this phrase out of context, to satisfy all conditions. The most ridiculous example I can think of is the one that the people who run public education promote the stupid and the idle along with the industrious—because all men are created equal, educators will gravely tell you, the children left behind suffer terrible feelings of inferiority" (Lee 205). The opinion in *Brown* notably, and controversially, used the argument of "inferiority" against racially segregated schools.[1] *To Kill a Mockingbird,* then, immense as it is in the American cultural memory of learning to read, of reading an entire book, of remembering the first lesson in equality, also twists Moebius-like to reveal its historical side—the side where resistance to integration struck deep, even into the rhetoric of an iconic champion of legal (if not social) justice.

If there is a writer better than Harper Lee to provide another example of the nuances of personal memory and its Moebius flow into history, it might be Vladimir Nabokov. Here is an excerpt from *Speak, Memory* (rev. ed., 1966). According to Nabokov, this moment, an evocation of his governess, is the germ of his memoir:

> A large woman, a very stout woman, Mademoiselle rolled into our existence in December 1905 when I was six and my brother five. There she is. I see so plainly her abundant dark hair, brushed up high and covertly graying; the three wrinkles on her austere forehead; her beetling brows; the steely eyes behind the black-rimmed pince-nez; that vestigial mustache; that blotchy complexion, which in moments of wrath develops an additional flush in the region of the third, and amplest, chin so regally spread over the frilled mountain of her blouse. (95–96)

No one, not even Nabokov's brother, has exactly *this* memory, although surely the younger Nabokov knew Mademoiselle too. No one but Vladimir Nabokov is Vladimir Nabokov, and no one can possess his foundational memory. No one else can stand in his place in his time. In the practice of personal memory, history vanishes ("There she is"). There is no need for the past tense; moments in 1905 are narrated in the present. Nabokov vetted the translation (9).

Cultural factors barge into Nabokov's memory almost immediately. There is a cultural psychology of memory that inflects individuating sensory details, turning them from personal to social almost before we become aware of the transformation. Memory science has a category for Mademoiselle's height and girth and coloring, and in the continuation of this passage the sounds her bulky movements make. They are called, in the whole, "bottom-up (stimulus-driven)" information. "[T]he clarity of the sensory input," memory science continues, ". . . would amplify the bottom-up component" (Kazdin, 164). From the literary studies point of view, we might prefer to say that "clarity of sensory input" depends on the skill of the writer, not only the rememberer. The ability to take in and store such stimuli we humans share, in some degree, with all living organisms. Learn from experience or die. "Collective" or "cultural" memory in humans leads to survival, though, when sensory intake is "processed" or "coded," and coding can only occur if and when "top-down (conceptually driven)" processing arranges stimuli along lines of "the perceiver's expectations" (Kazdin 164). Those expectations come from top-down codes formed because humans are social animals and we learn how to think about sensory input by imitating other humans around us who react to stimuli in certain consistent kinds of ways. Thus, in Nabokov's case, the unmediated sensory stimuli of Mademoiselle are processed as "female," "not mother," "employee"—each refinement of the raw sensory stimuli placing the self more deeply and tightly into a social formation: "male," "young," "privileged," "Russian." Just as the plot of *To Kill a Mockingbird* flows seamlessly from memory to history, the narrative Nabokov constructs moves from the intimately personal to the collective, social, historical.

One more example illustrates the relationship between sense memory and history, literature and science, and gives it a more accentuated historical/traumatic character relevant to the upcoming investigation of memory in the raveling and unraveling of the southern identity. The passage is lifted from *In Search of Memory: The Emergence of a New Science of Mind* (2006), by Eric R. Kandel, recipient of the Nobel Prize in 2000 for his work on the biological processes enabling memory in the human brain. Kandel's memoir is especially important to this investigation because he actually connects intimately personal memory scientifically to the biochemistry of the human brain, the work for which he won the Nobel, and culturally to a childhood trauma that clearly initiated him into the sadness of history; the Moebius strip once again. Kandel remembers his ninth birthday, November 7, 1938, when his parents gave him something he had "craved endlessly, a battery-operated, remote-controlled model car. This is a beautiful, shiny blue car" (Kandel 1). Almost seven decades later, this toy, like Nabokov's Mademoiselle and Scout's trove of small objects, still "is." Sense memory never accepts the past tense, never becomes history, although it coexists with history, because who we are depends on what we remember. Soon after the boy's birthday, Nazi policemen arrive at the Kandel apartment in Vienna, arrest Eric's father, and send the rest of the family away. When the Kandels, father fortunately included, are reunited in their apartment a few days later, Eric finds most of their ransacked possessions but no "shiny blue car." "The memories of those days," Kandel writes almost seventy years after the fact, "—steering my car around the apartment with increasing assurance, hearing the bangs on the door, being ordered by the Nazi policemen to go to a stranger's apartment, finding ourselves robbed of our belongings, the disappearance and reappearance of my father—are the most powerful memories of my early life. Later, I would come to understand that these events coincided with Kristallnacht, the calamitous night that shattered not just the windows of our synagogues and my parents' store in Vienna, but also the lives of countless Jews all over the German-speaking world" (3).

Which is more significant in this passage: the very particular and palpable memory of the "shiny blue car" connecting pre- and post-traumatic rememberer as one self (the Nobel Laureate Eric Kandel who remembers), or the "[l]ater" connection of that rememberer to the discourse of history where "Kristallnacht" displaces the "shiny blue car" and takes the splendidly fulfilled boy at one with his craving and delivers him into the disenchantments of history? And into the traumatic but necessary collective memory and identity of "Jews all over the German-speaking world." I don't have an answer; I only want to highlight the simple word "later" as the barely perceptible hinge where memory swings into history, the personal into the collective. Southern history connects with southern memory, the one unthinkable without its other, in just these ways. Sometimes the hinge-points are detectable, often they are not.

History and memory are not an unlikely couple in southern studies, and there have been many times in the writing and revising of this book that I have thought that one more iteration is one too many. I justified continuing with the project by visualizing, again, the Moebius strip: I have chosen spots of history-and-memory where the strip seems to begin its twist and the stretch of the continuous play between the two seems to undergo some disturbance.[2] *The South That Wasn't There* explores disturbances of "textual practice" manifest in novels, poems, memoir and autobiography, and film produced in and about the culture of the U.S. South in the twentieth and very early twenty-first centuries by means of what Scott Romine, in *The Real South: Southern Narrative in the Age of Cultural Reproduction,* rightly says "occasionally looks like a retro practice . . . literary analysis" (17). Much contemporary wariness about "literary analysis" flows from the fear that in most implementations it amounts to little more than the imposition of one hegemonic narrative upon another because the literary interpreter or critic forgets to examine his/her own race, class, gender, and national position. In fact, in the chapter on the image of Haiti in the southern imaginary, I try to mobilize that very argument within and against my own literary position. At the risk of being totally "retro," though, I offer the readings of a range of literary texts in the chapters that follow on the grounds that to describe a continuous process one ought to use a continuous process. I have looked for, or perhaps been found by, situations in which southern cultural memory is both direct and implied, situations as well in which "South" is not the sole or even the most potent cultural marker or term, situations of the practice of memory that may be examined for their workings rather than for their meanings. Another way to situate this project is to say that my curiosity here is widely focused, on cultural or collective memory and the various "media" in which its practices may be detected and scrutinized, but that, like the aging Godfather Michael Corleone, just when I thought I was clearly in the collective, I was pulled back toward the personal. That is to say, who the writers were, and when and where they lived, makes a difference.

The South, like the Germany that roots the Max Planck Society and figures traumatically in Kandel's personal memory, has better reasons than many freestanding national states and cultures to think about history-and-memory accessing, repealing, revising, and forgetting empirical history for what Kandel knew as "the shiny blue car" of eternal presentness. As we shall see in what follows, there is a holocaust (*not* by analogy) in southern history-and-memory, an engine of both trauma and guilt. In chapter 1, for example, I offer a reading of Toni Morrison's *Beloved* as the holocaust novel of American and southern fiction.[3] This is hardly a new insight, but framing *Beloved* with documents on traumatic memory reveals the gaps, splices, and elisions Morrison had to make in order to restore continuity to the strip of slave memory-and-history. There are cultural practices and behaviors issuing from the messy and inconclusive termination of that American holocaust—the Jim Crow South that succeeded the slave South—that have served as bad memory that individuals have struggled, in print and in fact, to forget. The cost and processes of forgetting, as I hope to show in a chapter on the ways Robert Penn Warren coped with being racist and recanting, draw heavily on personal and cultural identity accounts (insured by deposits of memory) in ways that, in Warren's case, trigger some creative bookkeeping. A putative genre, related to the confessional genre reserved for former sinners like Augustine of Hippo who were lost but then were found, has been suggested by Fred Hobson as a category for the wide array of southern literary works on this matter. I will offer a reading of Warren's *Who Speaks for the Negro?* as a way of getting at the cultural work done by individual texts that genre as a whole might not capture.[4]

The Max Planck Research Award reminds applicants to include some investigation of the ways history-and-memory is "produc[ed] and distribut[ed] through media," and *The South That Wasn't There* recognizes a recent episode in which the term "media" operates in a wide range of applications. *Gone With the Wind* is arguably the most widely recognized southern "product" in the world. Coca-Cola probably is, in fact, but more culture consumers choose *GWTW* when they crave the "taste" of southern history-and-memory. The publication of Alice Randall's parody of the *GWTW* brand, her novel *The Wind Done Gone* (2001), awakened legal and critical awareness of just how commodified the *GWTW* franchise had become. One of the chapters that follows addresses the legal drama in which protectors of the *GWTW* copyright—and of the money it annually generates—jousted with (and eventually lost to) the champions of freedom of cultural expression and revision of southern history-and-memory. In the language of the Moebius analogy: one side wanted to stop the strip's circulation, the other wanted to keep it moving. The *GWTW* brand continues to be distributed, however, and the chapter in this book itself might actually testify to *GWTW*'s market power. Randall's novel was strategically aimed at the close hyphenation of history-and-memory, and the shock waves emanating from the epicenter of the legal battle reveal memory "media" at work throughout the late capitalist culture of which *GWTW* is a major part.

The South That Wasn't There also attempts to address the broad issue of history-and-memory at work in "social groups and communities." The study of the embedding and fashioning of collective memory in social expressions (texts,

THE SOUTH THAT WASN'T THERE

built monuments and memorials, festivals and heritage events, etc.) grounds this investigation in memory work, with a somewhat longer history than the Max Planck Society acknowledges, that runs from Maurice Halbwachs's *The Collective Memory* (1950) through Pierre Nora's "Between Memory and History: *Les Lieux de Mémoire*" (1989).[5] Both Halbwachs and Nora base their analyses of collective memory on the practices of memory in twentieth-century France. Halbwachs's point of departure was his dissent from the Bergsonian position that memory is "a personal, subjective experience," as it seems so strongly to be in the examples above from the writing of Nabokov and Kandel. On the contrary, Halbwachs found memory to be "socially constructed and present-oriented, an instrument of reconfiguration and not of reclamation or retrieval" (Davis and Starn 4). I share the conviction that collective memory is "present-oriented," summoned by social groups and communities who find themselves in troubled waters and in need of reassurance that the present is indeed continuous with a past in which their origins were unambiguously established fact and that history is nothing less than the story of their (our) foreordained triumph. The-way-we-were is the-way-we-are.

Nora's configuration of history-and-memory in practice merits at least a summary here, even though I will refer to his essay repeatedly in the chapters to follow. Nora begins with the assumption that, unlike "archaic societies," their modern counterparts struggle against the "acceleration of history" (7), too many events reported too quickly, overwhelming the social means for organizing them to such a degree that modern societies become forgetful (8). Failing to organize all that happens, we memorialize what we need to survive in the present. Ruptures inevitably occur because history ("all that happens") is "in fundamental opposition" to memory (that which we choose to organize out of all that happens).

> Memory [Nora writes] is blind to all but the group it binds—which is to say, as Maurice Halbwachs has said, that there are as many memories as there are groups, that memory is by nature multiple and yet specific; collective, plural, yet individual. History, on the other hand, belongs to everyone and to no one, whence its claim to universal authority. Memory takes root in the concrete, in spaces, gestures, images, and objects; history binds itself strictly to temporal continuities, to progressions, and to relations between things. Memory is absolute, while history can only conceive the relative. (8–9)

History being, in Nora's view, always already otherwise, only memory can bestow upon an individual, a group, a region, a nation, an identity imaginable as constant through time. That is why memory is so important, and so valuable to those (southern) communities bound by the sharing of it, and why the practitioners of memory in any social community (here: mostly that community's writers) are important to it. In *The South That Wasn't There* I have settled focus on several situations in which the rivalry between history and memory is crucial, in which the practice of memory reveals the stresses wrought upon it by the various living, present interests it is expected or drafted to serve.

One of the most powerful stresses collective memory is expected to assuage is, of course, the stress of war. When peoples wage wars, there is always more in jeopardy than physical lives. In fact, merely thinking and typing that previous sentence indicates the totalitarian amnesia of memory over history: the dead leave histories behind them, but do they leave their memories? I try to autopsy history-and-memory in the longest chapter in this book, a mildly obsessive and melancholy study of the ways southern warrior collective memory, a staple of Old South identity commemorated in the New and even virtual "Souths," was used to treat the wounds and shocks to the American history-and-memory system inflicted by the Vietnam War. The premise of this chapter can be simplistically condensed, although working it out is more difficult: faced with an immediate, present space-time overcrowded with images the American psyche could not accept—and still maintain our best national image—the southern warrior image entered, or was pushed, into the maelstrom in the hope that it might tame the unthinkable. In fact, I think the chapter shows that the inner tumult wrought by Vietnam was so wide and deep that the ideal of the American warrior, clean hands and pure heart, did not survive the practical application of the southern tourniquet and, moreover, that our subsequent military expeditions both before and after September 11, 2001, have been motivated at least as much by the desire to renovate the warrior image and psyche (yet again) as they have by quasi designs to extend U.S. hegemony after the end of the cold war or to secure a steady supply of the world's oil. In the throes of the Vietnam War, the larger U.S. public called upon and accepted the good offices of a constituent group and its myth—southern novelists and their fund of the honorable warrior narrative—as a means to "remember," very nearly in the moment of initially processing the incoming images of Vietnam, an alternate version of that war presented by history.

Hegemonies can occur in fields of literary study as well as in geopolitics, and in recent years something like colonial outreach has altered the domain and practices of southern literary study. This "outreach" operates under a range of metaphors. One is the metaphor of "exchange." *Transatlantic Exchanges: The American South in Europe—Europe in the American South* (2007), edited by Richard Gray and Waldemar Zacharasiewicz, covers a wide range of comparative topics (thirty-four) arranged under eleven headings. Most of the individual critical essays in this compilation of conference presentations deploy the apparently neutral practice of comparison by which (as the palindromic play of the subtitle suggests) Europe can be read in the terms of the American South, and vice versa. Those terms are, however, seldom if ever cross-examined before, during, or after engaging in the comparative practice. The net effect of field-altering efforts like *Transatlantic Exchanges,* then, is subtly to change the arena of southern history-and-memory by suggesting that something noticeably like it has occurred elsewhere in other social communities. In *Look Away! The U.S. South in New World Studies* (2004), edited by Jon Smith and Deborah Cohn, comparison is pushed in a southern direction (the Caribbean, Latin America, and Africa), and although several of the essays in *Look Away!* run on comparative tracks, others operate on the seldom-queried assumption that "southern" cultural thinking is exportable to island or Caribbean cultural thinking.[6] Escalating *Transatlantic Exchanges, Look Away!* is more clearly hegemonic in its attempt to colonize new territory for southern history-and-memory. In a chapter investigating this topic area, I push the practice of exporting literary-critical paradigms into the discourse of "remembering." That is, if William Faulkner in the 1930s can write about Haiti in the 1820s without ever having been there, and Madison Smartt Bell can write at least the first volume of his trilogy on Toussaint Louverture and the Haitian wars for independence without having been there, what memory practices enable textual representations of an unexperienced, unvisited place? And do those practices result in the recovery of the real thing (as if Nabokov, writing about the Caribbean rather than his governess, had said: "There Haiti is"), or do they expose U.S./American/southern cultural memory as an arm of hegemonic appropriation? In other words, what are the limits to the practice(s) of literary-critical memory when it moves beyond the place and time in which it was sown? Nora, suspecting that in modernity "there is no spontaneous memory, [so] that we must deliberately create archives, maintain anniversaries, organize celebrations, pronounce eulogies, and notarize bills because such activities no longer occur naturally" (10), leads me to suspect that apparent similarities in history (both the Caribbean and the U.S. South were plantation economies and cultures) tempt us to assume similarities in memory: what I know about the U.S. South through representations of it in history and literature is convertible to what I can know about the "global South." But, if the literary critic has no "bottom-up" sensory experience of a place, can she/he substitute a "top-down" paradigmatic knowledge?

The South That Wasn't There emerges at a particularly bubbly time for southern literary and cultural studies, a protracted moment during which postcolonial theory, leading the way for other theoretical projects, is evicting an earlier critical practice or technique—primarily, but not exclusively, the "literary analysis" Scott Romine eulogizes in *The Real South,* as well as the foundation myth of the "South exceptional in history." Gestures to Europe and the Caribbean have indicated new and invigorating directions for an academic field whose bloodlines (and practices) go back at least a century in institutional memory. The New Southern Studies, a movement restlessly pushing the old academic boundaries and agitating for innovation in critical practices, has gained sufficient strength to sponsor special issues of established journals and to publish its own series of scholarly books.[7] Leigh Anne Duck's *The Nation's Region: Southern Modernism, Segregation, and U.S. Nationalism* (2006) launched the University of Georgia Press series "The New Southern Studies." Duck's book covers the middle years of the twentieth century, years dominated by Agrarian and Fugitive social and literary ideologies, by the Depression and the "problem" South, by the blockbuster novel and film *Gone With the Wind,* by the enigmatic Faulkner of *Requiem for a Nun,* by the tangled cultural currents of the Harlem Renaissance and Zora Neale Hurston. This is the familiar ground of the Southern Renascence, but Duck's interpretive apparatus is new. The "segregation" of Duck's tripartite subtitle might be read as the familiar evil—an American apartheid based on hoarded white economic and social power—but Duck's analysis of the maintenance of segregation within "southern" cultural modernism and U.S. nationalism takes her inward where Freudian theories connect the maintenance of social power with the shoring-up of self. My own reading of Robert Penn Warren's coming-to-terms with segregation connects with Duck's, but where she sees modernism and nationalism at work, I see memory.

One book in particular in the recent phalanx of New Southern Studies seems to have anticipated some of what *The South That Wasn't There* hopes to say, and in the same stride to have gone further than this book and its author wish to venture into new territory and discourses. Scott Romine's *The Real South: Southern Narrative in the Age of Cultural Reproduction* (2008) is an elegantly theorized and stylishly written study of the "post-South," what the South as content and temper becomes when it is read as "produced by and distributed through media" where literature shares space with theme parks, lifestyle real estate developments, TV sitcoms, film, and other forms of consumer entertainment. Indeed, *The Real South* seems to have anticipated the Max Planck Society. Romine's critical temper is as important as his subject matter, and in the following excerpt from his introduction both are apparent:

> One of the recurring questions of this study is whether a mechanically reproduced South is preferable to an authentic one. Another is whether [Walter] Benjamin's liquidation of culture and detachment from tradition actually operate in an age of reproductions, counterfeits, and simulacra that hardly liberate reality in the way Benjamin predicted. The South is full of fakes—Civil War reenactments and plantation tourism, to name two—infinitely preferable to their originals and arguably descended from them. Even so, faking it acquires, almost inevitably, the negative connotations associated with the work of Benjamin's longtime antagonist Theodor Adorno, in his pessimistic critique of the culture industry. (2)

Between the pessimism of Adorno, for whom culture had become a bazaar of the inauthentic in which the individual happily consumed all-but-worthless knock-offs of "real" culture—and who would know better about all of those issues than Adorno, living in southern California after fleeing from Nazi Germany—and the melancholy resignation of Benjamin, Romine leans to the latter, arguing that since "culture was never organic in the first place" (2) it has always been a game all of us play. "Play" is the operative word for Romine, but he does not mean "play around." In his prologue to a chapter on representations of the murder of Emmett Till, for example, in which he carefully grants that in history a teenaged African American boy from Chicago was indeed tortured and killed by white men in Mississippi who were subsequently acquitted by a jury of like-minded white men, his attention is focused on the types, tropes, simulations, and narrative codes through which "the South" plays in its own, and the wider, U.S. (and global) imaginary. I am interested in that same apparatus or systematized media, but I am calling it rather "history-and-memory." Unlike Romine, but without contesting his claims, I am more concerned with collisions in which the tidy hyphenated compound actually elides or disappears into its parts: when/where, in the case of *GWTW,* real property and text do not coincide, or when/where, in the case of appropriating the Caribbean, the prey swallows the predator and what started as an experiment in outreach results in a reinscription of colonializing clichés. I think there are more casualties on the road to the post-South than Romine is ready to record.

Another work in the genre of New Southern Studies that preceded Romine's *The Real South,* and together with it helps to frame my own work, is Martyn Bone's *The Postsouthern Sense of Place in Contemporary Fiction* (2005). Titles can be revealing in themselves. Bone, like Romine, plays with orthodox assumptions, under which his project might have been titled: "The Postmodern Sense of Place in Contemporary Southern Fiction." "Postmodern" usually takes precedence in critical formulations, and "southern" usually modifies (and marginalizes) "fiction." Bone disrupts our expectations, destabilizing the space-time configuration in which time ("postmodern") trumps space ("South").

Bone is acutely aware of "the moment" he helps to punctuate, and since it is a proximate moment to *The South That Wasn't There,* I will quote him: "In the last few years, there has been much talk of a 'transnational turn' in American Studies. . . . I have noted (especially in my analysis of Atlanta and its literary representations) that there is compelling evidence that 'the South' is now comprehensively integrated into a globalized economy dominated by multinational corporations that have transcended or circumvented the physical boundaries of the nation-state" (250–51). The "South" of Bone's work is no longer the distinctive enclave protected from the ravages of time and history (as it was before "the turn," in the mind's eye of Agrarian criticism), and his "historical-geographical materialist approach" (45), though rolling off the tongue with distant echoes of Polonius, turns out to be supple rather than pedantic. Like Romine, Bone can play like a virtuoso, but his score is different. Compare Romine's discussion of Atlanta, and the menagerie of Tara namesakes that radiate outward from it like the detritus of a culture bomb, with Bone's densely textured discussion of Atlanta municipal history that underlies his reading of fiction by Anne Rivers Siddons, whose novels of Atlanta (*Peachtree Road* [1988] and *Downtown* [1994]) evoke a still-southern city that seems to have existed between the Atlanta of Margaret Mitchell and the striving world city of the Olympic Games and Ted

Turner. Bone on the one hand and Romine on the other describe the amplitude the Planck Society envisions between the extremes of history and memory, as they play out in the New Southern Studies.

Bone does what many literary critics are leery of doing: he takes up "mass market" fiction and peels back the layers of the obvious without condescension to reveal its meaning as artifact. Perhaps Siddons's novels will not bear the weight of a full-bore historical analysis derived from Georg Lukacs, but in Bone's hands they are not inert blobs of time-killing pulp. He is equally adept with Tom Wolfe's *A Man in Full* (1998), but that is an easier task since Wolfe himself natters on relentlessly in his books about the meaning he means to convey. Compare, again, Romine's brief treatment of Wolfe's novel (Romine 21–22) with Bone's: Romine is drawn to the semiotic system(s) generated by the "mechanically reproduced" culture in *A Man in Full;* Bone is interested in where the money came from and where it went in making Atlanta a world city. I take from Martyn Bone's work on Atlanta a kind of answer to one of the questions inchoate in the Planck Society announcement: "Yes, history does have a memory, and its traces can be read in places shaped by material circumstance. Just look at Atlanta."

Bone's sense of the "place" of southern studies is compatible with Barbara Ladd's state-of-the-field essay in the March 2005 *PMLA.* Bone deals with "sociospatial" (Bone 28) place and relations (following Fredric Jameson, David Harvey, and Edward Soja), while Ladd remaps the sturdily place-oriented southern field with Caribbean and hemispheric coordinates. Because the Caribbean and Latin America suffered forms of race-based slavery, Ladd carries over themes and practices (and authors and texts) from the field as defined by earlier generations. Ladd "turns" in geography, but not so sharply in themes and methods. In *Nationalism and the Color Line* and *Resisting History,* Ladd carefully extends the horizon of the "former" southern studies southward into the islands of the Caribbean on the pontoons of U.S. southern authors who have tried to deal with that material. Her measured "turn" has riled at least one fellow critic.[8] Here Bone diverges from Ladd: *The Postsouthern Sense of Place in Contemporary Fiction* is not haunted by the specters of race and slavery, nor by the gender biases of earlier generations.[9] Perhaps because Bone was born and educated in Great Britain, and teaches in Denmark, our native regional reflexes don't hamper his thinking. Bone is not oblivious to these sources of power, but his case (as it develops in the penultimate chapter on Toni Cade Bambara) is that "the postsouthern sense of place" has eclipsed even these twin obsessions of the mind (and body) of the South. Bone might be correct; globalizing economies may have buried "the South" too deep for recovery by history or memory or by anyone but the archaeologist. If he is right, then the sedimentation did not begin yesterday. Michael O'Brien's magnificent two-volume intellectual history of the Old South, *Conjectures of Order: Intellectual Life and the American South, 1810–1860* (2004)—winner of the Bancroft Prize—is amply attentive to the European, Asian, and Caribbean reach of southern minds and bodies before the Civil War.

Memory in cultural studies is an elusive quarry. As the Max Planck Award announcement shows, it is often compressed and elided with history. In the context of cultural study, the aims and accomplishments of history and memory are distinct, and often antagonistic. Tony Judt, in *Postwar: A History of Europe Since 1945* (2005), bars the hyphenation of history-and-memory, preferring the "disenchantment" of history to the "inherently contentious and partisan" dynamics of the memory (829–30). Judt the historian takes the often-paraphrased words of Renan to be the keynote to his epilogue in *Postwar*: "Forgetting, I would even go so far as to say historical error, is a crucial factor in the creation of a nation; thus the progress of historical studies is often a danger for national identity. . . . The essence of a nation is that all individuals have many things in common, and also that they have forgotten many things" (803). What results, according to Judt, in a cultural metabolism on a heavy diet of memory is, paradoxically, a lot of forgetting. First, he reasons, the "process of remembering and acknowledging" typically requires at least two generations and several decades. Witnesses die, impressions wane. Even France (crucial to the memory work of Halbwachs and Nora), Judt proposes, a nation with a highly developed program in national, cultural memory, has achieved only a "serially incomplete" one. And enterprises designed to "memorialize the past in edifices and museums [are] also a way to contain and even neglect it—leaving the responsibility of memory to others" (812, 815, 829). Judt would seem to have an ally in southern studies in Robert H. Brinkmeyer, Jr., whose *The Fourth Ghost: White Southern Writers and European Fascism, 1930–1950* (2009) concludes with the admonition: "Remaining haunted by long memories of anguish and guilt, they [white southern writers of the World War II South] have learned that the fears and obsessions of their ancestors are in many ways their own, however much history separates them" (326) from the physical and moral destruction Judt massively records in *Postwar*.

Judt's insistence on "responsibility" is a useful antidote to Nora's surrender to "a historical past that is gone for good" (Nora 7) and to Romine's satisfaction with "faking it."[10] As Romine employs the concept of faking in the performance of culture, it tallies closely with the "memorialization" phase of memory. Like nations that memorialize their pasts in "edifices and museums," Romine might argue, individual consumers of (southern) culture "fake" a memory they cannot have, and at the same moment "contain and neglect" one (Civil War and plantation slavery) by no means to be actually relived (Romine 2). Romine's *The Real South,* I would then argue, is about memory—so deep, in the Benjaminian postmodern, into "forgetting" that what Judt might see as the give-and-take relating history and memory is fundamentally all "taking" from history.

The slippery relationship of history and memory is amply present in the published record of southern literary criticism, now metamorphosed into southern cultural studies. Two important texts by Richard Gray, separated by three decades, illustrate the point. In the preface to *The Literature of Memory: Modern Writers of the American South* (1977), Gray explains his general purpose. "I have written this book," he explains, "in the belief that literature is closely related to history and, in many cases, to historiography as well, and that I have tried, however tentatively and occasionally, to consider these relationships" (ix–x). And, Gray asserts, the relationship between the literary text and an extraordinary southern consciousness of history accounts for the "unique[ness]" of southern society and its literature (*Memory* ix). For Gray, what a culture remembers shapes it as "unique" more completely than do its rituals of forgetting. Significantly, even though "memory" appears in the title to Gray's earlier study, "history" dominates his interpretive apparatus and practice. The word "memory" does not appear in the preface where the schema of *The Literature of Memory* is justified. Gray's more recent *A Web of Words: The Great Dialogue of Southern Literature* (2007) is presented, by way of the Bakhtinian concept of dialogism (*Web* ix), as a study of the broad intertextuality that knits southern literary texts from the antebellum period to the present into a knowable canon. Implicit in Gray's use of Bakhtin—as I see it—is that southern literary texts do have memory, and we call that memory "intertextuality." In a sense, this answers, in the affirmative, one of the questions raised, pages ago, in my cross-examination of the Max Planck Society's call for proposals on History and Memory. But as much as the dialogics of Bakhtin function as the skeleton of *A Web of Words,* memory is its cardiovascular system. Gray's sense of the practice of memory in a cultural community and its literary canon differs from the sense I hope to present in this study, but the practice is there under one of its various aliases. The way, for example, southern memory handles the Vietnam War, in Gray's view, differs substantially from the way I see the same practice. Both of us read novels written by southern women in the 1980s, Bobbie Ann Mason's *In Country* (1985) and Jayne Anne Phillips's *Machine Dreams* (1984), but come to different conclusions as to the ways each text represents cultural memory colliding with the present trauma of Vietnam.

In the chapters that follow I have, I think, located six cultural situations in which southern memory-and-history reaches the crossover point at which, Moebius-like, the one becomes the other. As in the example taken from Gray's *Web of Words,* I see memory working under its own name and various aliases. The final chapter speculates on a South without memory that looks and feels a lot like a memory without a South. Readers will have to move through all or most of *The South That Wasn't There* before this promised reversibility will make much sense.

1

"SOMETHING OF AN OBSTACLE"

Remembering Slavery in Morrison's *Beloved*

∞

Slavery is the site of black victimage and thus of tradition's intended erasure. When the emphasis shifts towards the elements of unvariant tradition that heroically survive slavery, any desire to remember slavery itself becomes something of an obstacle.

—PAUL GILROY, *The Black Atlantic*

W e speak so much of memory," Pierre Nora writes, "because there is so little of it left" (7). Writing of communities of memory and their rituals for creating and rehabilitating identity at the end of the twentieth century—the same era in which Toni Morrison made *Beloved* (1987) a major and complex exploration of obstacles between memory and slavery— Nora explores a twentieth-century *fin-de-siècle* in which the dominant mood is nostalgia for diminished histories and the stable identities they might have ensured for the communities we imagine to have preceded our postmodern sea change. Rushed away from the present and the past, posthistorical communities resemble the victims of special-effects films like *The Matrix* (1999): there are no reliable signs by which we can distinguish between the real and the virtual, with the result that we suspect meanings are only virtual. Or that simulations will have to do in the absence of anything more verifiable. In such a world, where does experience rank in the hierarchy of meaning, and what can it matter in what Paul Gilroy, in *The Black Atlantic,* calls the "practice [of] remembrance" (212)? Heraclitus's river becomes a computer-generated flow of the deceptively real: and we flow with the river. "The acceleration of history," Nora intones, "[a]n increasingly rapid slippage of the present into a historical past that is gone for good, a general perception that anything and everything may disappear—these indicate a rupture of equilibrium" (7).

For the moment, let's suspend the begged question of whether, at any moment serving as the present to a human consciousness, "equilibrium" was an attribute of the real world. But let us also assume there is a real world continuous with the one in which slaves suffered, and concentrate on the crisis of "slippage," or worse: "a historical past that is gone for good." If Nora's dire diagnosis is accurate, the loss of "real environments of memory" (7) and their replacement by "*lieux de mémoire,*" culturally constructed sites of memory, augur a human future of inevitable amnesia, a kind of nostalgic longing for a sense of past and origins increasingly conflated with simulations of themselves. Rushed by the "acceleration of history" and the "slippage" of the past into the realm of constructed effects, Nora theorizes an age of constructed "sites" (official texts and editions, actual real estate set aside for remembrance, rites of heritage, to name a few).[1]

In the category of real estate set aside for remembrance is the National Underground Railroad Freedom Center on the "free" bank of the Ohio River in Cincinnati. The façade of the building, clad in copper sheets, faces Kentucky, the slave state of such *lieux de mémoire* as Harriet Beecher Stowe's *Uncle Tom's Cabin* (1852) and, more to the point, of Toni Morrison's *Beloved.* On the Kentucky side, in a now-trendy neighborhood of brunch places, sports bars, and local crafts galleries, is a historical marker reminding us of the importance of Margaret Garner, the slave woman on whom Morrison's Sethe is based. There are no physical sight lines from the marker on the Kentucky side of the Ohio River to the museum in Cincinnati, but for slavery to be rememberable, the absence of sight lines cannot remain "something of an obstacle."

The Underground Railroad Freedom Center, whose interior exhibit space was laid out by the same designer who planned the U.S. Holocaust Memorial Museum in Washington, D.C., struggles to "remember" slavery, to reconstruct sight lines. Its most tactile space is an actual slave pen, moved from a farm in Kentucky and reassembled in the museum. Filled with scrubbed and conditioned air, however, the pen falls short of summoning the full sense of enslaved black bodies. The wide and tall atrium design of the interior of the gallery lobby also works against the feeling of confinement, and the gift shop—ubiquitous appendage to the contemporary "site of memory" or museum—can extend the experience by way of logo refrigerator magnets, t-shirts, and other tchotzkes.

Nora predicted most of the postmodern commercialization of memory as souvenir. He described it as a clash between history and memory. An extended passage from his essay is pertinent here:

Memory and history, far from being synonymous, appear now to be in fundamental opposition. Memory is life, borne by living societies founded in its name. It remains in permanent evolution, open to the dialectic of remembering and forgetting, unconscious of its successive deformations, vulnerable to manipulation and appropriation, susceptible to being long dormant and periodically revived. History, on the other hand, is the reconstruction, always problematic and incomplete, of what is no longer. Memory is a perpetually actual phenomenon, a bond tying us to the eternal present; history is a representation of the past. Memory, insofar as it is affective and magical, only accommodates those facts that suit it; it nourishes recollections that may be out of focus or telescopic, global or detached, particular or symbolic—responsive to each avenue of conveyance or phenomenal screen, to every censorship or projection. History, because it is an intellectual and secular production, calls for analysis and criticism. Memory installs remembrance within the sacred; history, always prosaic, releases it again. Memory is blind to all but the group it binds—which is to say, as Maurice Halbwachs has said, that there are as many memories as there are groups, that memory is by nature multiple and yet specific; collective, plural, and yet individual. History, on the other hand, belongs to everyone and to no one, whence its claim to universal authority. Memory takes root in the concrete, in spaces, gestures, images, and objects; history binds itself strictly to temporal continuities, to progressions and to relations between things. Memory is absolute, while history can only conceive of the relative. (8–9)

If Nora is correct, and we are "between memory and history," between on the one hand the absolute of memory and on the other the contingent of history, faced with an either-or choice, then the temper of our age partakes of systemic divisiveness, of foreclosed alternatives. Our cultural productions, in fiction, in criticism, in copper, stone, and glass, might be identified as signs of the times: a nostalgia for wholeness, a yearning for identity in real communities who feel their verification in history withdrawn, an anxiety about carrying tradition in the universalizing and progressive narrative of history.

Nora's diagnosis prepares us to read these signs. "Memory is blind to all but the group it binds." Shared, collective, cultural memory marks groups *as groups,* confers upon the individual members the identity of the collective and distinguishes them among throngs threatening dissolution in the acceleration of history. "We" is necessarily psychologically preferable to "them" since among "them" "we" have no standing. Memory confers identity, an "absolute," by witnessing to a "we" durable over time. Such witnessing confers reality upon experience then and now: the collective assent of the group is the criterion of reality.

History cannot confer identity—at least, in Nora's view, history as practiced in the modern West—because it is too "pragmatic," too "plural" (10). Speaking of his own nation, France, Nora writes: "That we study the historiography of the French Revolution, that we reconstitute its myths and interpretations, implies that we no longer unquestioningly identify with its heritage" (10). In other words, as what happens to a people inevitably becomes the official record of what happened, it loses the capacity to confer identity because history might have been (or even could still be) otherwise. The large and comprehensive nation-group once bound by a collectivizing and "unquestioned" knowledge of what had happened to it in time becomes a dance of smaller groups and groups-within-groups—southerners, African Americans, Log Cabin Republicans, Generation X'ers, sixties types, baby boomers—each with its consensual, collective memory; each with its own swatch of history.

To mobilize these disparate groups into a facsimile of "nation," Nora proposes, official groups commission, sustain, valorize *lieux de mémoire,* "sites of memory." No less do literary texts perform the heavy lifting of memory. Here it is important to insert Gilroy's considerably less absolutist take on the flows of history and memory. In Gilroy's equation, the forward historical thrust of the African diaspora is not total loss but a gaining as well as a losing: the knowledges, cultural forms, even memories of "the intellectual heritage of the West" (2) are partly absorbed by, even as they absorb, those of "Africa." The result is not one-way acceleration away from identity, but rather a "stereophonic, bilingual, or bifocal [ensemble] of cultural forms" creating a new hybrid contemporary (Gilroy 3). To signify this condition of reciprocal annexing, Gilroy chooses the chronotrope of the slave ship in the middle passage (4). Hopefully for this discussion, the divergent energies of the moving ship—the central space of Charles Johnson's *Middle Passage* (1990)—and the fixed, even tomblike enclosure of the house on Bluestone Road in Toni Morrison's *Beloved* may serve as polar coordinates for an exploration of remembering and slavery.

Following Nora's theory, a wide and diverse cadre of professional scholars and critics from several fields—history, literature, anthropology, sociology, political science, psychoanalysis, and more—have coalesced around the proposition that at the point of origin of identity, or the core of values, beliefs, patterns of under-standing and behavior, is a foundational event, a trauma, violation, or rupture. This trauma, happening to certain bodies in time, marks those bodies as primary carriers of identity. Bodies not so physically marked substitute memory for the actual wound, and work to validate that memory by preserving a continuous line of witnessing (telling and listening) from past to present.

The overwhelming trauma of the twentieth century was, and still is, the Holocaust. In *Testimony: Crises of Witnessing in Literature, Psychoanalysis, and History* (1992), literary critic Shoshana Felman and psychoanalyst Dori Laub explore the interstices of witnessing and narrating where the complex phenom-enon of cultural memory is created. Himself a child-survivor of the Holocaust, Laub conducted psychoanalytic sessions—ceremonies of telling and listening, despite (or maybe because of) the clinical protocols—that equipped him to make a range of useful conclusions about traumatic experience, its effects on the original bodies and minds, its residual or acculturated effects on communities of memory derived from those original survivors, and—on the outer borders of his conclusions—the viability of the Holocaust as a metaphor or analogy in cul-tural studies that propose as their field the origin and maintenance of identity.

What made the Holocaust out of the myriad individual deaths of imprisoned Jews and others was, Laub writes, "the unique way in which, during its historical occurrence, *the event produced no witnesses.* Not only, in effect, did the Nazis try to exterminate the physical witnesses of their crime; but the inherently incom-prehensible *and* deceptive psychological structures of the event precluded its own witnessing, even by its very victims" (80). In other words, the trauma of the death camps at the time of the event(s) both erased the victims bodily and so far outstripped the ability of the survivors to say to another human being what was happening that no public, communal discourse was established—no "witness-ing" in the formal sense of communal certification of the event took place. Nev-ertheless, though there were millions of victims, the identity "the Jewish people" was not annihilated. Ritualized remembering—what Gilroy in another but re-lated context terms "remembering socially organized" (212)—filled the absence made by so many dead.

For Laub, and for traumatic memory generally, the survival of identity amid the destruction of bodies is a crucial situation that communities of memory after the fact exist to make palpable. "[I]t was not only the reality of the situa-tion and the lack of responsiveness of bystanders or the world," Laub continues, "that accounts for the fact that history was taking place with no witness: it was also the very circumstance of *being inside the event* that made unthinkable the very notion that a witness could exist, that is, someone who could step outside of the coercively totalitarian and dehumanizing frame of reference in which the event was taking place, and provide an independent frame of reference through which the event could be observed" (81).

Thus, survivors take upon themselves the coupled burdens of history and identity, responsible for the identities of those who perished, who "disappeared," and for the identities of those in the continuous though interrupted line that runs through the trauma into the present. Laub writes: "The absence of an empathic listener, or more radically, the absence of an *addressable other,* an other who can hear the anguish of one's memories and thus affirm and recognize their realness, annihilates the story" (68). Laub, as both survivor and analyst, fulfills the role of empathic listener ideally—he possesses some foreknowledge of what is to be related since he suffered it—but his formulation challenges us to imagine less biographically ideal but still strategically useful stand-ins for the "addressable other." If we were, however, to insert the word "reader" for "addressable other," is it both safe and valid to assume that any reader of the survivor-narrative-as-text qualifies as "empathic" and "addressable?" What is the politics of reading what must be an "unvariant tradition" in an age of variants; that is, if no members of original sufferers-in-the-body survive, what constitutes a permissible and adequate substitute for the slipped-away trauma? An answer would bring Nora's work on public memory and Laub's on the Holocaust into a collision: is the U.S. Holocaust Memorial Museum in Washington, D.C., for example, a site of memory, a witnessing? Or a monument to our failure to achieve either one? Or, to the point here: can a museum devoted to slavery witness slavery?

The form(s) witnessing might take poses a less immediate problem for Laub; he is a psychoanalyst, and "the session" serves almost self-evidently as the form for the narration of experience into memory. Historian Eva Hoffman, in *Complex Histories, Contested Memories: Some Reflections on Remembering Difficult Pasts* (2000), alerts us to the questions of form indicated by the two terms: site of memory and witnessing. At the outset, there is the question of representation itself:

> The attempt to identify with the older generation's experience—the insistence
> that we can identify with it through memory—can verge on a kind of appro-

priation, or even bad faith. The experience was emphatically not ours, and in our desire to merge with it, to bridge the distance through a sheer claim of memory rights, one can perhaps detect a sort of envy, a fascination with the elemental drama that the previous generation has lived through with a knowledge garnered from extremity. The pasts we attempt to "remember" were terrible, but they had *terribilitas* and a dark grandeur. (Hoffman 7)

That the past "was emphatically not ours" is the starting point of the historian, but not of the community of memory. Historian David Novick, for example, in *The Holocaust in American Life* (1999) attempts to disentangle the "not ours" from the "ours," the recoverable past and our present designs upon it. Hoffman takes the question further:

> But the question is: What should we, in the second generation, do with the received, transferred memories? Do we have the right to touch upon them, so to speak, to dis-identify from them, to examine them from different viewpoints, or insert them into a coherent narrative or structure of interpretation? My answer is that not only do we have the right, we have the obligation to do so. . . . Surely if we are to understand the legacy of the Holocaust, and other disturbing pasts, we must stand in an investigative relationship to memory; we must acknowledge our distance—both generational and cultural—from the events we're trying to comprehend. But it seems to me that if we are to deepen our comprehension, we need to use that distance to try to see aspects of the past that may not have been perceptible at other moments and from other perspectives. (8–9; my ellipsis)

Representation of the data of memory is always compromised, Hoffman's argument seems to admit, with the inflections and interests of the present. We see ourselves seeing the past through memory—which, far from being a demerit on memory is in fact the process by which we are connected to it. Acknowledgment of this connection distinguishes memory from history, enlivens the work/text of memory in the question of form. It might even operate, on some level, in the adoption of the alternate history or counter-factual narrative: one strategy for overcoming the barriers to repossession of one's history is simply to transport oneself there.[2]

This double-echoed or multifaceted enterprise, however, troubles investiga-tors of collective memory little. In fact, Iwona Irwin-Zarecka, in *Frames of Re-membrance: The Dynamics of Collective Memory* (1994), stresses that collective memory is meaningless as a concept without focus on the reasons in the present for remembering a certain past: "To understand how collective memory works, we cannot restrict our inquiries to tracing the vicissitudes of historical knowl-edge or narratives. We must also, and I believe foremost, attend to the construc-tion of our emotional and moral engagement with the past. When looking at public discourse, this translates into questions about how the past is made to matter" (7). And the past is made to matter, for the public in its ongoing life, only to the extent that it sheds light on the problems of the present.

The great analogy to the Holocaust as a "difficult past" in U.S. history is slavery, and many, if not all, of the issues are the same: witnessing, testimony, experi-ence, memory and history, narratability, representation among a finite array of forms. Stanley Elkins, in *Slavery: A Problem in American Institutional and Intel-lectual Life* (1959), was one of the first to use emerging analyses of the Holocaust as a way to think about slavery, to mitigate the problematic status targeted by his title.[3] Scholars and writers have been at the center of an ongoing conversation as to whether the analogy linking U.S. slavery and the Holocaust brings us closer to, or takes us further from, an understanding of either event. Both events included the violent oppression of one population by the power and usage of another; both entailed the erasure of the victims and witnesses to the event; both have produced survivors needful of testimony and the recovery of identity and com-munity. Most important for this essay, both events have challenged the "post-" generation to represent what could not be, or was not, witnessed.

The problem of representing slavery arises as a formal, or structural, prob-lem in literary criticism and literary history. Is there an existing structure with formal properties adequate to the representation of slavery? If so, what is it? Is the history of this discursive structure the same as the history of slavery? Is it unique to the experience of slavery and the identity of the subjects? Is "com-parative study" in any way a forfeiting of identity in the first place? In "Chang-ing the Letter: The Yoke, the Jokes of Discourse, or, Mrs. Stowe and Mr. Reed," Hortense J. Spillers frames the problem of history, memory, and representation within a comparative study of Stowe's *Uncle Tom's Cabin* and Ishmael Reed's *Flight to Canada*. The problem of achieving an adequate representation of slavery, Spillers finds, is

> that every generation of systematic readers is compelled not only to reinvent "slavery" in its elaborate and peculiar institutional ways and means, but also, in such play of replication, its prominent discursive features. . . . This field of enunciative possibilities—its horizon, its limits, its enabling postulates, and its placement in perspective with other fields of signification—constitutes the discourse of slavery, and, as concretely material as the "institution" was, as a natural historical sequence and as a scene of pulverization and murder, "slavery," for all that, remains one of the most textualized and discursive fields of practice that we could posit as a structure for attention. (28–29)

Setting the word "slavery" within quotation marks creates a problematic relationship between the thing (Spillers does not deny its historical existence) and the layering series of representations ("discursive fields of practice") that, over time, have left the residue of successive groups' and generations' attempts to remember the actuality. Reading Reed and Stowe within a comparative field energizes these living discourses, Spillers argues, when "the real, rich, 'thing' itself before discourse touched it" might not be recoverable (29).

Spillers's passionate doubt about a pure representation of slavery draws a bold line between it and the Holocaust. Slavery in the New World spanned so much more historical time than the Holocaust in Europe—centuries rather than years—and occurred to a people prevented (until relatively late in the history of the institution) from producing a written or otherwise transferable record of their experience. Can we, here and now, know slavery as we can, albeit approximately, know the Holocaust? Elkins was confident enough to use the analogy between the slave plantation and the concentration camp. Spillers would seem to answer no; too many other discursive fields, representing the interests of several groups and generations, have intervened between the experience and the memory. Unlike Dori Laub listening to his fellow survivor, the "post"slavery writer must imagine much of both subject and discourse. This situation produces such aggressively parodic texts as Reed's *Flight to Canada* (1976), Alice Randall's parody of *Gone With the Wind, The Wind Done Gone* (2000), and the cut-paper works of African American artist Kara Walker, who takes conven-

tional scenes from plantation discourse and fills them with violent sex and dismembered bodies.[4]

Toni Morrison's *Beloved* was published in this milieu, as Hazel V. Carby
writes in a footnote to her essay "Ideologies of Black Folk: The Historical Novel
of Slavery," as "a remarkable exploration and revisioning of the limits of conventional historical narrative strategies for representing slavery" (143). Multiple
discursive fields overlap in *Beloved,* representing slavery as a contested site of
memory that even Morrison herself negotiates—at least partially—by analogy.

One of the discursive strategies for representing slavery in *Beloved,* signaled
consistently by Morrison's deployment of a third-person, omniscient, and historical voice, is informed by Orlando Patterson's influential comparative study
of slavery in human history, *Slavery and Social Death* (1982), published only
five years before Morrison's novel and influenced substantially by Elkins's work.
"Certainly," Patterson begins—perhaps less than certain himself—"we know
next to nothing about the individual personalities of slaves, or of the way they
felt about one another. The data are just not there. . . ." (11). Yet Patterson, like
Dori Laub, affirms the importance of testimony:

> Slaves differed from other human beings in that they were not allowed freely to
> integrate the experience of their ancestors into their lives, to inform their un-
> derstanding of social reality with the inherited meanings of their natural fore-
> bears, or to anchor the living present in any conscious community of memory.
> That they reached back for the past, as they reached out for the related living,
> there can be no doubt. Unlike other persons, doing so meant struggling with
> and penetrating the iron curtain of the master, his community, his laws, his
> policemen or patrollers, and his heritage. (5)

Like Laub who offered himself as an active agent in the forging of a "community
of memory" by investing in the experiences of the survivors he interviewed,
Patterson—even allowing for his more distant and "objective" status as historian
—valorizes connection between experience and witnessing. He notes the damage done by the prohibition of memory under slavery: slaves were prevented
from integrating past, present, and future, and hence were left with neither
community nor self.

For Patterson as well as for Laub, erasure of identity was not only physical,
the annihilation of the physical body of the enslaved on such a scale as to elimi-

nate life itself as an object of thought, but also psychological or, in a sense, linguistic or semiotic. Masters removed the language or symbols by which the enslaved integrated themselves into "social reality" and inserted their own instead:

> The symbolic instruments [by which the master controlled the slave] may be seen as the cultural counterpart to the physical instruments used to control the slave's body. In much the same way that the literal whips were fashioned from different materials, the symbolic whips of slavery were woven from many areas of culture. Masters all over the world used special rituals of enslavement upon first acquiring slaves: the symbolism of naming, of clothing, of hairstyle, of language, and of body marks. And they used, especially in the more advanced slave systems, the sacred symbols of religion. (Patterson 8–9)

For slavery, then, experience came in a deliberate variety of cultural forms. The forms have survived, and mutated, while the original experience has not: "The data are just not there . . ." (11). Patterson constructs a magisterial comparative field of data drawn from slave societies other than the United States, hoping, perhaps, that the surplus of other slaveries might trickle into the relative absence called "U.S. slavery."

Beloved is not daunted by Patterson's lament for absent data, unrepresented experience and identity, but rather addresses the full range of questions concerning slave experience and the adequacy of forms for its expression. *Beloved* does not furnish a full range of answers, and that has kept critics busy with the text for twenty years and more. Like some works by William Faulkner, to which Morrison's fiction is often compared, *Beloved* has been subjected to a myriad of critical approaches, producing one of the most extensive critical bibliographies in U.S. literary criticism. Memory work has not been omitted in the panoply of approaches. One of the most arresting essays on *Beloved* and memory is Avery F. Gordon's "not only the footprints but the water too and what is down there," chapter 4 of her book *Ghostly Matters: Haunting and the Sociological Imagination* (1997). My chapter, like Gordon's, argues that *Beloved* enacts collective memory rather than describing or analyzing it. But my sense of *Beloved* is that Morrison is much more conflicted than Gordon about what makes the past matter now. By featuring contested voices and shifting interests, crucial elements of the collective memory process, and leaving the question of representation ultimately unanswered, Morrison creates power through irresolution.

Ironically, approaching *Beloved* (and beyond it the subsequent pair of novels Morrison named to fill up the trilogy—*Jazz* [1992] and *Paradise* [1998]) as a novel significant for its problems in coming to closure links it more intimately with the issues raised in survival and memory studies.

Beloved is dedicated to "[s]ixty million and more" slaves brought in captivity to the New World and their issue born here whose lives and experience have been "lost," or recorded paradoxically under erasure in ledgers and account books like the one Faulkner imagines in "The Bear." Some masters record the presence of some black physical bodies, but fail to comprehend the human experience of those bodies in their times and places.[5] This is not to say that the experiences, individual and collective, of those sixty million and more did not register on the consciousness of the masters or of the world. Sethe's theory of rememory maintains that physical places hold the traces of what happened to the human beings in them (Morrison, 36).[6] As sensitive (and conflicted) a gauge as Thomas Jefferson detected such human presence and the durability of memory when he tried to explain the imbricated patterns of slavery and race in *Notes on the State of Virginia:*

> It will probably be asked, why not retain and incorporate the blacks into the state, and thus save the expence of supplying, by importation of white settlers, the vacancies they will leave? Deep rooted prejudices entertained by the whites; ten thousand recollections, by the blacks, of the injuries they have sustained; new provocations; the real distinctions which nature has made; and many other circumstances, will divide us into parties, and produce convulsions which will probably never end but in the extermination of the one or the other race. (138)

More than most white witnesses to slavery, Jefferson felt the human presence of the slave; his prediction of a race Armageddon is predicated on the slave body carrying not only the injury but the recollection of it. Transgenerational memory communicated by physical bodies thought, by Orlando Patterson and others, to have left no "data" opens the discourse of slavery history to ghosts. Gordon appreciates the extent to which Morrison feels the ghostly "life world of those with no names we remember, with no 'visible reason' for being in the archive" (150). With no other means of recording "data," the slave body itself became an archive. If Patterson claims that the "data [of individual slave personalities] are just not there," it is in part because as historian he is restrained from believing in what he cannot see. Morrison—focusing relentlessly on the slave body tortured, working, being raped, suckling, giving birth, performing fellatio, bloating, shrinking—corrects Patterson's myopia. For she can see the body of the disappeared slave in every (black) woman's body.

Beloved must first recreate the experience of slavery and the individual human personalities encased within it, *and* forge a modern form or instrument for conveying the substance and meaning to a late twentieth-century, now twenty-first, reading audience. One burden of the author in the "post-" generation (discussed by Eva Hoffman in her comments on Holocaust survivors) is the knowledge that earlier forms will not suffice. The autobiographical narratives of Frederick Douglass and Booker T. Washington, for example, have long been recognized as problematic because of their appropriations of (or by) the white man's tropes and language.[7] Where does irony stop and ventriloquism begin?

Morrison establishes a familiar modernist time line: historical chronology fragmented and reassembled. The "events" of *Beloved* are both historical and imagined, and the novel covers primarily the historical years from 1850 (the year of the Fugitive Slave Act) to 1873, three years before the official end of Reconstruction and the beginning of Jim Crow.[8] Some characters are framed in deep memory, others by verifiable historical event. The main character, Sethe, an escaped slave living in southern Ohio on the outskirts of Cincinnati, equally accepts her memory of killing her baby daughter in 1855 and that daughter's return as a ghost in 1873.

The novel opens in 1873 at the house in southern Ohio. 124 Bluestone Road is owned by a former abolitionist, rented by Sethe (who works in the kitchen of a Cincinnati restaurant), occupied by Sethe and her second daughter, Denver (born during Sethe's flight to freedom in 1855), and haunted benignly by the memory of Baby Suggs (Sethe's husband's mother, who dies while Denver is a child) and then more violently by Beloved (the ghost of Sethe's first daughter). The ghost of Beloved has driven Sethe's two sons, Howard and Buglar, to leave home, and 124 Bluestone becomes a community of women, a site crucial to the power and limits of the novel—and the premise by which Morrison runs the memory of slavery on the fuel of gendered body consciousness. It also becomes—in contrast to the moving chronotrope of the slave ship adopted by Gilroy and by Charles Johnson in his novel *Middle Passage*—a static interior from which Beloved is exorcised and Denver flees.

Into this haunted community comes a former slave, Paul D, bringing with him the memory of the plantation, Sweet Home, on which Sethe, her husband Halle, and several other slaves—some dead, some dispersed—were held in seeming historical suspension. At least early in their captivity, their bondage seemed deceptively liberal and "enlightened":

> He [Paul D] grew up thinking that, of all the Blacks in Kentucky, only the five of them were men. Allowed, encouraged to correct Garner [their owner, his surname linking the novel to historical "data"], even defy him. To invent ways of doing things; to see what was needed and attack it without permission. To buy a mother [one of the six, Halle, buys his mother, Baby Suggs, out of bondage], choose a horse or a wife, handle guns, even learn reading if they wanted to . . . Was that it? Is that where the manhood lay? In the naming done by a whiteman who was supposed to know? Who gave them the privilege not of working but of deciding how to? No. In their relationship with Garner was true metal: they were believed and trusted, but most of all they were listened to. (Morrison 125; my ellipsis)

Garner dies, under suspicious circumstances never clarified in the novel; the slaves suspect he was murdered to erase his liberal views and to finagle his property. The liberal master out of the way leaves room for the regime of a racist, Schoolteacher. Under his rule white children are schooled in the animal characteristics of the slave, and his nephews inflict the central trauma on Sethe when one holds her down while his brother suckles at her breasts swollen with milk for her child, Beloved. Other manifestations of trauma are named in *Beloved*: Paul D is shackled in a brace, Sixo is burned to death, several others hanged. Sethe's rape, however, is the central image, linking the "ten thousand recollections" of injury to the female body primarily—proposing a route to the original trauma of slavery through the physical fact of being in a female body.

Trauma reaches further than Sethe knows at the time, for her husband Halle is forced to witness her rape but is dishonored by being prevented from halting it or exacting revenge upon Schoolteacher's nephews. Being forced to witness injustice and dishonor, Orlando Patterson writes, is as traumatic as suffering torture in one's own body; either way the slave has no rights in his/her body and is rendered socially dead (8). Halle's trauma is real, although not immediately physical, and he shames himself by smearing clabber on his face. And yet, a real distinction exists: in the language of bodies, male trauma is remembered differently, and the community founded by sharing it seems—in the novel—less permanent. For example: having escaped the chain gang in Alfred, Georgia, the black, male inmates separate, while the community of 124 Bluestone endures in one place.

The narrative voice Morrison uses to explain such events as Halle's shame utilizes Patterson's formulae of trauma, honor, memory, and social death. This voice is historically informed, analytically adept, in many respects echoing the authorial voice in *Slavery and Social Death*. In this voice slavery is perceived as a system of power relations involving race but not restricted to it. Class inflects the racial mores of the white people on Sweet Home and outside it: the Garners aspire to a higher level of refinement than Schoolteacher, his mossy-toothed nephews, and the patrollers he hires to hunt down runaways. The Garners flatter themselves with the illusion that they treat their slaves more humanely than their fellow white slave owners, and are therefore superior to their neighbors. They flatter themselves that they do not own slaves merely to indulge in the pleasure of exercising complete power over another human being. More than once Morrison has Garner insist that his "niggers is men": "'Y'all got boys,' [Garner tells other white farmers], "[y]oung boys, old boys, picky boys, stroppin boys. Now at Sweet Home, my niggers is men every one of em. Bought em thataway, raised em thataway. Men every one'" (10). The text's irony is patent: horses and cattle are bought and raised, not men. The names of the Sweet Home men give the lie to Garner's self-congratulation: Paul D Garner, Paul F Garner, Paul A Garner, Halle, and Sixo. Of the five only Halle, Sethe's eventual husband, knows his mother, Baby Suggs. He buys her out of slavery and succeeds in moving her to Ohio. Inside the locked box of slavery, Halle sees what Patterson called the symbolic and physical "whips" of slavery (Morrison 8–9). It is Halle who witnesses the rape of Sethe when Schoolteacher's nephews steal her milk (69) and, as Patterson notes, suffered the social death of those slaves forced to witness injustice and dishonor. It is Halle who cleverly manipulates an argument with Schoolteacher over a butchered shoat, yet is beaten anyway because, as the narrator explains the white man's motive: "definitions belonged to the definers—not the defined" (190). And it is Halle, when the scheme for fleeing the Schoolteacher regime at Sweet Home is initiated, explains the catch-22 of slavery economics. Schoolteacher has embargoed all off-site slave work and income. No "new money" will come to the plantation, and therefore there will be no surplus to use for the buying out of slave labor. "If all my labor is Sweet Home," [Halle tells Sethe], "including the extra, what I got left to sell?" (196). Halle's conversation with Sethe is brief and definitive, evincing the central Pattersonian contention about New World slavery: the market value of the product was always secondary to the pleasures of power. Realizing as much, Halle gives up hope; no one sees him again.

The slave men of *Beloved,* as a group, surrender to despair. Morrison's portrayal of them implies that their knowledge of slavery as an affront to intellect and honor (Halle) and their experience of slavery in history (Paul D) have much to do with their (relative) failure to assimilate experience to self and memory. Stolen mother's milk proves a more durable correlative for memory than lost (male) honor.

Paul D is the survivor of Sweet Home, and of slavery; his response to the call for memory is to try to forget. Paul D has undoubtedly suffered torture and indignity. He has been locked in chains for eighty-three consecutive days (18), subjected to forced labor and compelled to perform fellatio on his white captors while on a chain gang (108), permitted a kind of historical mirror when he meets up with remnants of the Cherokee Nation during his escape from the gang (111), and battered with Civil War and Reconstruction history (267). In addition to Paul D's lessons in slavery as a historical practice, he knows what Halle knew about the psychological and economic double bind. Like Patterson's reconstruction of the African slave in the New World, Paul D remembers a blank: "He had already seen his brother wave goodbye from the back of a dray, fried chicken in his pocket, tears in his eyes. Mother. Father. Didn't remember the one. Never saw the other" (219). When Paul D does meet a black family with known intergenerational relationships—with what Patterson describes as a means "freely to integrate the experience of their ancestors into their lives" (5)—he hones in on an experience of self wholly lacking in his own consciousness. "He watched them with awe and envy, and each time he discovered large families of black people he made them identify over and over who each was, what relation, who, in fact, belonged to who. . . . Nothing like that had ever been his. . . ." (219). Identity, even that of others, for Paul D is like water to a man dying of thirst.

What he does remember from growing up at Sweet Home is the dehumanizing realization of being seen, thought of, in the consciousness of the white people, as a thing:

For years Paul D believed Schoolteacher broke into children what Garner had raised into men. And it was that that made them run off. Now, plagued by the contents of his tobacco tin, he wondered how much difference there really was between before Schoolteacher and after. Garner called and announced them men—but only on Sweet Home, and by his leave. Was he naming what he saw or creating what he did not? (220)

"The contents of the tobacco tin," then, symbolize the fragmented elements of manhood lying inert in the emotional memory of the male slave. No integrated, intergenerational family life as a child and adolescent, and no prospect of a stable sexual and community life as adult, husband, and father, fill the absence at the felt center of the male slave's identity. Clearly, this is a formulation of slavery addressed to a contemporary audience honed to attention by scholarship such as Patterson's. When Jefferson wrote of "injuries" he, arguably, meant something more clinically traumatic.

At moments like this, *Beloved* announces itself as a collective memory project, for past and present "matters" cohabit. Gordon notes this characteristic as well:

The presence of the ghost [in *Beloved*] informs us that the over and done with "extremity" of a domestic and international slavery has not entirely gone away, even if it seems to have passed into the register of history and symbol. Haunting the post–Civil War and by allegorical reference the post–civil rights era, the presence of a ghost who is herself haunted tells us that although we may not be able to grasp all of what the ghost is trying to communicate to us, "taking the dead or the past back to a symbolic place is connected to the labor aimed at creating in the present a place (past or future)." (168)

Gordon's idea of the present condition that makes the past matter is the present condition of market capitalism in which we all suffer commodification, even if that commodification is not overtly marked as it was in slavery. Gordon's reading is elegant: slavery enunciates the bodily but unspeakable trauma, capitalism the speakable but invisible (183). Therein lies the link to the postmodern community.

Paul D may indeed represent the commodified body, but that body is sexed, and his sexual and sexist presence in the novel suggests another allegory rooted in the present. Until he meets Stamp Paid he is incapable of expressing his need and pain—except in a kind of proprietary sexual takeover of Sethe, Beloved, and the all-female household of 124. Stamp Paid tells him his own memory story. Married to Vashti, another slave on the same plantation, Stamp Paid (then named Joshua, apparently by his owner) is robbed of his wife by the young master, "seventeen, twenty maybe" (Morrison 233) who takes Vashti as his mistress. Seeking revenge the only way a slave can—indirectly—Joshua insinuates to the master's white wife what she apparently already knows or senses: that her husband has a slave mistress. Vashti reappears at Joshua's cabin soon thereafter, and the insulted slave husband remembers trembling on the brink of snapping his wife's neck in retribution. Instead, he changes his name to Stamp Paid, walks to freedom, and becomes what he is when Paul D meets him: an active agent on the Underground Railroad.

The lesson of Joshua-Stamp Paid's memory story seems clear, in context. The condition of slavery fundamentally alters the universe of behaviors and expectations—although not the gut yearnings—of the male and female human beings trapped within it. Extraordinary acts become ordinary, the most basic of which is incorporating the past (memory) into the present. Paul D is moved by Stamp Paid's suggestion more deeply than he was by the ghost of Beloved:

> A shudder ran through Paul D. A bone-cold spasm that made him clutch his knees. He didn't know if it was bad whiskey, nights in the cellar, pig fever, iron bits, smiling roosters, fired feet, laughing dead men, hissing grass, rain, apple blossoms, neck jewelry, Judy in the slaughterhouse, Halle in the butter, ghost-white stairs, choke-cherry trees, cameo pins, aspens, Paul A's face, sausage or the loss of a red, red heart.
>
> "Tell me something, Stamp," Paul D's eyes were rheumy. "Tell me this one thing. How much is a nigger supposed to take? Tell me. How much?"
>
> "All he can," said Stamp Paid. "All he can." (235)

The catalog of images and memories that speeds across Paul D's memory in the shuddering moment is the dislocated contents of his "tobacco tin," a container of experience without the living ("red, red") power to shape and reconcile disparate and even self-contradictory experience into an integrated person. But, Morrison insists, that person is gendered as well as enslaved, and memory carries forward insults to both conditions of the body.

The novel's course to a happy ending might be clearly and directly charted from this moment. Indeed, approximately forty pages later Paul D does return to 124 and Sethe's bed. Beloved subsides; in fact, she drops from memory. These two survivors, Sethe and Paul D, would seem to provide witness for each other, not so much in an analyst-analysand relationship as in a recreated heterosexual one in which Paul D grows out of his predatory phase and into the arguably more mature phase represented in the novel by the Sweet Home slave Sixo, who walks fifteen miles each way to visit—only for minutes—the Thirty-Mile Woman because she was a "friend of his mind" (272).[9]

In Part Three of *Beloved,* the forty-page delay and redirection between Paul D's moment of breakthrough and his reunion with Sethe at 124, Morrison makes her own bold attempt at rememory: a process not just of attempting to record past events in the order in which they occurred, but to rethink them into the advancing present in such a way as to energize them with a sense of living urgency: to remember, as it were in Jefferson's fearful terms, the wounds of slavery in the living bodies of the survivors: to witness. Morrison's central strategy for accomplishing this type of witnessing is to render the experiences of the female in slavery in a kind of special category such that the religious and mythic world of Baby Suggs moves undeterred from her through her daughter-in-law Sethe, and then into Sethe's daughter Denver. In a fundamental way, the men and women enslaved in the United States do not travel the same path.

One effect of *Beloved*'s modernist structural blending of fragmented chronology and the braiding of historical event and magical realism is that the primacy of history is interrupted at the outset. *Beloved* tells one story, but more than one way. The pivotal event, drawn from a historical account, on which the novel is balanced—Sethe's murder of her child Beloved rather than surrender of her to Schoolteacher and his slavecatchers—is delayed in the plotting. And that event significantly functions as a sign of the simultaneity of the layered stories in *Beloved:* the killing of Beloved throws slavery as the essential story of the novel into collision with gender, for the event simultaneously explores slavery and the mother's "special" responsibility for her children.

Part One of the novel systematically establishes 124 as a community of women. Sethe's two sons, Buglar and Howard, have departed, leaving the house to the women: "Within two months, in the dead of winter, leaving their grandmother, Baby Suggs; Sethe, their mother; and their little sister, Denver, all by themselves in the gray and white house on Bluestone Road" (3). Before we know more about him, we are told that Halle, Sethe's husband, left the day Beloved was born. When Paul D arrives, he brings, therefore, an ambivalent masculine presence. On the one hand, Sethe has been starved for sexual companionship for eighteen years, and Paul D's reverent sympathy for the whipping scars on her back and his magical understanding of women make him a kind of savior for Sethe: "Not even trying, he had become the kind of man who could walk into a house and make the women cry. Because with him, in his presence, they could. There was something blessed in his manner. Women saw him and wanted to weep—to tell him that their chest hurt and their knees did too. Strong women and wise saw him and told him things they only told each other" (17). On the other hand, the remembered voice of Baby Suggs reminds Sethe that men "encouraged you to put some of your weight in their hands and as soon as you felt how light and lovely that was, they studied your scars and tribulations, after which they did what he had done: ran her children out and tore up the house." "A man ain't nothing but a man," is the sum of Baby Suggs's experience (22, 23). And the summit of her expression is the sermon that she delivers to the survivor community of ex-slaves. Her message is stern and concentrates on recovering the body from the control of the white man. "She did not tell them to clean up their lives or to go and sin no more. She did not tell them they were the blessed of the earth, its inheriting meek or its glorybound pure. She told them that the only grace they could have was the grace they could imagine" (88). And, as the rest of Baby Suggs's sermon exhorts, that imagining takes place in the flesh first. Pointedly, Morrison says this is not the Sermon on the Mount, echoing a cue from Patterson: even the sacred symbols of religion could become "symbolic whips" (Patterson 9).

Although the men enslaved at Sweet Home, and among the sixty million and more, suffered in the body, the first part of Morrison's novel stresses communal suffering in the female body. Even granting the erasure of family relations under slavery, the mother-daughter bond survives. Sethe remembers her mother only partially, but "[o]ne thing she did do," Sethe tells Beloved and Denver. "She picked me up and carried me behind the smokehouse. Back there she opened up her dress front and lifted her breast and pointed under it. Right on her rib was a circle and a cross burnt right into the skin. She said, 'This is your ma'am. This,' and she pointed. 'I am the only one got this mark now. The rest dead. If something happens to me and you can't tell me by my face, you can know me by this mark'" (61).

The scar that marks the white man's possession and the breast of her mother are nearly conflated in Sethe's memory, and carry in the novel the heaviest burden of the particular suffering and identity of the woman enslaved. Sethe's rape by Schoolteacher's nephews is not conventional penetration, but an enforced suckling. And, after Sethe kills her "crawling already baby" to prevent the slave-catchers from returning her to Sweet Home, she immediately takes up Denver to nurse:

> "It's time to nurse your youngest," she [Baby Suggs] said.
> Sethe reached up for the baby without letting the dead one go. Baby Suggs shook her head. "One at a time," she said and traded the living for the dead, which she carried into the keeping room. When she came back, Sethe was aiming a bloody nipple into the baby's mouth . . . So Denver took her mother's milk right along with the blood of her sister. (152)

Blood, milk, memory, and sisterhood therefore make Denver the emergent character in *Beloved,* for it is in terms of her eventual outcome that the outcome of memory and survivorship is calculated.

Denver knows Beloved more intimately, completely, than she would if her older sister had survived, for Beloved is the direct path to Sethe's unmediated memory, the memory of the escape from Sweet Home—Denver in her mother's womb—and her birth on the road to freedom. "Denver was seeing it now and feeling it—through Beloved. Feeling how it must have felt to her mother. Seeing how it must have looked" (78). What Denver sees and feels is not so much the chronicled history of slavery, the slavery lived and suffered by Paul D, for example—as it is her symbolic birth out of history. Denver sees and feels her birth, midwived by a white woman for whom she is named, into a community with the potential to transcend the racism that holds slavery to the body in time and replaces it with gender solidarity.

Denver resists Paul D's re-entry into the life of 124 at least partially because his return makes slavery, her mother's life before Denver's miraculous birth, the "data" of Sethe's memory. When Sethe takes Paul D upstairs and into her bed, the integrity of the community of women is reordered. Indeed, Paul D shatters it almost terminally when he takes on Beloved as a sexual partner too. Paul D's intercourse with the ghost is as traumatic to Denver as the memory of her sister's death, because it brings back into the picture not just slavery but a semblance of "natural" masculine sexual hegemony over community and family that Denver has never known. Unlike the slaves among her ancestors, Denver builds a private, imaginative, inner life (28). Again unlike her forebears, Denver has access to literacy. Morrison dwells upon Denver's year at Lady Jones's school with extraordinary attention to detail in a novel about slavery and memory. It is as if literacy is the map to the future, and Denver's progress is only suspended, not stopped, when a boy classmate brings up the issue of history with a question about her mother and, by extension, the past. At stake with the character of Denver and the character of her memory is the basis for the foundation of the survivor community. Shall the survivors endure, reestablish the connections that Patterson and others have identified as the sustenance of human, social existence, on the foundation of shared memory of the trauma to the innumerable bodies of slave ancestors? Or will Denver emerge from the past with the issues of identity and memory rooted in her needs as daughter, sister, woman?

In Part Three of *Beloved* the voices contesting for representation of slavery, for the privilege of rememory, come formally and thematically into collision. Whereas getting Beloved out of 124 was the problematic accomplishment of Paul D in Part One, getting Denver out is the concern of Part Three. The terms of her eviction are crucial to the meaning of the novel.

Beloved's claustrophobic repossession of 124 carries the ideal of the community of women to a drastic extreme. Sethe teeters on the brink of being sucked dry by the rememory of her murdered baby, and Denver, albeit nurtured deeply by the all-enveloping sisterly knowledge of Beloved, hovers perilously close to a kind of autistic disorder. The joys of Lady Jones's school, prominent in Part One, return in the final part of the novel. It is Denver's grandmother, Baby Suggs, holy spokeswoman of memory in and of the flesh, who almost literally pushes Denver off the porch of 124. Denver remembers a verbal fencing match over memory and racial identity between Sethe and Baby Suggs in which, for every grant of amelioration to the whites Sethe ventured Baby Suggs countered with an accusation of more heinous evil. "There's more of us they drowned than there is all of them ever lived from the start of time. Lay down your sword. This ain't a battle; it's a rout" (244). Baby Suggs declares the kind of victory that vaporizes the obligation for interracial nostalgia. She seems to be saying: this is not about being black in a white world, but rather about being with and because of the memory of the sixty million and more.

"Remembering those conversations and her grandmother's last and final words, Denver stood on the porch in the sun and couldn't leave it." Her grand-mother's voice comes into her through memory, offering to repeat the story of forced migration, bodily usage and torture—all of which Morrison records earlier in the text. Baby Suggs's words seem to paralyze Denver, but there is no way through the tangle of memory except by the existential stroke: "Know it, and go on out the yard. Go on" (244). The language is evocative, for although the story of slavery quilted into *Beloved* by way of several voices is not one to pass on, the way to live the memory is to "go on out the yard," to act in the world of the present and future with the embedded memory of the past. Denver is the woman of the (diasporic) present, imagined in the historical present of the novel as a New Woman—educated (by the conditions of the late nineteenth century), independent, economically self-supporting, and therefore possessing some measure of autonomy in the labor and marriage market.

Morrison's plotting in Part Three underscores this projective conclusion to a novel so concerned with rememory. As a foil to Sethe, whose story absorbs much of Parts One and Two, Morrison elaborates the character of Ella, introduced earlier and marginally. Ella is the antithesis of Sethe:

> She was a practical woman who believed there was a root either to chew or avoid for every ailment. Cogitation, as she called it, clouded things and prevented action. Nobody loved her and she wouldn't have liked it if they had, for she considered love a serious disability. Her puberty was spent in a house where she was shared by father and son, whom she called "the lowest yet." It was "the lowest yet" who gave her a disgust for sex and against whom she measured all atrocities. . . . Whatever Sethe had done, Ella didn't like the idea of past errors taking possession of the present. Sethe's crime was staggering and her pride outstripped even that; but she could not countenance the possibility of sin moving on in the house, unleashed and sassy. Daily life took as much as she had. The future was sunset; the past something to leave behind. And if it didn't stay behind, well, you might have to stomp it out. Slave life; freed life—every day was a test and a trial. (256; my ellipsis)

Quite clearly Morrison mobilizes Ella to represent life without memory, or at least life with memory in check to the necessities of the oncoming present. In keeping with one of the strongest thematic patterns in the novel, Ella's experience of slavery is her experience of sex—her body sexualized as it is enslaved.

She is Denver's surrogate mother, the one whose life imprints the possibility of the memory of slavery lived in the material circumstances of a woman in the present.

One of the plotted climaxes of *Beloved* enacts this collection of meanings and representations, while reprising the central event: the intrusion of the white man, Sethe's killing of her child to prevent a return to slavery. *Beloved's* occupation of 124 has locked the place into a paradoxical image of a death camp. Sethe becomes more emaciated in body and alienated in mind as Beloved bloats. Denver ventures off the porch, into the world of work and social intercourse, both to save herself and to rescue her mother from her crippling addiction to memory. Denver finds domestic work in the home of the Bodwins, an elderly white brother and sister, lifelong abolitionists and landlords of the property at 124 Bluestone. Ella hears about Denver's work and home situation on the local grapevine, and sets out to 124 on a quest to exorcise the ghost. Her quest takes place on the same day that Edward Bodwin drives by 124 to pick up Denver for her first day of work at his home. The convergence repeats the arrival of Schoolteacher and his slavecatchers that traumatized Sethe, triggered the killing of Beloved, and laid down the pattern for the life of 124. When Bodwin enters the yard at 124, Sethe slips out of the present and into the eternal return of traumatized memory: every white man is Schoolteacher, every approach is an approach to violate, every confrontation is mortal self-defense. Sethe attacks Bodwin with an ice pick, Denver and a collection of women led by Ella pile on Sethe to prevent her from repeating with tragic and uncalled-for results the trauma of the past, and Beloved hovers apart "smiling" (262).

The thematic indications of the plotted repetition seem clear. Sethe's total and unremitting identification with traumatic memory dooms her to relive the past in the present; in fact, she is doomed to misconstrue the present as the past. Her emaciated and exhausted flesh is the sign that there is no nourishment in memory cut off from its usage to the present. Ella and Denver comprise the surrogate mother-daughter pair who emerge from the scrum at 124. Sethe survives and is reunited with Paul D, who returns to 124. But the man's return is problematic. As he and Stamp Paid "remember" a "scene neither one had witnessed," they jocularly misconstrue its origins and its meaning:

> "Every time a whiteman come to the door she got to kill somebody?"
> "For all she know, the man could be coming for the rent."

"Good thing they don't deliver mail out that way."

"Wouldn't nobody get no letter."

"Except the postman."

"Be a mighty hard message."

"And his last."

When their laughter was spent, they took deep breaths and shook their heads. (265)

Morrison's decision to omit attributions in the dialogue is archly significant: it does not matter which man says what, for male slave anguish and trauma, as tropes in the novel, are not as durable vehicles for identity and memory as mother's milk and childbirth. Humorous one-upmanship may act as a salve for the hurt, or the men may be dissing what appears to them to be a symptom of female trouble. Whatever the reason, the trauma of the female slave's history, and its continuation in memory, are too powerful for the male to take without deflection.

Part Three triggers profound, and profoundly ambiguous, contested meanings. Once Beloved is exorcised again, and Sethe and Paul D are reconnected in domestic peace, a new grounding for sex and gender relations is paved. The much younger Paul D who, with his fellow Sweet Home men, first saw Sethe in a rutting fever ("All in their twenties, minus women, fucking cows, dreaming of rape, thrashing on pallets, rubbing their thighs and waiting for the new girl—the one who took Baby Suggs' place after Halle bought her with five years of Sundays" [11]) has matured into a partner and friend with a pledge of future care and attention. This climactic stasis in shared memory, passion subdued to understanding, and a projected future of domestic tranquility follows immediately upon a digest of Paul D's wanderings between the time he left Sweet Home and the moment he found 124 (267–70). Parts of the digest are implanted in *Beloved,* variations on the thicker network of the slave women's less chronological and less public narrative. His reunion with Sethe suggests a reconciliation of the narratives and the competing constructions of memory and identity embedded in each.

If this were the final scene of *Beloved* the novel might be thought to address the issues of memory and forgetting, witnessing and testimony along the lines of more conventional holocaust fiction. Charles Johnson's novel *Middle Passage,* we will soon see, a novel to which *Beloved* is sometimes contrasted, leaves its picaro-hero safely in the arms of his lost and found lover after a series of elaborate adventures—arguably reducing the narrative of the sixty million and more to a half-serious parody of a seagoing yarn. Johnson suggests that the analogical narrative for slavery is not the Holocaust but *Tom Jones.* Perhaps recognizing that domestic stasis is not the resolution to the rigors of rememory, Morrison concludes *Beloved* with a two-page prose meditation on memory and forgetting:

> They forgot her [Beloved] like a bad dream. After they made up their tales, shaped and decorated them, those that saw her that day on the porch quickly and deliberately forgot her. It took longer for those who had spoken to her, lived with her, fallen in love with her, to forget, until they realized they couldn't remember or repeat a single thing she said, and began to believe that, other than what they themselves were thinking, she hadn't said anything at all. (274)

As conclusion to a novel seriously aimed at retrieving the memory of the experience of slave trauma, reconstituting the "ten thousand" insults to the bodies of the innumerable slaves lost to memory, Morrison's sense that the community of memory lives not on a continuous channel to the past but on here-and-now pragmatic constructions sufficient to the day is a breath-taking supposition. And powerfully registers the contradictory dynamics of communities of memory.

In *The Black Atlantic,* Paul Gilroy calls out Charles Johnson's novel *Middle Passage* (1990) to complement *Beloved.* Morrison's novel is crucial to Gilroy's investigation of "modernity and double consciousness" because in it he finds her "moving excursion into the relationship between terror and memory, sublimity and the impossible desire to forget the unforgettable," crucial to his sense "about the way modernity operates" in collusion with forms of rationalized slavery (plantation slavery and the Holocaust) (Gilroy 217). Gilroy's thesis in *The Black Atlantic* is that "anti-textual, vernacular forms" in black expressive cultures have been successful in "respond[ing] to the aporetic status of post-emancipation black art" because these forms, unlike the novel, are less encumbered by the inadequacies of form and language; form and language being, as Morrison shows amply well in the figure of Schoolteacher, the very instruments of the "terror and memory." The "aporia" confronting the black novelist, then, is how to use language to manage a trauma that the language itself inflicts. Morrison strives to break the aporetic showdown by replenishing an exhausted novelistic language with resources drawn from her female communities, chiefly the memory realized in the blood and breast milk Sethe's mother bequeaths to all slave women.

Stanley Crouch, notoriously, objected to what he saw as the takeover of African American memory-and-history by a "feminist ideology" droning on about "the horrors wrought by the priapic demon of sexism" (38–39). These ideologues (Morrison and Alice Walker are the central agents) replaced history with "their own inclination to melodrama, militant self-pity, guilt-mongering, and pretensions to mystic wisdom" (39). *Beloved* especially irked Crouch: "For all the memory within this book, including recollections of the trip across the Atlantic and the slave trading in the Caribbean, no one ever recalls how the Africans were captured. That would have complicated matters. It would have demanded that the Africans who raided the villages of their enemies to sell them for guns, drink, and trinkets be included in the equation of injustice, something far too many Afro-Americans are loath to do—including Toni Morrison" (40). Among the alternatives to Morrison, Crouch advances Charles Johnson. *Middle Passage* was yet to be written, but it can certainly be read as a rejoinder to *Beloved,* countering Morrison's alleged feminist ideology with an aggressively masculinist one, and dismissing the so-called exhaustion of literary language in the face of slavery to make way for a narrative, sometimes, all about literary language.

Gilroy all but names *Middle Passage* early in *The Black Atlantic* as the case-in-point to illustrate the viability of his study of double consciousness and modernity: "But it is the struggle to have blacks perceived as agents, as people with cognitive capacities and even with an intellectual history—attributes denied by modern racism—that is for me the primary reason for writing this book" (6). Gilroy's point is more temperately made than, but essentially the same as, Crouch's grouchy objection to the acclaim Morrison's fiction had been accumulating up to and including *Beloved:* "For *Beloved,* above all else, is a blackface holocaust novel. It seems to have been written in order to enter American slavery into the big-time martyr ratings contest, a contest usually won by references to, and works about, the experience of Jews at the hands of Nazis" (Crouch 40). Leaving aside the tone of bruised masculine whining in Crouch's review, his point about historicizing the memory of slavery is significant to Gilroy's pivotal question: "How do black expressive cultures practice remembrance?" (212). If

Morrison's way is the only way remembrance can happen, then more than male privilege is superseded; among his huffing and puffing, Crouch insists that history be at least co-equal to memory in what Gilroy names "any desire to remember slavery" (189).

Johnson's *Middle Passage* is thematically built to move the story of African slavery out of the control of memory—and African American memory out of the control of the slave woman—and into a narrative molded by history, and by rational rather than magical thinking about events in which all stories are "sayable" if the writer has the "courage to face the ambiguities of the human soul, which transcend race."[10] Johnson's fictional narrator, Rutherford Calhoun, introduces himself as "a newly freed bondman" (1), not a former slave, and he is clearly intended to be read as a type of Henry Fielding's picaresque hero Tom Jones rather than Nat Turner. (Johnson sets the novel in 1829–1830, the years of the incubation of Turner's insurrection.) Clearly, Johnson's Calhoun is a premeditated study in African American agency grafted to the oppressor's literary canon; what Calhoun remembers of earlier life as a slave is that he never identified as one, even though his father and elder brother did. Victimage is not the soil of his identity, and he blithely carries a name redolent of white genealogies.

If the woman's body carries the memory of slavery in *Beloved,* Johnson promptly introduces the main female protagonist, Isadora Bailey, as, in Calhoun's view, a "pudgy," "prim, dry, flat-breasted" free black woman from Boston boarding with a houseful of "beautiful" Creoles (6). Far from being a sexualized victim like Sethe, Isadora is a kind of predatory spinster, targeting Calhoun from their first meeting as the man who will rescue her: not from slavery but from celibacy. Isadora's problem, as Johnson sets it, is not that she might be raped at any moment by an oppressive white, male population, but that she cannot seduce the one man she wants, Rutherford Calhoun. Whether or not Johnson purposely intended to counter the victimage of Sethe with Isadora Bailey, the two female characters function as foils in an intense literary-political bout. Failing an actual seduction, Isadora has the local mulatto godfather, Papa Zeringue, buy up Calhoun's debts. Mixing tropes of finance and romance that will play out problematically in the conclusion to *Middle Passage,* Papa presents the rake-hero with a choice between equally unattractive fates: debtor or husband.

To escape actually saying no to either, Calhoun stows away on a ship bound he knows not where. As Johnson's allegorical design will have it, the ship (the *Republic*) is a slaver under the command of Ebenezer Falcon, a homosexual dwarf born "but a few hours" after the American republic for which his ship is named (49). Falcon will never find his bust carved on Mount Rushmore, but he impersonates a Founding Father nonetheless—another indication that Johnson will use the historical record. In their initial encounter, Calhoun tries out the narrative of slave victimage on Falcon, who responds to each stanza in the litany of black suffering with "So?" (27–28). Falcon's *Republic* might be a rotting and leaky rendition of the United States (36), each leak representing a gap between republican ideals and actual performance, but once Calhoun learns the lesson that "affirmative action" is not shipboard law (31), he finds a place among the motley, macho crew and eventually adjusts.

The *Republic*'s voyage takes it eastward to the coast of Africa and metaphorically inward to the putative origins of African identity and memory, where Falcon picks up a cargo of slaves, the Allmuseri. The Allmuseri embody a Western myth of pre-Enlightenment African humanity that Gilroy describes as the "crude opposition" of "Africa, authenticity, purity, and origin" against "the Americas, hybridity, creolisation, and rootlessness" (Gilroy 199). Their language is not analytic but rather onomatopoetic (C. Johnson 77). Their synthetic communal consciousness erases individuality along with history, and remains as inscrutable to Calhoun as his version of republican ego is to them (61). Calhoun, boasting knowledge of the mind of the West (he has read Kant and Proudhon [50]), is blackmailed by Falcon into spying on the Allmuseri. Falcon (even Captain Queeg was right about one conspiracy) fears an uprising by his slave cargo and wants an agent in their midst to warn him of the actual time and place. Calhoun is not only trapped between a white master (with whom he shares, albeit distastefully, a national identity) and fellow blacks (with whom he shares skin color but, initially, little else), but also psychologically torn between his American black self (a "poaching" improvised self [162]) and the assumption by the Allmuseri of his essential Africanness (163). When the mutiny finally occurs—staffed with characters lifted from Herman Melville's "Benito Cereno" —Calhoun finds himself, by default, more American than African. By borrowing freely from the (white) literary canon, Johnson's text argues that the master's narrative is not the site of a "primary historical oblivion" (Handley 29) but rather a rich, if ironic, intertextuality reflecting a rich, if ironic, African American identity. Calhoun, reluctantly, pleads before the Allmuseri mutineers for the life of a white crew member, on the grounds that the Allmuseri are not seamen and will need their former captor's expertise to sail the *Republic* back to Africa.

Calhoun, like the Allmuseri, wants to go home, but his home is to the West, away from Africa (179), and he plots to lure the Allmuseri, ignorant of navigation (Calhoun assumes), into thinking they are sailing eastward when in fact their course is for the New World.

Calhoun's epiphany occurs when the uprising of the Allmuseri teaches him that he is American, not African. The myth of pure, transhistorical African identity is a casualty of the Allmuseri uprising. Johnson poignantly depicts the despair of Ngonyama, the leader of the Allmuseri, when he realizes the fatal dilemma he faces. Taking up arms against the white captors dragged the Allmuseri into the narrative of the captors: history. In the synthetic unity of pre-contact, there was no possibility of, or word for, the Other in the Allmuseri tongue. Now that the Allmuseri have drawn blood to regain their freedom, Ngonyama, at least, realizes that they have lost their organic connection to the world (140). The implications for Calhoun, the modern black man, are clear: what is the use of trying to remember an identity that can neither be recovered nor replicated?

Leadership of the "liberated" Allmuseri passes from Ngonyama to the demagogue Diamelo, who propagandizes on the theme of victimage (153–54). Calhoun turns away from the politicized identity of victim, thinking to return to an America where the past and memory will wear upon him more lightly. But Falcon, before he dies in the mutiny, reveals to Calhoun the secret identity of the *Republic:* Papa Zeringue, the money behind the Creole façade of New Orleans, is the financial principal among the voyage's backers. How could a man such as Papa Zeringue, labeled black by white America, buy and sell his fellow black human beings? Capitalism, Falcon reveals, is the water we all swim in; profit does not care what color the buyers and sellers are, and the currents are always east to west, past to future (147–50). The Middle Passage, Johnson's text suggests, was indeed "sayable" as a chapter in the history of capitalism.

If my reading of *Middle Passage,* so far, seems bent to an either/or framework, Gilroy reads Calhoun as a "'creolised' double consciousness," between the Allmuseri, who "stand . . . as persuasive symbols of an Africa that remains stubbornly incompatible with the modern world" (221), and the entrepreneur Zeringue, figure of modernity. Yet Gilroy does not fully allow for Calhoun's ambivalent attraction to Papa Zeringue, the capitalist father-surrogate who displaces victim-memory embodied by Calhoun's biological father, on whom the son had thought to turn his back (C. Johnson 169–71). On the figure of the father, *Middle Passage* downshifts from cruising allegory to a laboring negotiation of contesting father figures. For a moment Calhoun thinks Papa might be a trailblazer out of victimage, but Johnson's language is conflicted:

> Aye, for many he [Papa] was a patron of the race, a man who lent money to other blacks, and sometimes backed stage plays written by Negro playwrights in New Orleans. Could evil such as his actually produce good? Could money earned from murder, lies, and slave trading be used for civic service? These questions coursed through me as I paused before his cabin, and I saw how a man such as Papa might hunger for an heir, particularly a son raised by a woman as refined as Isadora—a teacher, indeed, a nursery-governess by trade. As the boy matured, he might feel a twinge of shame at his father's bloody fortune, but he would toast his old man's portrait some nights, for those crimes had carried their family from the fields to the Big House, from the quarters to the centers of finance. (198–99)

Implicit in Calhoun's interior interrogation is an unasked question in direct competition with the overt question of *Beloved*. In Morrison's novel the black body is the remembering carrier of slavery and identity. In *Middle Passage* the carrier is money—untouched by trauma, money circulates unstained from transaction to transaction, from trade in human beings to art patronage. Money is the ultimate amnesia. Memory, it seems, is always someone's politics. In Papa's cabinful of things there is no memory at all, only the traces of money having passed through.

Still, *Middle Passage,* novel and allegory, ends with a less than clear-cut set of alternatives. Out of the wreckage of the mutiny on the *Republic,* Calhoun has rescued one Allmuseri child who becomes a memory talisman to him. He and the child are two-thirds of a nuclear family in the New World where they survive. The symmetry of family seems to be fully restored when Isadora and Calhoun fall into bed as the novel closes. *Beloved* closes with the image of erotic regeneration in bodies scarred by slavery, but *Middle Passage* stalls. Calhoun and Isadora postpone lovemaking, and instead of desire Calhoun's "memory of the Middle Passage kept coming back" (208), its questions unanswered.

2

ROBERT PENN WARREN

The Real Southerner and the "Hypothetical Negro"

∞

Therefore, a vast amount of the energy that goes into what we call the Negro problem is produced by the white man's profound desire not to be judged by those who are not white, not to be seen as he is, and at the same time a vast amount of the white anguish is rooted in the white man's equally profound need to be seen as he is, to be released from the tyranny of his mirror.

—JAMES BALDWIN, *The Fire Next Time*

For so many white men in the twentieth century, "the tyranny of the mirror" was memory. For a significant number of these twentieth-century southerners (most of them male), *having been racist* is a memory so anguished as to call for amnesia. Jimmy Carter, a good example of the wiles of amnesia and memory, remembers growing up in rural Georgia in the 1930s but seems not to remember much racism in himself—except as southern traditions forced it on him. He portrays himself as more Huck Finn, less Tom Sawyer. Mississippian Willie Morris, growing up in the Delta in the 1940s, remembers being sadistically racist as a boy, alienated from his traditions on visits home from the University of Texas during the "massive resistance" to school desegregation in the 1950s, and finally ambiguously absolved (but without the right penance) as an expatriate in Manhattan in the 1960s. Anne Moody, growing up in Mississippi a few years later than Morris, knew nothing but white racism—until she joined the civil rights movement.[1] Fred Hobson has tried to deal with remembered southern lives and remembered racism by suggesting that "the White Southern Racial Conversion Narrative" be added to the canon as a "Southern literary subgenre" (*But Now I See* 120). His survey of the texts and his analysis of their shared constituent parts in *But Now I See* (1999) are persuasive.[2] There may, however, be limits to what generic formalism can reveal about the inter-play of identity and memory when guilt is added to the mix.

For most southern writers coming of age during the rise and fall of Jim Crow, there was no other subject matter, no other crisis—social or psychologi-cal. If not the whole world, then at least the nation was watching for the confes-sion, the conversion, the road-to-Tarsus bolt of lightning. What could possibly block the South from the joyous relief of penitence? Senator Fred R. Harris, in his brief foreword to *Black Rage* (1968), spoke for many Americans when he counted up "five civil rights bills since 1957 . . . the erosion of legal supports for segregated institutions . . . greater acceptance of Negroes into our major institu-tions . . . [but] it is still no easy thing to be a black person in America" (Grier and Cobbs vii). How could circumstances change so much yet remain the same? How could the same public that made *Gone With the Wind* an iconic cultural experience also embrace *To Kill a Mockingbird* barely a generation later?[3]

Perhaps public and private, cultural and psychological flows of memory do not work in tandem, and the narratives of those flows are roiled by undertows and countercurrents genre criticism too often muffles. An episode in Carter's memoir, *An Hour Before Daylight,* serves as an apt example. Archery, Georgia (his boyhood home—even smaller than Plains), and the Carter household, as the future president remembers them, formed an enclave of humane (almost prelapsarian) calm in the race-baiting Georgia of "Gene" Talmadge. Jimmy played with A.D., his sidekick, and other African American neighbor boys ut-terly free from racist awareness until he ventured beyond the boundaries of Eden. The closest movie theater was in Americus, a local train ride away, and when he and A.D. got to the theater they had to split up, the white boy to the choicer seats, the black to the balcony. They rode home, too, on a Jim Crow train. In spite of the patent racism, Jimmy can't remember being a part of it: ". . . I don't remember ever questioning the mandatory racial separation, which we accepted like breathing or waking up in Archery every morning" (*Hour* 95–96). Who is "we"? In the immediate context, Jimmy speaks for A.D. What did he think, exiled to the balcony? What would it cost the white southerner to listen to what A.D. has to say for himself?

Indeed, in many cases public rituals of confession, recantation, or conversion and the narratives socially and historically shaped around them (shaped around presence and absence both) actually work to camouflage an obstinate—even desperate—clinging to the status quo. Unlike many other sins, racism seems to involve personal and communal identity: you are in sin before you do anything. The southerner (of a certain generation) cannot *be* without being racist. Genuine penance and contrition require exile. In the Roman Catholic rite of penance, absolution is accompanied by the confessor's soothing benediction to "Go, and sin no more." But where is the southern penitent to go, in terms of psychological identity, when his sin *is* that identity?

One modern southern writer above all lived and worked in the crosscurrents of that psychological and cultural storm: Robert Penn Warren. Warren's conversion is crucial to the narrative of southern cultural "awakening" and progressive growth; he is the biographical "fact" that grounds so much faith in a fictional-cultural character like Harper Lee's Atticus Finch: the white southern male who is deeply identified in his people and his place, but is also able to rise above and move onward from "the sins of the fathers." But it is with Warren as it is with Finch: the will to believe that racism can be overcome by those whose cultural memories and identities have been made by it outruns the evidence of the narrative. In Warren's case, the narrative we have defaulted to is the one he created in fiction, *All the King's Men*. What I suggest is a longer arc, one in which the potent novel is only a part.

In *A Southern Renaissance: The Cultural Awakening of the American South, 1930–1955,* Richard King, testifying to the cultural importance of Robert Penn Warren to an intellectual and ethical history of the South, places him at the transition in a narrative from a "first generation of the Southern Renaissance [to] the post-1954 South" (277). Crucial to King's narrative of progressive transition is the belief that the earlier South could not or would not fully acknowledge its racism, but that awakening to a new order became a possibility after the legal abolition of segregation. Warren's rebirth is central to King's narrative; Warren's textual trail from "The Briar Patch" in 1929 to *Who Speaks for the Negro?* in 1965 is the confessional narrative: "From today's perspective Warren's essay ["The Briar Patch'] represents an arrogance few would now dare in trying to fathom the complexities of race relations or the needs and desires of black Southerners. Yet one cannot too readily dismiss Warren for the extremity of his opinions. As he later claimed, no one in the South, at least no white person, was calling for an end to segregation in 1930" (R. King 277–78).

King takes Warren's first published version of *Brother to Dragons* (1953, not the revised version of 1979) and his assessment of the condition of race relations just after *Brown* in *Segregation: The Inner Conflict of the South* (1956) as the trace of a personal conversion, and the paradigm for a cultural "awakening." King is wary of overplaying the hand: "The question must be left open," he writes, "as to whether Warren's own self-division is moral or psychological—or both. But much of Warren's moralizing seems to be a cover for something else, a fundamental fear of appearing moral or committed to a cause beyond the individual" (286).

Here my view of Warren diverges from King's. "Cover," yes. Not, however, a modesty curtain behind which Warren might be an agnostic moral hero—one who declines to believe in constants or imperatives but acts out their consequences anyway (like Atticus Finch, for example)—but rather a decoy against the inevitable surrender of identity (white, southern, male, privileged) that any acknowledgment of his (our) racism would require. In my view, Warren did not exactly fear the "appearance" of being moral, but rather the actual and psychological dues for "being" moral. Warren's career, then, is propelled by the psychological imperative to "speak for the Negro" (as Jimmy Carter so effortlessly does) when the moral imperative is to let the Negro speak for himself.

Something like this approach has been attempted before. Forrest G. Robinson's essay on Warren, "A Combat with the Past: Robert Penn Warren on Race and Slavery" (1995), called the certainty and fullness of Warren's racial conversion into question. Although Robinson relies almost solely on a close reading of Warren's big novel *All the King's Men* (1946), his conclusions are provocative. Drawing back from his close reading, Robinson ventures a broader appraisal. "[I]t appears," he writes, "that Warren's enduring preoccupation with questions of identity was an evasive strategy permitting him to address racial themes, as he felt compelled to, without facing directly or for long their painful moral implications" (526). The psychological model that Robinson seems to have in mind—once sin is confronted, the "moral implications" of reform are clear and obvious—is complicated, as Baldwin suggests in the epigraph to this chapter, by "questions of identity." Deception is native to the process of identity formation, just as construction is inherent in the memory process.[4]

The program of deception and evasion was obvious at the time of Warren's deepest immersion in southern racism—if not to Warren himself or his fellow white, male southerners. Drs. William H. Grier and Price M. Cobbs, who psychoanalyzed black men and women in *Black Rage*, are clear: "White Americans have developed a high skill in the art of misunderstanding black people." This "misunderstanding," Grier and Cobbs argue, is public as well as private. "The hatred of blacks has been so deeply bound up with being an American that it has been one of the first things new Americans learn and one of the last things old Americans forget. . . .The nation has incorporated this oppression into itself in the form of folkways and storied traditions, leaving the individual free to shrug his shoulders and say only: 'That's our way of life'" (210, 204–05). "Being American" is the larger category of identity into which "being Southern" fits, and Warren was hyperconscious of the interplay of both related identities.[5] What fascinates me about Warren is not that he might not have faced the moral implications of racism directly—I am sure he did—but rather the ferocious complexity with which he fended off the inevitable surrender of whatever part of identity had to listen to, rather than speak for, the Negro.

Warren's first and recurring antagonist in this bout was W. E. B. Du Bois. In "The Souls of White Folk," as well as in other writings, Du Bois demonstrated the ability to get inside the "folkways and storied traditions" that bolstered white identity. "Mine is not the knowledge of the traveler or the colonial composite of dear memories, words and wonders," Du Bois begins. "Nor yet is my knowledge that which servants have of masters, or mass of class, or capitalist of artisan. Rather I see these souls undressed and from back and side. I see the workings of their entrails. I know their thoughts and they know that I know" (*Writings* 923). In other words, it is not merely Du Bois's polemic that unsettles white thinking on race; it is his ability to dismantle the premises of whiteness as *one* (not *the*) identity:

> Slowly but surely white culture is evolving the theory that "darkies" are born beasts of burden for white folk. It were silly to think otherwise, cries the cultured world, with stronger and shriller accord. The supporting arguments grow and twist themselves in the mouths of merchant, scientist, soldier, traveler, writer, and missionary: Darker peoples are dark in mind as well as body; of dark, uncertain, and imperfect descent; of frailer, cheaper stuff; they are cowards in the face of mausers and maxims; they have no feelings, aspirations, and loves; they are fools, illogical idiots,—"half-devil and half-child." (931)

Du Bois was not willing to play any scene in the racial farce over which he had no script approval. This refusal to play a part, even for expediency's sake, made Du Bois a formidable rival; he would not be spoken for.

Warren's first encounter with Du Bois provides a vivid sense of the crossfire of identity's demands. Early in his career, Warren was almost haughty in his seeming possession of all there was to know about race, slavery, the South, and the intellectual equipment required to discuss them all. His *hauteur*, as I hope to show, was the product of a directed amnesia—Warren's refusal to acknowledge in any overt way the presence of W. E. B. Du Bois, manifested as his (Warren's) preference for Booker T. Washington as the only African American intellectual whom he needed to engage. Warren's early work, *John Brown: The Making of a Martyr* (1929) and "The Briar Patch" (1930), are crucial to understanding his apparent recantation and change of heart in *Who Speaks for the Negro?* (1965).

"The Briar Patch" is Warren's contribution to *I'll Take My Stand* (1930), the southern manifesto organized by John Crowe Ransom, Donald Davidson, and Allen Tate. It has been discussed many times, in many contexts. Warren argued, in 1930, for the agenda of Booker T. Washington as a way for white southerners both to acknowledge the presence of race within their traditions and to absolve themselves of any responsibility to share power or agency with those across "the color line." "Let the negro sit beneath his own vine and fig tree," Warren concluded, while the white man owned the vineyards and orchards (*Stand* 264). Washington's separatism seemed to the young Warren the best course for race relations in the South; after all, he reasoned in what he later confessed was ignorance, total equality now was an option that even the Negro race itself had declined to accept.

The process by which Warren arrived at his conclusions in "The Briar Patch" is full of echoes and shadows of a phantom engagement with Du Bois in which Washington looms artificially larger than Du Bois—the adversary who cannot be named. Warren launches his essay with a brief, confident, but selective excursion into the historical record on slavery. Post-Emancipation Proclamation Negroes, he asserts, "found [themselves] in a jungle as puzzling and mysterious, and as little answering to [their] desires, as the forgotten jungles of Africa" (247). Furthermore, "The negro was as little equipped to establish himself in it [the post-emancipation American world] as he would have been to live again, with spear and breech-clout, in the Sudan or Bantu country. The necessities of life had always found their way to his back or skillet without the least thought on his part; the things had been only the bare necessities, but their coming was certain" (247). Warren's breezy dismissal of the psychological and

physical hardships of slave life (about which there was abundant, available historical evidence in, for example, Du Bois's *The Suppression of the African Slave-
Trade to the United States of American, 1638–1870* [1896] and *The Souls of Black
Folk* [1903]—and about which Warren himself wrote graphically and movingly
later in *Band of Angels* [1955]) positions white southern memory and tradition
directly in the path of actuality. If Warren overtly names Washington, the mod-
est trades program of Tuskegee, and the subservient message of the "Atlanta
Exposition Address" as the constituent parts of a wise and pragmatic gradualism, he also acknowledges, by obvious omission, Du Bois and the claims of "the
Talented Tenth." Our attention should be focused on what Warren chooses to
forget (the presence of Du Bois), not what he might like us to remember (that
many Americans and southerners were more racist than the young author of
"The Briar Patch").

The process of creating a careful amnesia around Du Bois and his intellectual project begins generally in "The Briar Patch" but becomes more contorted
as the essay moves to its conclusion. After approvingly citing Washington on
his conciliatory point that "my [Washington's] race will succeed in proportion
as it learns to do a common thing in an uncommon manner," Warren quickly
disparages an unnamed African American for "creat[ing] a small group of intellectual aristocrats in the race" (*Stand* 250). Warren, here, alludes to Washington's allusion to Du Bois's call in "The Talented Tenth" (1903) and in *The Souls
of Black Folk* for a black intellectual elite, "college-bred" and therefore fit to lead
modern civilization whatever the race.[6] Du Bois's position is undermined, first,
because Washington leaves its source anonymous, and, second, when Warren
claims that "the masses of negroes" agreed with Washington "that little was to
be gained" by following the path to "The Talented Tenth" (*Stand* 250).[7]

Unlike most of the Twelve Southerners who joined in *I'll Take My Stand*,
Warren was willing to think, albeit carefully, of a class of African American in-
tellectuals like the one to which he belonged in the white population. "There are
strong arguments in favor of higher education for the negro," Warren admitted,
"but those arguments are badly damaged if at the same time a separate negro
community or group is not built up which is capable of absorbing and profit-
ing from those members who have received this higher education" (*Stand* 251).
It is difficult to imagine that Du Bois, recipient of a B.A. from Fisk University
(a few blocks from the Vanderbilt campus in Nashville, where Warren attended
college) and of the B.A., M.A., and Ph.D. from Harvard (and by 1930 the author

of several books and cofounder of the NAACP), was not the target of Warren's anonymous criticism.[8] In other words, if Warren knew Washington's arguments in favor of "uplift" and accommodation to the white man's fiction of the black, then he must have known Du Bois's dissenting narrative.

Much of *The Souls of Black Folk* is devoted to Du Bois's argument that between African American history and culture and the world-dominating cultures of Europe there was and ought to be no barrier or veil. He writes at the beginning of chapter 9, "Of the Sons of Master and Man": "The world-old phenomenon of the contact of diverse races of men is to have new exemplification during the new century. Indeed, the characteristic of our age is the contact of European civilization with the world's undeveloped peoples" (133). Behind Du Bois's argument with Washington was a larger disagreement about the full partnership of the African American in emerging modern civilization: Washington, Du Bois maintained, wished to keep the African American subservient to the white by keeping the race a peasant or folk people. Du Bois insisted that his people be admitted to the modern age with full rights and privileges, and without delay (*Writings* 842–61).

Warren took Washington's side. "Let us," Warren proposes at the outset of a long hypothetical example in "The Briar Patch," "take the case of a negro who has satisfactorily prepared himself for a profession" (*Stand* 252–53). This professionally trained (Du Bois would have written "college-bred") African American would gravitate to modern civilization and away from the folk. In real terms this would mean gravitating to white institutions and practices.

> He has money in his pocket [Warren elaborates], but he is turned away from the white man's restaurant. At the hotel he is denied the bed which he is ready to pay for. He likes music, but must be content with a poor seat at a concert— if he is fortunate enough to get one at all. The restrictions confront him at every turn of his ordinary life. But his answer to another question might do something to clear both his and the white man's mind. Does he simply want to spend the night in a hotel as comfortable as the one from which he is turned away, or does he want to spend the night in that same hotel? A good deal depends on how this hypothetical negro would answer the question. (254–55)

The "hypothetical negro" Warren uses in his example can scarcely veil the identity of Du Bois, who argued for all of the rights and privileges Warren interprets, in this parable, to be the "eccentric" wishes of "the negro radical" (254). To Warren such equality is "millenarian" in its dreaminess, not pragmatic but "doctrinaire" (254, 255). To Du Bois it was nothing less than his birthright: "I sit with Shakespeare and he winces not" (*Soul* 90). Warren had made the point that the Negro was naturally suited to physical rather than intellectual labor more crudely in "Pondy Woods," a poem from 1928: "Nigger, your breed ain't metaphysical."[9] Not to belabor the point, but if Warren's statements in "The Briar Patch" needed recanting, then they were not the only ones. Such statements were not appendages to Warren, the real southerner, but integral to his identity.

The paths of Warren and Du Bois had, however, crossed before "The Briar Patch."[10] Warren wrote *John Brown: The Making of a Martyr* (1929) while in graduate school at Yale, before he went to England as a Rhodes scholar. Brown was, and still is, central to the memory of race in the South, and a catalyst for American thinking on racism and the range of actions permissible in its eradication.[11] If slavery was monstrous, then violent means were justified in combating it, and John Brown becomes a hero. This is, in a nutshell, Thoreau's argument in "A Plea for Captain John Brown" (1857). If slavery was in practice "humane," however, and the human beings enslaved therefore disinclined to want (or benefit from) freedom, then Brown was something else: an agitator, a murderer, a thief, a terrorist. Warren called him all or most of these names.

If *John Brown* was simply about staking out the territory of the southern partisan, then Warren might have opted for a more southern subject—as did Allen Tate in his *Jefferson Davis* and *Stonewall Jackson,* and Andrew Lytle in his *Nathan Bedford Forrest* within a few years of Warren's *John Brown.* By accepting the Brown assignment, Warren made an aggressive move into enemy territory, for the subject matter itself and his accumulated research on Brown made it possible for Warren to skirmish behind enemy lines with New England intellectual, cultural, and historiographical traditions. As much as Warren belittled Brown, as a literary guerrilla he resembled him.

The fiftieth anniversary of Brown's hanging in 1859 was the occasion for reevaluations. Oswald Garrison Villard's *John Brown: A Biography Fifty Years After* (1910) was the locus of most of Warren's research. Villard, Du Bois's sometime antagonist, expressed the (ultimately futile) hope that "fifty years later, it is possible to take an unbiased view of John Brown and his achievements" (586). He was privately and publicly critical of Du Bois's *John Brown* (1909) (Lewis, *Biography*, I, 357–62). Villard, unlike Du Bois, insisted on seeing Brown in multiple perspectives. In his view Brown "atoned for [the murders in] Pottawatomie by the nobility of his philosophy and his sublime devotion to principle, even to the gallows" (Villard 586). "It was the man on the scaffold sacrificing, not taking life, who inspired," Villard's ringing epilogue claims; the years of social failure and criminal violence from 1850 through October 1859 were balanced (on Villard's moral scales) by Brown's weeks in prison before his execution in December 1859.

Warren appreciated and understood Villard's thorough research, but he had no patience for Villard's encomium. Such thinking, Warren maintained, is symptomatic of the New England penchant for floating off into blurry abstraction, and moreover misses Brown's "elaborate psychological mechanism for justification which appeared regularly in terms of the thing which friends called Puritanism and enemies called fanaticism . . ." (*Brown* 446). There was nothing morally transcendent in what Brown did during his life, according to Warren, nor was there in Brown's time or in the present of Warren's writing any doorway to transcendence. "Elaborate psychological mechanism[s] for justification" filled Warren's field of vision—perhaps because he himself was absorbed in them.

Despite his public acknowledgment of Villard in the path to Brown, Warren's ghostly antagonist in his Brown project was W. E. B. Du Bois. Du Bois's *John Brown* is listed in Warren's bibliography but otherwise ignored. In his "Bibliographical Note," where Warren takes issue with Villard by finding several flaws in his research and interpretation, he nevertheless credits Villard's book with making "all other books on the subject which had appeared before 1910, seem as mere trifling with the matter" (*Brown* 442). Again, Warren deals with Du Bois by indirection: he might be "named" by being listed in the bibliography, but that is as far as Warren will go.

Warren's John Brown is a hothouse intensification of the errors Warren located in New England and Transcendental thinking and politics—a theme that would develop in Warren's prose and poetry. Brown, the ungrounded paragon of this culture, was strongly motivated by a certain set of historical circumstances; but so overpowering was his habit of abstracting significance away from the concrete and immediate that he never knew what those real circumstances were. For Warren, Brown was a born loser who panted for the material and social comforts of the upper class but never understood he was always the pawn, never the knight:

> When John Brown was fifty-seven years old [two years before Harpers Ferry] and had discovered that he possessed no head for getting along in the world and had passed through many lawsuits and bankruptcy, he wrote of those early griefs as the beginning of a much needed course of discipline, which had ended by teaching him that the Heavenly Father saw best to take out of his hands whatever little thing he might place in them. At the time he was living on the generosity of some New England gentlemen who had comfortable businesses or owned factories, believed in a high protective tariff, and felt that the Southern States would be a better market if there the people did not hold slaves. By that time also, John Brown had in mind the project that was to end at Harper's Ferry. (*Brown* 17)

Warren's sarcasm is regionally specific: if Brown thinks God is boxing him in the trials of Job, Warren thinks there is a capitalistic economic system that has exactly the same effect.[12] If Brown thought abolition a moral imperative, his funding sources saw it as opening markets.

Du Bois's Brown could not, perhaps, be more different from Warren's. If Warren perceived Brown as the thick-headed dupe of capitalist bosses—a "useful idiot" before Lenin is said to have coined the term—Du Bois sees Brown as a kind of Christian socialist by instinct: "No sooner did John Brown grasp the details of the wool business than he began to work out plans for amelioration. And he conceived of this amelioration not as measured simply in personal wealth. To him business was philanthropy. We have not even to-day [1909] reached this idea, but, urged on by the Socialists, we are faintly perceiving it" (*Brown* 61). Warren sees Brown as far from ameliorative socialist, much nearer slave owner. Enjoying some success in his tanyard (before embarking on the wool business), Brown, Warren recounts, hired a laborer to build his house. The man had been caught with stolen property: "As long as the fellow stayed with John Brown and did his work he was not to be handed over to the law, but while he was there no person on the place was to speak to him not even to answer a practical question. The man stayed about two months and endured his punishment" (24). The implication is that Brown could run a forced-labor establishment as sternly as any slave master. Between such strong-minded antagonists as Du Bois and Warren, it is no surprise that the actual Brown fades into one or the other ideology.

Warren's Brown is ever the puppet of stronger forces, and the inner psychological forces that fire Brown interest Warren (a future novelist) as much as the very real social and economic strings of this or that regime. To Warren, Brown was damaged goods when he came to Kansas in 1856:

> He and his family had tried each time [in several failures and restarts] to regain their fortune by pioneering in some new region—in Ohio, at Richmond, at North Elba—and each time he had come out just a little poorer, and a little older, from that hard speculating with crops, drouths, storm, and disease. Nature had been as perfidious as the Canal Company, or Mr. Chamberlain, or the New England Woolen Mills. A little older. Pride at seeing his name in print, when the Lawrence [Kansas] *Herald of Freedom* mentioned the arrival of his party, must have been tempered by another feeling. "An aged gentleman from Essex County," that paper had called him. And the neighbors spoke of him as Old Brown. (*Brown* 126)[13]

Warren's Brown is chiefly motivated by public shame as a failure in the marketplace. Brown's recuperative strategy, according to Warren, is simplistic and utterly lacking in honor: if he cannot become wealthy by hard work or luck or financial acumen, he will just steal what he covets. Kansas was apt territory for financial recovery, not the ground of transcendental moral action. "The cause of freedom and the plunder business were thriving side by side," Warren sardonically notes (189). And he leaves no doubt that Brown went to Kansas to speculate in "the plunder business."

As determined as Warren was to roll John Brown into ordinariness and away from what Villard called "Greek tragedy" (Villard 586), Du Bois was determined to make him a model of the suppressed, denied, white racial conscience. Born in 1800, for Du Bois, means that Brown "was born just as the shudder of Hayti was running through all the Americas, and from his earliest boyhood he saw and felt the price of repression—the fearful cost that the Western world was paying for slavery" (Du Bois, *Brown* 75). The economic nexus did locate Du Bois's Brown, but it located him outside his personal ambitions and within a wider, world-historical awareness that positioned slavery not only as a personal moral failing, but also as an excess of the Western commodification of labor. Warren and Du Bois might have found common ground on this point, for Warren too saw market capitalism as one of the forces controlling Brown's fate.

Du Bois interpreted Brown's youthful religious fervor as a special calling. He heard voices, but they were not chimerical or ventriloquized versions of baser

ambitions—as they were for Warren. Through the incantatory power of a frequent refrain in his biography, "The price of repression is greater than the cost
of liberty" (*Brown* 12, 76, 140, 395), Du Bois builds Brown into what today we
would probably call a "jihadist," a terrorist in means but a prophet by virtue of
ends (338).

Du Bois's reasoning is stark; it lacks the sardonic shadings of Warren's and
suffers grievously in the post-9/11 temper. If Brown and his sons and their associates murdered opponents to free Kansas in the prelude to the Civil War, it was
because nonviolent resistance to slavery had proved futile (Du Bois, *Brown* 153).
The end, a free Kansas, justified the means, the cold-blooded execution of slave
proponents (157). The raid on and occupation of the federal arsenal at Harpers
Ferry, the final act of Brown's anointed enterprise, was, according to Du Bois,
carried out by "a veritable band of crusaders" (286). Slavery was an evil of such
magnitude, and it had such a psychological and legal grip on American people
and institutions, that in Du Bois's view, it could only be eradicated by violence:

> The forcible staying of human uplift by barriers of law, and might, and tra-
> dition is the most wicked thing on earth. It is wrong, eternally wrong. It is
> wrong, by whatever name it is called, or in whatever guise it lurks, and when-
> ever it appears. But it is especially heinous, black, and cruel when it masquer-
> ades in the robes of law and justice and patriotism. So was American slavery
> clothed in 1859, and it had to die by revolution, not milder means. (340–41)

Du Bois, clearly, takes an absolutist position on slavery, and John Brown is
his model of a kindred moral conscience intolerant of intermediate, pragmatic
stages on the gradual way to perfection. The central example of the pragmatic,
situational moral conscience in American myth is Huck Finn, who settles for a
series of temporary, pragmatic lies ("stretchers") until he is faced with the climactic either/or: surrender Jim back into bondage or venture forward on the
wings of his own, personal moral feeling. "All right," Huck says, "I'll go to hell."
Du Bois casts John Brown in a similar drama; but once Du Bois's Brown reaches
the conclusion that legal conscience is false and private is true, he becomes
proactive, taking arms against the apparatus of legal morality rather than, like
Huck, winning a reprieve from action when he learns that Jim has been a free
man all along thanks to the Widow Douglas. Du Bois's ideological force, in *John
Brown,* is to eliminate all excuses for direct, moral action.

The contrast between Du Bois and Warren on John Brown throws into high relief Warren's contingent universe and sense of history. Du Bois indeed possesses a sense of history, and he makes Brown receptive of the currents, for example, let loose by the slave rebellion in Haiti. But for Du Bois there is existential meaning over and above history; individual actions taken in the ether of absolute moral conflicts exert history-changing forces. Warren's world is both, in the literal sense, more mundane and more complex.

"More mundane" in the sense that he sees Brown's antislavery violence in Kansas as simple murder (Warren, *Brown* 162). "More complex" in the sense that the world Brown thought he inhabited was a much more tangled net of forces (interior and exterior), interests, and plain chance than his simplistic mind could grasp. Extremists like Brown, Warren comments, "could not understand the philosophy that one must live in an imperfect world and should try to do what one can with the imperfect institutions devised by other imperfect men; they were so sure that they knew the truth" (317–18). Specifically, Brown and his abolitionist "crusaders" were so sure they knew the truth of the South and slavery and the slave: "But there was another fundamental error in the plan of conquest. John Brown, along with the greater number of Abolitionists, thought of slavery in terms of abstract morality, and never in the more human terms of its practical workings. They saw a situation which violated all justice and they firmly believed that every victim of the situation was ready to avenge himself by cutting a throat" (331–32).

The mistake Du Bois and his forerunner abolitionists made was reducing the South to one institution, then viewing that institution in moral rather than "practical" and historical terms. And yet Warren's realistic and practical rendition of the South rapidly becomes a convenient myth too:

The slave himself was at the same time more realistic and more humane; he never bothered his kinky head about the moral issue, and for him the matter simply remained one of convenience or inconvenience. Since the system did not involve that absentee ownership, which had caused the horrors of West Indian slavery, and since immediate contact existed between master and slave, an exercise of obligation reached downward as well as upward and the negro's condition was tolerable enough. The system was subject to grave abuse, but economic considerations bolstered whatever little decency the slaveholder possessed, for the slave was very valuable property and it was only natural that the master would take care to give his property such treatment as would not jeopardize its value. There was, by consequence, no great reservoir of hate and rancor which at the least opportunity would convert every slave into a soldier . . . (332)

To anticipate the title of one of Warren's later works on racism in the United States, it is clear "who speaks for the negro" in this passage. It is a white man appropriating to himself all subjectivity, supremely sure that every human person in a dark skin is satisfied with the status of being a commodity, comforted to know that "its value" would protect *it* from abuse "grave" or venial. The early Warren almost perfectly answers to Grier and Cobbs's "high skill" in white misunderstanding of the African American.

Du Bois used his *John Brown* to inveigh against such unreflective dehumanizing—such reduction of individual black human beings to "the hypothetical negro." Du Bois would not allow Warren, or any other writer, to advance the theory that "immediate contact . . . between master and slave" would "natural[ly]" result in black affection for and deference to white. If Warren argued that the antebellum South was an imperfect but realistic society in which all participants were reasonably content with the cards fate had dealt them, Du Bois insisted on a far darker, even gothic, dystopia in which "imperfection" had escalated into a carnival of the Seven Deadly Sins:

As a school of brutality and human suffering, of female prostitution and male debauchery; as a mockery of marriage and defilement of family life; as a darkening of reason, and spiritual death, it [the South] had no parallel in its day. . . . Society there was of a certain type—courtly and lavish, but quarrelsome; seductive and lazy; with a half Oriental sheen and languor spread above peculiar poverty of resource; a fineness and delicacy in certain details, coupled with coarseness and self-indulgence in others; a mingling of the sexes only in play and seldom in work, with its concomitant tendency toward seclusion and helplessness among women. Withal a society strong indeed, but wholly without vigor or invention. (Du Bois, *Brown* 76, 78–79; my ellipsis)

Du Bois's Brown struck not only to free bondmen and bondwomen, but also to redeem a society wallowing in a slough of sensuality and ease: "His [Brown's] childhood had little formal pleasure, his young manhood had been serious and filled with responsibility, and almost before he himself knew the full meaning of life, he was trying to teach it to his children" (41–42). Presumably, if Brown had succeeded at Harpers Ferry, the armed revolution would have swiftly given way to a revolution in American civilization generally, with the more refined and disciplined individuals of all races rallying against the indolent.

By the 1960s, Du Bois had become more radical, in some ways, than he had been in his earlier brushes with Warren.[14] In the late 1940s he publicly doubted the wisdom of NATO and became enmeshed in the controversy over the end of Paul Robeson's performing career in the United States. The 1950s had not been kind either. Du Bois questioned the Korean War. Anti-Communist fervor had led to charges of anti-Americanism against him, outright blockage or restrictions on his international travel, even indictment under a federal law requiring members of certain international organizations to register as agents of foreign governments. The charge was eventually dismissed. Du Bois was skeptical of the NAACP's strategy against segregation, then had to eat crow after *Brown*. In 1956 Du Bois challenged William Faulkner, a powerful voice in the South for gradualism in desegregation after *Brown,* to a debate, an invitation that Faulkner declined. In 1961 Du Bois moved permanently to Ghana, where he died two years later.

Du Bois, the first antagonist, the first "hypothetical negro," had died two years before Warren undertook his great soul-searching reassessment of his and his region's attitudes on race: *Who Speaks for the Negro?*[15] If Du Bois is not the principal ghost in this project, haunting Warren's attempts to control the dialogue on a racial situation that is more nuanced than the status quo, there is a successor to the original "hypothetical negro." As Du Bois fades from *Who Speaks for the Negro?* Malcolm X looms more ominously and eventually appears. Grier and Cobbs had seen Malcolm X as the way out of the tragic tangle of "black rage." "History may well show," they predict, "that of all the men who lived during our fateful century none illustrated the breadth of the grand potential of man so magnificently as did Malcolm X." He was "indeed the only universal black hero" (Grier and Cobbs 200). Not solely for the constructive impact he may have had on the psyches of black men and women, but crucially also for the unsettling effect he would (and did) have on white America: "Alarmed white people see him [Malcolm X] first as an eccentric and later as a dangerous radical—a revolutionary without troops who threatened to stir black people to riot and civil disobedience. Publicly, they treated him as a joke; privately, they were afraid of him" (201). A Toussaint Louverture for the twentieth century.

The Warren in *Who Speaks for the Negro?* proves out much of the Grier-Cobbs prophecy. Warren rests his claim to be able to listen to the African American, and in many ways to speak for him, on his pedigree: he is a white southern male of a certain generation, and his memory of having been a racist has given him, he claims, a key to the vocabulary of race. *Who Speaks for the Negro?* begins with a rush; before Warren introduces himself, we hear him ventriloquizing the voice of a fifty-five-year-old black minister from West Feliciana Parish, Louisiana. Rev. Joe Carter is close to Warren's age in 1965, and he tells his story of trying to "red-ish" (register to vote) in a mixture of standard English and Louisiana black dialect: "Deppity," "thowed," "fixen." Warren interprets for his white readers: "His speech is careful and slow. He is anxious to say things just as they had been, now and then pausing to let the word come right in his head. And there is always that careful use of detail or circumstance, that attention to things that the unlettered man achieves by his very unletteredness, by his need to hang on to the specificity of things; for the image in his head, not any written word or abstraction, is his fundamental contact with reality" (10). The overture with Rev. Carter establishes boundaries for black identity. Not coincidentally, those boundaries generally coincide with Warren's own thinking: concreteness over abstraction, a black intellect still as unfamiliar with "metaphysics" as it had been when he wrote "Pondy Woods" almost four decades earlier with the mentality he now recants.

Warren lays claim to Rev. Carter:

> I have seen this old man somewhere before. Of course, I had seen aging Negro men like him [he is a few years younger than Warren at the time of the meeting], back in my boyhood in Kentucky and Tennessee. And I had seen them in Louisiana, up in West Feliciana, long ago, when I used to go there to stand in the silence of the moss-draped oaks of the old graveyard at Saint Francisville. That palpable silence, the never-violated shadow of the spreading live oaks and the windless gray garlands of moss, had seemed to absorb everything into a Platonic certainty—even human pain. (10)

Rev. Joe Carter is, however, not a Platonic certainty but a citizen attempting to claim his political right to vote in the United States, and in the State of Louisiana after the passage of the Voting Rights Act and the Civil Rights Act of 1963 and 1964. Warren's writerly evocation of the atmosphere of his youth and memory clearly dilutes the history in which Rev. Carter is a man with rights, and fills in as upon a palimpsest a "Platonic" or archetypal old Negro man: unlettered, anachronistic in the modern world of rights and written language: the controversial Negro figure of "Pondy Woods." By virtue of leading off the book, he becomes the type against which the subsequent African American men in *Who Speaks for the Negro?* are to be measured and judged.[16]

Memory, too, clothes the narrator. Warren establishes his *bona fides* by first recanting "The Briar Patch," the essay he had written for *I'll Take My Stand,* an essay he acknowledges not by its title but only as "an essay on the Negro in the South." "I never read that essay after it was published," he claims, and remembers that even in the writing of it something felt "fake" and incomplete (*Who Speaks* 10–11). Warren's strategies of evasion and distancing seem egregious: Why not acknowledge his essay by its title? Why claim never to have read the essay he was now disavowing?

If what Warren had written in 1929–30 about "the Negro in the South" had been in several ways uncooked, a deeper memory was far more legitimate. As a boy Warren remembers the "decrepit, shoe-box size jail" of the town where he was born, and the oak tree that stood near it.

> But that scene is very vivid in my memory, for when I was a child I scarcely ever passed down that street—which was only a piece of country road that had somehow got mislaid in town—without some peculiar, cold flicker of feeling. The image of that tree which I still carry in my head has a rotten and raveled length of rope hanging from a bare bough, bare because the image in my head is always of a tree set in a winter scene. In actuality it is most improbable that I ever saw a length of rope hanging from that tree, for the lynching had taken place long before my birth. It may not, even, have been that tree. It may, even, have been out in the country. (*Who Speaks* 11)

Memory (specifically, memory of the racist milieu of the South) works to legitimate Warren's credentials to "speak for the Negro" while simultaneously becoming so porous that "actuality" never lodges long enough to create complicity. These five sentences, receding stealthily yet in plain sight from actual lynching to an image long ago and far away, were written by the same Warren who indicted John Brown and his Yankee sponsors for their "abstracting" habits of mind.[17]

Yet it is not as if nothing remains. There is guilt for "something men might do, might mysteriously have to do, put a rope around a man's neck and pull him up and watch him struggle"; and there is the complex "shame" Warren feels knowing he could not do what the men of his community could do and did (11–12). As close as he had come to a lynching is stored, again, in a narrative memory. Sitting alone in his car in Baton Rouge in 1939, he saw a white man seize a black teenager and begin to whip him with his belt.

> What was clear, in the speed-shutter instant, was my own complex reaction. I had felt some surge of anger, I had put my hand on the latch of the door, and then had, in that very motion, stopped. Let us not discount what simple cowardice there may have been in the hesitation. But what I actually felt was not fear—it was something worse, a sudden, appalling sense of aloneness. I had never had that feeling before, that paralyzing sense of being totally outside my own community. (13)

Warren is rescued, the moment of psychological exile put off. But the glimpse of "being totally outside my own community" by, presumably, intervening in the "storied tradition" of white beating black seems to make the Warren of *Who Speaks for the Negro?* heed the warning implicit in racial conversion: lose guilt and forfeit identity. A burly LSU student wanders into the scene, asks the white man, "[W]hat you doen to that nigger?" and breaks up the drama. The system, it seems, self-adjusts; but only if the power to rescue is the power—attached to the word "nigger"—to possess (13).

Warren's overture to *Who Speaks for the Negro?* shapes the narrative to come in deeply significant ways. Looming over Warren's representative racial identity is the figure of the unlettered, primordial black man—the figure represented by Rev. Carter—who gropes toward the lodestar of rights and personhood without the constant aid of the modern consciousness. The "nigger" figure of Warren's work is not unfamiliar to his readers and critics, some of whom find it nothing more or less than his unreconstructed racism. There is also the unfinished persona of the white man, dangling between ambiguous belonging to a community where men might have to do savage violence in the name of that community, and the paralyzing yet urgent need to act for the self regardless of that community. Warren might have recanted the comparatively simple racist perspective of "The Briar Patch," but it did not get him out of a thornier one.

Du Bois gradually gives way to the unlettered African American of Warren's memory and imagination. That Warren is relentlessly chasing him is clear in the first formal interview in *Who Speaks for the Negro?* Warren's discussion with Dr. Felton Clark, president of Southern University in Baton Rouge. After sit-ins had effectively closed down Southern in 1964, Clark had required all returning students to reregister. Many had not. Clark endured criticism that he had purged Southern of its best and brightest, its "talented tenth." The intersection with Du Boisian thinking (and perhaps with Du Bois's part in the Fisk student strike of 1924–25) is not lost on Warren, who seizes the word "identity" and frames "the question of identity for the Negro" in terms of Du Bois's thinking on "double consciousness" in *The Souls of Black Folk* (Warren, *Who Speaks* 17). It is important to Warren that the identity "Negro" is not something the white man has constructed and imposed on the African American, and he seems satisfied when Clark agrees with him that Du Bois fell short of "true greatness" because he "got trapped, not in his race, but in the race problem" (20). It is almost as if Warren wants to believe that "the race problem" is something the African American creates when he thinks too much about being black. Here we see the significance of the figure of Rev. Carter in the overture: a model of an African American, unlike Du Bois, who was content and comfortable wholly inside the identity familiar to Warren, even constructed by him through the repeated traditions of his community. The presence of Du Bois always suggests the desire for and possibility of autonomy in the identity of the African American—a consciousness coequal to but independent of Warren's.

The third section of *Who Speaks for the Negro?* "The Big Brass," is delicately balanced on major elements of the Washington–Du Bois debate. Meetings with Adam Clayton Powell, Roy Wilkins, Whitney Young, and James Farmer set up the dramatic meetings with Dr. Martin Luther King, Jr., in Atlanta, and with Malcolm X in Harlem. Warren undercuts Du Bois's influence in the making of African American character and institutions in the twentieth century. He was not central to the founding of NAACP in 1909, Warren notes (145). Nor is "the talented tenth" crucial to the work of CORE, James Farmer's organization; participation of "the rank and file," Warren reports, is closer to the heart of Farmer's agenda (191). In general, Warren approves of Wilkins, Young, and Farmer because they can be seen to agree in general that the Negro is an American, perhaps even an older American than many whites because of a simpler faith in the nation's founding principles (152). In Warren's thinking, an identity so American, even deep and suppressed, heals the double consciousness at the keystone of Du Bois's theory of racial identity.

Indeed, Warren badgers Martin Luther King, Jr., to disown the concept of double consciousness in favor of an overarching American identity. "What do you feel," Warren asks, "about the danger of the psychic split that Du Bois wrote about—the pull, on the one hand, toward Negro tradition, or culture, or blood, and the pull on the other hand toward the white cultural heritage with, perhaps, an eventual absorption of the Negro blood?" (216). The question is loaded. Warren had been at pains in many of the preceding interviews to elicit a noncommittal reaction to "eventual absorption" of black into white culture and blood. He seldom got the unequivocal assent he seems to have wanted. When an interviewee, like Roy Wilkins for example, expressed comfort with being an American, Warren approved. In the interview with King, he seems intent on the same assent.

> [KING]: This [assimilation to the white majority in blood and culture] has been a problem, but I don't think it has to be. One can live in American society with a certain cultural heritage—African or what have you—and still absorb a great deal of this culture. The Negro is an American. We know nothing of Africa. He's got to face the fact that he is an American.
>
> WARREN: Some sociologists say that the American Negro is more like the old American—the old New Englander or old Southerner—than is any other kind of American. Does this make sense?
>
> KING: I think so.
>
> WARREN: A young lady at Howard—who stands high in her studies and has been on picket lines and in jails, too—said to me that she has hope for settlement in the South because of the common history on the land of the Southern white man and the Negro—because of some human recognition. And she added that she was frightened by the big anonymous city—the apparent lack of possibility of human communication. Of course, she was raised in Virginia. What about that?
>
> KING: I think there may be some truth in it. In the South you have a sort of contact between Negroes and whites, an individual contact that you don't have in the North. Now this is mainly a paternalistic thing, a law of servantry— (216–17)

At this point in the transcript, Warren notes a break for a change of tape. When the conversation resumes, the topic has changed. Before the break, Warren had been honing in on one of his own cherished ideas. American identity—when it is not racialized as white—is a detour from the ultimate realization of shared identity among black and white. Those activists and theorists who put race above national identity—in Warren's thinking Du Bois is the fountainhead of this kind of thinking, as Booker T. Washington is the antithesis—do not speak for the Negro.

Ultimately, Warren can "control" Martin Luther King, Jr. Malcolm X is not so easy. Warren confronts no "hypothetical Negro" when he meets Malcolm X in Harlem, the interview with which he closes "The Big Brass." Warren notes that he meets Malcolm X in the hotel where Fidel Castro stayed when he visited New York City to address the United Nations. And Warren is at pains to describe his audience with Malcolm X in the *mise-en-scène* of meeting an Oriental potentate:

> I cross to him, over the royal distance of floor, and with the slightest hint of a smile, he gives me his hand. The hand is large and strong-boned, but not heavy, and the fingers are long. The face is a pale yellowish brown, with a somewhat scraggly short beard, with reddish-cropped tints, the brow straight, squarish and high. The short-cropped hair of close, crisp kinkiness, set right on the skull like a cap or casque, is rather light in color, with reddish-copper glints.
>
> The most striking thing, at first, about that face is a sort of stoniness, a rigidity, as though beyond all feeling. When the lips move to speak you experience a faint hint of surprise. When—as I discover later—he scores a point and the face suddenly breaks into his characteristic wide, leering, merciless smile, with the powerful even teeth gleaming beyond the very pale pink lips, the effect is, to say the least, startling. But behind the horn-rimmed glasses always the eyes are watching, pale brown or hazel, some tint of yellow. You cannot imagine them closed in sleep. (245)

Warren's handling of Malcolm X in *Who Speaks for the Negro?* is symptomatic of his handling of the black intellectual subject in all of his writing. Years earlier, in *John Brown,* Warren portrayed Frederick Douglass with a similar strategy of marginalizing him from mainstream black and white alike. In the index to *John Brown,* Douglass is identified as "ex-slave and agitator" (Warren, *Brown* 466)—certainly two of the many epithets that might be attached to Douglass, but choices redolent of Warren's denial of the full scope of Douglass's meaning for African American and American history. In the dramatized first meeting between Brown and Douglass, Warren describes Douglass as the insurgent's "mulatto guest" (Warren, *Brown* 55), and in the climactic scene in which Douglass must choose to follow Brown to Harpers Ferry or decline what is surely suicide, Warren implies that Douglass "flinch[ed]" in the face of his commitment to support Brown (328). If rhetorical maneuvering is any indication of the deep psychological unrest felt by the author, then Warren wrestles with every African American (Du Bois, Douglass, Malcolm X) who knows enough about the white man's moves to slip or reverse them—who steps from the objectively physical to the subjectively metaphysical.

Warren's interview with Malcolm X is a wrestling match:

WARREN: Can any person of white blood—even one—be guiltless?

MALCOLM X: Guiltless?

WARREN: Yes.

MALCOLM X: You can answer it this way, by turning it around. Can any Negro who is the victim of the system escape the collective stigma that is placed upon all Negroes in this country? And the answer is "No." Well, the white race in America is the same way. As individuals it is impossible to escape the collective crime. (256)

Malcolm X's fencing clearly troubles Warren, who wants to be, among the echoes of the Old Testament story of Sodom and Gomorrah, one of the just worthy of saving. He constructs a hypothetical situation in which a white child of three is about to be run over by a speeding truck. Is that child guiltless? Malcolm X continues to spar, countering Warren's example with one of his own: a four-year-old black child who, Malcolm X insists, is always already immersed in the "stigma of segregation." What about a white man, Warren volleys, who leaps into the street and rescues the black child from death? Is he just? Still, Malcolm X will not answer: the white hero could not take the black child into many restaurants. "But what is your attitude toward [this hypothetical white man's] moral nature?" Warren pursues. "I'm not even interested in his moral nature," Malcolm X counters. "Until the problem is solved, we're not interested in anybody's moral nature" (256–57).

Like Du Bois, Malcolm X presents Warren with an African American sub-

jectivity, a kernel of self-consciousness around and through which a world circulates—a world tangential at best to Warren's fierce and insistent attempts to
appropriate it to the one he controls. Malcolm X, "in his symbiotic function,"
brings out "that hard, aggressive, assertive, uncompromising and masculine self
that leaps out of its deep inwardness to confront [him, Warren, the white man]
with a repudiation as murderous as his own. . . ." "He is the face not seen in
the mirror. He is the threat not spoken. He is the nightmare self. He is the secret sharer" (266). He was assassinated while *Who Speaks for the Negro?* was in
production.

Warren had, in a sense, encountered Malcolm X before they actually met in
Harlem. In his novel *Band of Angels*, a blend of tragic mulatta story and Civil
War melodrama more than faintly reminiscent of *Gone With the Wind*, Warren constructed the character of Rau-Ru, an imperious, autonomous Caribbean
black man who eerily foreshadows Malcolm X.

> . . . all at once, but without haste, [he] was there before us, the face of preter-
> natural blackness, like enameled steel, against the white of the loose blouse.
>
> For an instant he stood there, and I saw that his eyes were wide, large, and
> deep-set, his nose wide but not flattened, the under-lip full, if not to the comic
> fullness favored in the make-up of minstrel shows of our day, and the corners
> of the mouth were drawn back so that the effect of that mouth was one of ar-
> rogant reserve and not blubbering docility. A mustache of a few hairs hung
> wispily down below the corners of the mouth, in a kind of ambitious boyish-
> ness. (Warren, *Angels* 99)[18]

Rau-Ru is clearly outside the physical and symbolic field of the American Negro,
as Warren had usually remembered him. As civil war looms beyond the New Orleans venue of the plot, a creole, a competitor for Amantha (the mulatta heroine
and narrator of the novel), appears at the Hamish Bond plantation with a coffle
of slaves. Bond refuses to tolerate the slaves' presence, but in the torch-lit darkness they appear counter-symbolic to Rau-Ru: "The figures in the center were
Negroes, eyes bulging white and rolling in the light of the flares, big awkward fel-
lows, half crouching, near naked, breech-clout or ragged trousers, here and there
some sacking tied about shoulders, elsewhere black, slick shoulders . . ." (126).

Seen *en masse* rather than as individuals, these "Negroes" are summed up
in and limited to physical flesh. They are reprises of the cartoonish blacks "with

spear and breech-clout" of "The Briar Patch." Rau-Ru, by contrast, is body and mind. When Charles de Marigny Prieur-Denis, the creole villain of the novel, attempts to rape Amantha, it is Rau-Ru who defends her. And it is Rau-Ru who springs into violence when the white man invokes racial privilege over both of them, claiming his seigneurial right to rape Amantha and his right to punish Rau-Ru under the *Code Noir:*

> "Don't look at her," Charles said. "She may come to you behind the barn, but she can't help you now. Not against a white man. For she"—and he looked at me [Amantha] and drew his lips back—"she can't testify—she's a nigger, too."
> All that time Rau-Ru was looking at Charles, wide-eyed and blank. There simply wasn't a thing on his face. Then he struck him. (129)

Rau-Ru is soon caught by a white posse, but escapes after killing a guard. The advent of civil war affords him the opportunity to become the leader of a guerrilla band of black insurgents operating on the swampy borders of New Orleans, where he metamorphoses into the insurgent Oliver Cromwell Jones—an awkward appropriation of Eugene O'Neill's protagonist in *Emperor Jones.* In *Band of Angels* the significance of the "ex-slave and agitator" is molded with strong psychological tightness to the Conradian character of Hamish Bond—to whom the black subject, no matter how self-determining, is always to some degree in "bond." Rau-Ru/Jones executes Bond midway through the novel, a summary "justice" that might be construed as symbolizing inescapable white guilt for slavery. Rau-Ru/Jones is unfazed by the killing, and later says to a white character active in the Freedman's movement: "'As for me . . . I'm a Radical for only one reason, and that reason is that I can't be anything else. Not with this face.' And he stabbed a forefinger brutally into the flesh of his own cheek" (228). When Warren met Malcolm X, he must have come face to face with a version of his own imaginative construction, a fully autonomous black person, fully equipped with a sense of history and psychology and utterly uninterested in the moral nature of the white man.

In the wake of Malcolm X's murder, Warren allows him status as "the tragic hero . . . caught on the horns of the classic dilemma of tragedy" (*Who Speaks* 267). Surely, this is intended as tribute to a worthy antagonist, but Warren never resolves the dilemma Malcolm X, Du Bois, and Douglass raise up in his thinking. In subsequent interviews arranged later in *Who Speaks for the Negro?* James

Baldwin and Ralph Ellison supply a kind of depressurization. Baldwin, a writer with interests in the European classics, knowledgeable about white and black sharecroppers in the South, and willing to discuss shared psyches, even willing to appreciate white southern guilt (284–87), returns Warren to a familiar terrain.[19]

Warren has perhaps his most collegial conversation with Ralph Ellison. Remembering his worrying engagements with Du Bois, it must have been comforting for Warren to hear Ellison say, "The idea that the Negro psyche is split is not as viable as it seems—although it might have been true of Dr. Du Bois personally. My problem is not whether I will accept or reject American values. It is, rather, how I can get into a position where I can have the maximum influence upon those values" (327). In Ellison's voice "from the periphery" (268), Warren seems to find ideas and a temperament less disruptive to his assumptions than those he found in activist political leaders. Ellison does not want a separate game; he wants a place at the big table, and he will play the cards Warren deals. Warren and Ellison agree that the real clash in America in the early 1960s is not a clash of race but of class, and Ellison goes on to speculate that the white, middle class response to the civil rights movement is a crisis in middle-class identity (338). Warren readily agrees, citing flight from "the flatness of their middle-class American spiritual ghetto" (not a commitment to work for social justice) as the motivation for so many young white people going south for Freedom Summer (338).

The long, sonorous final movement of *Who Speaks for the Negro?* eventually returns Warren to Du Bois. By the middle 1960s, of course, Du Bois's long life had ended. He was not the "problem" he had been for *John Brown: The Making of a Martyr,* or for "The Briar Patch."[20] Malcolm X had been assassinated by the time the book was published; King would be killed a few years later. As Du Bois racialized and internationalized his outlook, and Malcolm X radicalized race in America and denied Warren a hold by way of Western, liberal-democratic cultural memory, Warren pulled inward toward the answer to his book's central question:

> But if he [the Negro] is to redeem America, he will do so as a creative inheritor
> of the Judeo-Christian and American tradition—that is, by applying the stan-
> dards of that tradition—the standards of Western civilization developed and
> elaborated here. He will point out—as he is now pointing out with anger and
> irony, with intelligence, devotion, and distinguished courage—that the white

man is to be indicted by his own self-possessed, and self-created, standards. For the Negro is the Negro American, and is "more American than the Americans." He is, shall we say, the "existentialist" American. He is a fundamentalist of Western culture. His role is to dramatize the most inward revelation of that culture. (442)

Warren's peroration would seem to exclude Malcolm X and Du Bois—those who came to the conclusion reluctantly or readily that a flawed culture could not be corrected from within.[21] Warren's project was to keep the system in the hands of the insiders, having both the sin and the penance in one cultural liturgy "developed and elaborated here." This is either/both a sincere act of contrition or/and a strenuous act of denial and counterappropriation, for as courageous as Warren could be in confessing his own "cowardice" or "defensiveness" or "callowness," he was not about to surrender "here" nor the identity that functioned as his title to it.

3

ARMS AND THE MAN
Southern Honor and the Memory of Vietnam

∞

The real war will never get in the books.
—WALT WHITMAN, *Specimen Days*

Even by Walt's own hand, a civil war did get into "the books," a war to be sure of gruesomely maimed male bodies, but also one of "fascinating sights" of battlefield carnage (Whitman 577) and of warriors who glowed in the bardic poet's imagination as "fine specimen[s] of youthful physical manliness" even as they died slowly and painfully, "shot through the lungs" (583). They were, in Whitman's imagination, both the mortal bodies buried in commemorative cemeteries and the idealized heroes in the monuments installed above them. My question here is how a "real war" is "booked"—converted from history to memory—specifically, how the strong and pervasive memory of "honor" in the southern cultural imaginary reconciled, by way of all-but-ubiquitous narratives and seminarratives of Lee and Jackson and Stuart, the shock of the Vietnam War. The topic area is vast, and at many points flows over the boundaries of regionally specific southern into American cultural memory more generally. But the contemporary submission of history to memory is compelling, and the range of media in play is wide and diverse. In *American Myth and the Legacy of Vietnam,* John Hellmann suggests the vast reach of this process of conversion by tracing the image of the American frontier hero from Leatherstocking and Daniel Boone to John F. Kennedy, where the disintegration (and U.S. military involvement in Southeast Asia) began in earnest. Hellmann begins with John F. Kennedy's insertion of military "advisers" into Vietnam in the early 1960s, moves through the fall of Saigon in 1975, and ends with what he sees as a more or less deliberate cultural project to renovate the image of the American warrior with the debut of the original *Star Wars* trilogy of films in the late 1970s, stories in which honor, courage, and technology wielded by earthlings who look and sound suspiciously like Americans overcome a powerful totalitarian empire and befriend smaller, outgunned peoples in the process (209–20). A pop epic of re-remembrance devoutly to be wished. Hellmann's archive is composed mainly of fiction and popular film, but he never for a minute forgets that real shots are fired at real people who go to war for intangible reasons like "honor" and "service," embracing myths that they think will make them bulletproof—or make their lives "mean something."

Within the American community of meanings and meaners defined in Hellmann's exploration, southerners—especially southern men—identify as a subgroup most likely to affirm the identity of the honorable warrior. From the fall of Saigon, during the administration of President Gerald Ford, to the launching of Desert Storm, during the administration of President George H. W. Bush, southern fiction writers tried to reconcile the traumatic real-war experience of Vietnam with their collective memory of the South as an honor-bound culture, membership in which reciprocally required and conferred meaning upon otherwise destructive acts. In *Southern Honor: Ethics and Behavior in the Old South* (1982), historian Bertram Wyatt-Brown claims that southern cultural customs of behavior, at least as these are manifested in the Old South historical and literary records, affirm "primal honor" as a real imperative in cultural behavior. In Wyatt-Brown's view, "The sources of that ethic lay deep in mythology, literature, history, and civilization" and issued forth in real actions (3). Choices, options, reactions to present emergencies, then, had always already been framed by systems of thought and belief as ancient, in a "pagan" context, as the Indo-European, and updated in time by a "Stoic-Christian" ethic that took (some) of the raw edge off what could turn out to be more (pagan) violence than (stoic) restraint (26). In a real sense, then, southern honor is remembered as well as enacted because it comes with the authority of always having been "the way we were." It should not go without saying also that Wyatt-Brown describes an exclusively masculine honor; women could participate only as spectators and memorialists while the men performed on the altars of honor-culture and often died in the process. By the time of the Vietnam War, gendered "spheres" were in a process of reconfiguration across U.S. culture; still, the memory of honor emanating from an exclusively masculine heritage dominates southern writing about Vietnam—even in cases in which the author is a woman.

Southern honor, Wyatt-Brown theorizes, exists in a problematic relationship to history: it precedes it. "Honor came first," he claims (16). The specific case Wyatt-Brown summons as a demonstration of the precedence of honor over history concerns slavery. Slavery, in Wyatt-Brown's argument standing for historical circumstance writ large, is the effect—not the cause—of a cultural system already in place before plantations were staked out or crops planted. "The South was not founded to create slavery," Wyatt-Brown insists; "slavery was recruited to perpetuate the South" (16). The honor-bound South, then, is a kind of cultural system imprinted as meaning upon a people before the narrative of history fixes them in time and place. In the language of the psychology lab echoing from the introduction, southern honor is a fierce "top-down" organizer that precedes and manages sensory stimuli. In addition to claiming an ancient bloodline, this system is also comprehensive:

> The following elements were crucial in the formulation of Southern evaluations of conduct: (1) honor as immortalizing valor, particularly in the character of revenge against familial and community enemies (2) opinion of others as an indispensable part of personal identity and gauge of self-worth (3) physical appearance and ferocity of will as signs of inner merit (4) defense of male integrity and mingled fear and love of woman; and finally (5) reliance upon oath-taking as a bond in lieu of family obligations and allegiances. (34)

I want to suggest that Wyatt-Brown's synopsis of the operating character of southern honor culture, despite being open to a "top-down" versus "bottom-up" debate, is useful for exploring the memory of a once and future southern culture in the disintegrating times of the Vietnam War. The Vietnam War was not waged to create or rehabilitate southern honor, but southern honor was often "recruited" to treat the cultural wounds inflicted by that war.

The interplay of historical disintegration and remembered cultural integrity in the aftermath of a traumatic war is not the exclusive property of the South after the Civil War. Paul Fussell's *The Great War and Modern Memory,* "about the British experience on the Western Front from 1914 to 1918 and some of the literary means by which it has been remembered, conventionalized, and mythologized" (ix), sets about to study the forms through which post–World War I Britain coped with an experience potentially devastating to the image of itself it had projected over history. Fussell argues that what Great Britain experienced on the battlefields of 1914–1918 did not square with what it remembered of its past wars and warriors. War and memory, as Fussell abundantly shows, are codependent. The firsthand experience (the "real war" of trenches and mustard gas and "attrition"—a term, Fussell shows, that was invented for World War I) evades literary and psychological strategies of transformation in the immediate, blunt force of the moment. But remembering, conventionalizing, mythologizing (the "getting into the books"), according to Fussell, begin almost before the blood of the dead and wounded starts to clot. And like the clotting of blood, public patriotic memory eventually stops the psychic bleeding of the nation in whose name the war was fought.

Fussell's study of the literary means by which the actual brutality of the 1914–1918 war in Europe was eventually enfolded into British memory and national image was published in the year the Vietnam War finally "ended." Like Wyatt-Brown, Fussell studies a culturewide system of meaning *in extremis*. But Fussell traces the process, while Wyatt-Brown begins and ends with the product: southern honor. Fussell sees the Great War, indeed all wars great and small, as "written" first in facts—actual wounds inflicted upon the bodies of soldiers— and only retrospectively rewritten according to the habits of public memory. Individual sufferers remember their actual wounds, and, if they survive, are often reluctant to talk about them. Cultures rewrite such raw brutality only if and only when they can translate it into an ennobling narrative consistent with their best memories of themselves. Rewriting might not be completely conscious and manipulated, in Fussell's view, but it is never accidental, and it takes place in an aftermath. It uses all the resources of language, from the most particular niceties of vocabulary, syntax, and grammar of the national peoples who waged the war to the macronarrative connecting the living to their precursors. If the present cannot be made to connect to the past—the mechanism for "fitting" being some form of memorial reconciliation in a story of the present that can be made compatible with the past—then the community, the ultimate arbiter of virtue and identity, must choose between dishonor and amnesia (xii). The Great War in Europe stands out because of the problem it presented (to those who fought the war no less than to those working to remember it): how to reconcile the enormous waste of human life on battlefields—most of which scarcely qualified as "fields"—with collective public myth enshrining heroic pursuit of noble causes. Fussell suggests, disputing Wyatt-Brown's assertion that "Honor came first," that honor is actually the process of collective narrating and remembering, always deferred behind the act.

Andrew Bacevich, thinking more recently of the aftermath of Vietnam in American memory, agrees that our nation "contrive[s] a sentimentalized version of the American military experience and an idealized image of the American Soldier" (97) as a matter of course for all wars. Although the national ideal may be battered, it is never obliterated; cultural mechanisms of restoration and repair begin at once; some are as simple as disbelief. The acceleration of history, detected by Nora, seems apparent in the "aftermath" of Fussell and the immediacy of Bacevich. Bacevich further differs from Fussell because, whereas Fussell finds the process of "repair" in literary texts of several sorts, Bacevich locates the process in public policy and the documents and projects generated from it. We need to keep both in view. For Bacevich, correction comes in programmed efforts to imagine the next war in the ashes of the last one. Most of the contriving and mythmaking undertaken to erase dark images of Vietnam, Bacevich argues, can be found in public policy decisions taken in the eight years of the Reagan administration, as defeat and victory competed for control of the official narrative (98). Bacevich's reasoning is encoded in his subtitle, *How Americans are Seduced by War*: like all seductions, war bypasses conscious will and is, at least in part, desired by both parties. In this chapter I want to try to weave the southernness of Wyatt-Brown, the literary-ness of Fussell, and the military analysis of Bacevich into an interpretive net to cast over the subject matter of Vietnam in writing by southerners during the times of four U.S. presidential administrations: those of Gerald Ford, Jimmy Carter, Ronald Reagan, and George H. W. Bush. These regimes cover the "interwar" era from the end of the Vietnam War to the beginning of the first Gulf War, tracing an important arc in the reconciling of Vietnam to U.S. cultural memory.

The Vietnam War brought the United States close to the edge of political and social disintegration. Literary, visual (cinema and television), and photographic images interfered with official, "mythic" narratives of how and why "we" were waging this war, how we preserved morality in the process of killing an enemy we often could not distinguish from the civilian population, how citizens became soldiers and then citizens again through the draft, how the home front reconnected with its warriors when they came home. Wyatt-Brown's view of southern honor (albeit with reservations about violent excesses) touts the regional-cultural myth for the continuity of the individual warrior and community it preserves. At its best, southern honor integrates individual and community:

"[H]e knows no other good or evil except that which the collective group designates. He reflects society as society reflects him" (Wyatt-Brown 15). One of the early cultural casualties of Vietnam was that intimacy. Books like C. D. B. Bryan's *Friendly Fire* (1976) record the monolithic inertia of communal belief in the face of official lies and evasions, and the film adaptation (1979) starring Carol Burnett further testifies to the immense torque in the national belief system when myths of honorable and meaningful war are broken by facts, and the community becomes estranged from its uniformed icons. If a comedienne in the tradition of Lucille Ball can play the part of a disbelieving mother who resists the Pentagon's fiction of noble death in battle in the killing of her son, how far from orthodoxy has the myth of the continuity of home-front and foreign fields wandered?

By 1968, after the Tet Offensive, the massacre at My Lai, and political violence at home, "fear of national collapse peaked" (Turner 31). At the center of the fear of collapse was the fear of what had become of the American soldier in Vietnam. "As this society's representative on the field of battle," Fred Turner continues in *Echoes of Combat: The Vietnam War in American Memory* (1996), "they had come to stand for all that Americans were ashamed of in the war" (Turner 14). By the mid-1970s, the figure of the American soldier had devolved into a crazed, psychotic killer. Michael Herr's riff in *Dispatches* (1977) became a kind of mantra:

> In Saigon and Danang we'd get stoned together and keep the common pool stocked and tended. It was bottomless and alive with Lurps, seals, recondos, Green-Beret bushmasters, redundant mutilators, heavy rapers, eye-shooters, widow-makers, nametakers, classic essential American types; point men, isolatos and outriders like they were programmed in their genes to do it, the first taste made them crazy for it, just like they knew it would. (34–35)

Herr's profile of Deerslayer as a psychotic killer gradually occupied one pole in the national, military identity debate. The hyperpatriotic model of Robin Moore's *The Green Berets* (1965) and the idolatrous film version made by, and starring, John Wayne (1968) occupied the other in an attempt to preserve the traditional version.[1]

Mary McCarthy, reporting on the court-martial of Capt. Ernest Medina for war crimes alleged to have been committed at My Lai, saw the two extremes as one man. For McCarthy, the My Lai revelations highlighted the dichotomy between psychosis and honor as a false dichotomy. Captain Medina, she allowed, was the "classic essential American type," but the type was embedded in the fatally flawed norm. No need to look, as Herr had, among the crazies. McCarthy characterized the man who reported to Medina, Lt. William Calley (already court-martialed but free on a presidential [Nixon] commutation), as an "erratic character and malformed lieutenant who though not demented in the legal sense, was plainly unable to function in the Army or in American society, even though his strivings and failure to 'make it' . . . appeared horribly typical" (13–14).[2] If McCarthy was correct, and the "horribly typical" was in fact demented, American society had suffered an invasion more serious than the Tet Offensive. The seamless bond of honor that Wyatt-Brown professed to find in the DNA of southern culture could become, potentially, a life-saving graft.

Clearly, what Philip Beidler sees as "a collocation of experience and myth called Vietnam" (266) dominated war and memory in the American public consciousness from the moment news reports and images returned to the home front. Peter Arnett supplied the haunting subtitle to the Vietnam War in 1968, reporting the slogan of search-and-destroy tactics: "It became necessary to destroy the village in order to save it." Linguistic absurdity thus lurked at one end of the spectrum, and the public consciousness was mobilized to counteract it with a narrative of virtue and efficiency. By early 1991, the legions of counterattack were poised in Kuwait to exorcise the image of the American military as badly trained and officered. Although, as the aftermath of the first war in the Persian Gulf was to tell us, in Iraq we once again destroyed the village and failed to save it. Nevertheless, as Vietnam veteran Andrew Bacevich writes in *The New American Militarism* (2005), "Victory over Iraq [in 1991] vindicated a massive effort of recovery and renewal launched in the immediate aftermath of Vietnam" (35). With a kind of eerie symmetry, Gen. Norman Schwarzkopf, who as a lieutenant colonel figures prominently in Bryan's *Friendly Fire,* and was Lieutenant Calley's commanding officer, commanded U.S. forces in Desert Storm. The narrative of war and memory, it is vital to remember, runs continuously from printed text to video screen to actual battleground. And sometimes, in the service of memory, back the other way.

If there are few discernible agents of direction in the chaos of actual battle, there are the paths redirection takes in remembering it. That, as Bacevich says, Vietnam was a "formative experience" in late twentieth-century American military memory (civilian and professional) is a given (xiii). The agents of the transformation of experience, he argues, are many and diverse (6). Turner's question in *Echoes of Combat* is also germane: "How is it then, that in a little more than twenty years [1973–1993], the image of the American soldier as executioner should have vanished and that of the American soldier as victim should have taken its place?" (11).

Four U.S. presidents coped with the burdens and problems of the memory of Vietnam over the first two decades (1970–1990s) of the reinscription of Vietnam in the public narrative. Gerald Ford, Jimmy Carter, Ronald Reagan, and George H. W. Bush adopted different strategies in their policies and rhetorics for managing the "wound" of Vietnam. These four agendas of policy and rhetoric, reaching from defeat in Vietnam to the launching of Desert Storm in 1991, cover crucial years of memory work in which representations of the Civil War and the southern warrior of tradition played powerful, if often surreptitious, parts in the battle of the Vietnam War waged on the field of American memory.

GERALD R. FORD (1974-1976)

The presidency of Gerald Ford began in an aggravated traumatic state of shame brought on by defeat in Vietnam and the resignation (in response to articles of impeachment) of Richard Nixon. Ford and his advisers, haunted by more than one "national nightmare," prescribed amnesia to cover them all. The pardoning of Nixon was put forward as the beginning of wide-awake, ordinary daylight. The rhetoric of sheer forgetting was carried over from Nixon's impeachment to the fall of Saigon and defeat in Vietnam. In a speech at Tulane University scarcely weeks after the evacuation of Saigon, Ford put the present into the past: "Today [April 23, 1975] America can again regain the sense of pride that existed before Vietnam. But it cannot be achieved by refighting a war that is finished— as far as America is concerned. The time has come to look forward to an agenda for the future, to unity, to binding up the nation's wounds and restoring it to health and optimistic self-confidence" (qtd. in Turner 15). For a president who notably described himself as "A Ford Not a Lincoln," the echo of Abraham Lincoln's second inaugural address is a backdoor raid on the memory of an iconic president who, in the midst of the Civil War, succeeded in establishing a memory of that war that hallowed its cause and dedicated the nation to an equally noble future even before the war was won.[3] Ford's formula for dealing with the traumatic memory of Vietnam was simply to replace the past with a bright future—a popular bromide of American national thematics, a rhetoric of man-ifest destiny reborn in psychic rather than geographical space. It must have resonated with his audience. "The bleachers rocked," according to one report (Brinkley, *Ford* 91).

Some southern writers can be found outside the main course of Ford's "op-timistic self-confidence." Short stories in Barry Hannah's collection *Airships* (1979) reflect a 1970s in which the myth of southern warrior hero and the real-ity of Vietnam mix, but only satirically. In Hannah's short story "Testimony of Pilot," two southern friends from the same small town go through high school together playing music and loving the same girl. College splits them up. One, William, stays in Mississippi for college, and his friend Arden Quadberry (the "pilot" of the title) is accepted by the Naval Academy. Quadberry becomes a fighter pilot, but a virus in his education as a modern warrior infects the sweet soul he had shown leading the high school band, with his tenor saxophone, in their rendition of Ravel's *Bolero*. When Quadberry visits Mississippi on his way to Vietnam, his parting words to his girlfriend, before he thunders down the runway with afterburners blazing, is "I am a dragon, America the beau-tiful, like you will never know" (Hannah 37). Quadberry's thundering depar-ture, probably not accidentally, brings to memory an earlier southern aviator, Faulkner's John Sartoris, killed in action in the skies over France in *Flags in the Dust*.[4] In Faulkner's novel, the southern warrior memory of Lee, Stuart, and a host of additional heroes affects the Sartoris brothers Bayard and John in oppo-site ways. John, "spontaneous and merry and wild" (*Flags* 76), enlists with the Lafayette Esquadrille and is shot down over the battlefield in France in 1918 just a few months before the armistice. Bayard, condemned to survive, is ultimately driven to self-destruction by a "cold, arrogant sort of leashed violence" (76) that corrodes most of those around him. Wyatt-Brown's dichotomy of pagan and stoic seems appropriate for placing the Sartoris brothers in the scheme of south-ern honor.

What Faulkner imagined in dichotomous brothers, Hannah puts destruc-tively in one character. The war in Vietnam finishes the devolution of the south-ern warrior in Quadberry, turning him from a "spontaneous and merry and wild" saxophonist into a "dragon." Having shot the tail assembly off a North Vietnamese MiG, Quadberry feels compelled to pay chivalric honor to his foe, as if the code of the Lafayette Esquadrille that lifted John Sartoris still obtains fifty years later and many thousands of miles to the east. Quadberry circles until he is sure his foe's parachute opens. But the enemy pilot, rather than eject, tries to ram an air force B-52, and Quadberry has to blast what's left of the MiG (and his wished-for honor) out of the Southeast Asian sky. Not long after the kill, Quadberry's fighter is hit by a surface-to-air missile. He makes the return trip to the aircraft carrier where he is based, but in the crash landing of his damaged plane, his back is broken. Although the physical injury heals, Quadberry is never the same man or pilot. He returns from Vietnam literally and figuratively broken: "meek," "anemic," "shorter," and "sick," Quadberry seems more defeated than victorious (41). Eventually, he dies as a result of a risky surgery to cure the constant pain in his broken back. His abandoned girlfriend had died in the crash of a commercial jet on which she worked as an attendant.

Barry Hannah turns the iconology of southern warrior heroism inside out in "Midnight and I'm Not Famous Yet," another Vietnam story collected in *Airships*. In this story, General Robert E. Lee, the icon of southern honor, metamorphoses into North Vietnamese Army (NVA) general Li Dap, an urbane officer who speaks Parisian French, studies the campaigns of Napoleon, and craves nothing more than to *be* Jeb Stuart. The punch line of Hannah's story is abrupt and bloody: General Li might be an incompetent dilettante (and maybe Stuart was too), but he is also dangerous and Hannah's narrator (prefiguring Rambo) blows the Vietnamese general Li, and more than a few of his fellow NVA military, to kingdom come with an experimental phosphorus shotgun. The word "atrocity" dogs Hannah's narrator's action, but he is never court-martialed and comes home something of a hero (117).

President Ford's call for amnesia on the war in Vietnam is vivid, if background, texture in Michael Shaara's novel of the Battle of Gettysburg, *The Killer Angels* (1974). Classically unified in Aristotelian terms of place and time by the three days of the actual battle (July 1–3, 1863), *The Killer Angels* poses shadow answers to cultural-memory questions raised by the shock of Vietnam, suggesting that a particular past, rather than the bright but nebulous future recommended by President Ford, harbors the best hope for national consolation. By juxtaposing historical figures from North and South who embody different traditions—in fact, different "Americas"—Shaara implicitly puts Civil War military memory up against contemporary, Vietnam-era military shock: as brutal as Civil War battles surely were, our warriors fought them with honor and valor. Vietnam is not yet the new norm, as Michael Herr and Mary McCarthy and Barry Hannah had direly warned us, *if* Civil War memory can be implemented to postpone or derail it.

In one of his paratextual addresses ("To the Reader"), Shaara betrays an ambiguous desire to claim both the authority of historical circumstance and the security of myth. He characterizes the historical period of which he writes as naïve and sentimental; the "religiosity" of the mid-nineteenth century in the United States (North less so than South), Shaara claims, was a climate the mid-1970s can never know. From the margins of his text, Shaara kindles cultural memory: what we do not have now ("religiosity" and, therefore, a purer love of country) we can repossess vicariously, by historical proxy, by refloating the memory of a former war and seeing the present war through the screen of the past.

In his foreword to the novel, still another paratext attached to "the text itself," Shaara tries to shape reader response to *The Killer Angels* further. Here, the two Americas appear. Lee's Army of Northern Virginia, and by extension the Confederacy, was a homogeneous integrity; it could, Shaara insists, act as one, integrated people. In this claim, Shaara invests in Wyatt-Brown's theory of the honor community of the antebellum South. Anglo-Saxon, English-speaking, and Protestant, Shaara claims, Lee's army was a reflection and extension of its leader; and Lee was the faultless reflection of a people thinking with one mind and speaking with one voice. The Army of the Potomac, on the other hand, was an experiment in the "melting pot" America. With its revolving-door generals and polyglot languages and ethnicities, Shaara's Union army is, as a cultural symbol, what we had become (in Vietnam) foreshadowed by what we were in the process of becoming in the Civil War.

In *Echoes of Combat,* Turner makes a point of describing the barriers to comradeship in Vietnam that underlie Shaara's contrast of northern and southern armies: "Brought into their units one at a time, made to fight for twelve or fourteen months, and sent home alone, many grunts of the Vietnam era, unlike their fathers in World War II, saw little connection between their personal tours of duty and the aims and scope of America's national commitment to the war" (5). One of the first casualties of this polyglot army, Turner says elsewhere in *Echoes of Combat,* was the Vietnam soldier's "faith in the possibility of a community" (9). Bacevich pushes Turner's point further. Not only was community within the Vietnam unit undermined, but community between the uniformed soldier and citizens back home was shattered by the military's practice of assembling units with individuals from diverse places (Bacevich 27). Shaara's contrast between Lee's army and the Army of the Potomac reflects public anxiety about how armies mirror the collective identities of the communities who assemble them. It is not that war itself undermines the community of warriors in a collective cause, it is *this* war that poisons that myth in the American system because we have somehow forgotten that severing warriors from their home places damages their allegiances. Civil War/southern memory enables us collectively to counteract the fear that we are inescapably a flawed nation fighting this war this way in Vietnam by suggesting that it is the way the forces are organized, not the soldiers themselves or the policy, that causes the problem.

The Killer Angels is not a simplistic, costumed retreat into hackneyed Old South myth.[5] Even though honor binds the officers and men of the Confederate Army (M. Shaara xviii), and contractual agreements bind the Union soldiers to service, honor on the southern side is not without its limitations, and modernity as a temperament is not reserved to the Federal side. Shaara's James Longstreet is the modern man of logic and analytical—as distinct from traditional— thinking. But he is pledged to a premodern army and officer corps, a dichotomy that gives *The Killer Angels* a contemporary bite. Shaara's Longstreet is uncomfortable among the traditional men on Lee's staff; for him the battle at Gettysburg is not a Holy War but a problem of elevations, firing angles, and force calculations (63–65). As the battle progresses, Longstreet sees that honor without intelligence could, and probably will, lose Gettysburg and ultimately the war. Genius in war is not, as the legend of Lee would have it, the instinctive sense of what your adversary might or might not do, but successful adaptation to the facts on the field (138). Shaara's Longstreet, then, is a rebuke to officers up the Vietnam command chain to Gen. William C. Westmoreland—and back to Fussell's Field Marshal Haig—who saw success in terms of outdated rhetoric from an earlier war rather than analytical thinking about the one facing them in the present.

Longstreet feels a deep sadness at the thought of all the dying on both sides (206). And, as the frontal assault of July 3 clearly and surely fails from the outset, he is almost paralyzed with guilt and sorrow, torn between his obligation to execute an order and his certainty that Lee's decision to send his troops in a frontal attack fatally confuses the situation on the ground with a myth of invincible power and purity of motives (346). And yet that frontal attack, Pickett's Charge, remains hallowed in cultural memory.

An equally significant and problematic figure in *The Killer Angels* is the Union captain Joshua Chamberlain. In Chamberlain, Shaara imagines a secular warrior as a kind of foil for Lee (who invokes the name and presence of God frequently in *The Killer Angels*), standing upon a moral and ethical ground opposed to slavery and to the social class claims of the men on the southern side, but eschewing the naïve "religiosity" of his time (30). Shaara's Chamberlain feels the "excitement" of the battle but realizes that there is no metaphysical grounding to the killing (124). As a clear contrast to Lee, however, Shaara tries to redeem Chamberlain's wholly secular involvement in the killing. Chamberlain, Shaara claims, does love his comrades-in-arms—unlike Lee, who accepts the adoration of his men but never returns it (240). After repelling the final assault, as the sun sets on the evening of July 3, Chamberlain senses the battlefield as imbued with an "unspeakable beauty" (349). More factual descriptions of the aftermath of Gettysburg, and other Civil War battles, pay more attention to the stench and bloating of dead bodies, the desperate cries of the wounded and dying. Geoffrey C. Ward's illustrated companion book to Ken Burns's PBS documentary, *The Civil War: An Illustrated History* (1990), is a notable example.[6] But, the beauty of quick and dead bodies in battle, and the concept of the beauty of male sacrifice, which Shaara strives to represent in the figure of Chamberlain, create a thematic question: Does this warrior rapture somehow reimagine war with amnesiac rhetoric, or uncover in it something redemptive to the public at large that authorizes words like "sacrifice" and "altar"?

The Killer Angels, read as memory text in dialogue with images of Vietnam, insists that war can be fought with meaning—although not without mothballing sentimentality and "religiosity." In Shaara's remembered world, the higher up the chain of command the more abstract the sense of war, the more it becomes a play of words and less a contest in which real human beings lose their lives. For his Chamberlain and Longstreet, each caught by rank and temperament midway between modern grunt and antique field marshal, the conflict is acute, and thrusts both into a future not yet (in 1863) known as fully to his characters as it was to Shaara himself. Both Longstreet and Chamberlain struggle for an adequate feeling for what they have done and seen. In the context of the mid-1970s, the acuteness with which Shaara places these characters at odds with remembered warfare argues that a modern war probably cannot be fought with such "love" and "beauty."

As the southern army limps back across the Pennsylvania state line, Chamberlain surveys the site of so much bloodshed and his own bloodlust. Without his heedless but heroic charge that saved the Union position on Little Round Top (for which the historical Chamberlain won the Medal of Honor), the Battle of Gettysburg might have ended differently. Shaara's fictional Chamberlain feels full and sympathetic comradeship with the Rebel soldiers he has so recently tried to kill. His reaction is not unlike that of Walt Whitman, who reports in *Specimen Days* of feeling a great homosocial, sacramental aura on recently vacated battlegrounds where the dead still ooze blood and men fatally wounded cry out in vain for help. What the hallowing of the battlefield means, Chamberlain muses, will have to be postponed until a time in the future when the war is over and he can visit Gettysburg not as a field of battle but as a site of memory (M. Shaara 351). Of course, such a moment had arrived when *The Killer Angels* was published. In photographs and text Geoffrey Ward describes the fiftieth reunion of northern and southern veterans at Gettysburg in 1913. As southern survivors of Pickett's Charge hobbled on crutches and canes toward Union lines, they eventually fell into the arms of their victorious foes "re-united in brotherly love and affection" (Ward, *Civil War* 412). By having Chamberlain postpone meaning until memory begins, Shaara elides the moral questions of the present war, Vietnam, and suggests that wars are never over until they are remembered, that history is not the past—memory is.

JIMMY CARTER (1976–1980)

As the first southern president of the United States since Woodrow Wilson (Thomas W. Dixon's former classmate and promoter of *The Birth of a Nation*)[7], Jimmy Carter might have been expected to play a more nuanced part in the drama of the Vietnam War and southern memory than midwesterner Gerald Ford. But, whereas the bitter southern memory of civil war and reconstruction was a professional concern for Wilson as historian and politician, Carter distanced himself from Old South memory:

> Many older Georgians still remembered vividly the anger and embarrassment of their parents, who had to live under the domination of carpetbaggers and their Southern allies, who were known as scalawags. . . . My mother was the only one in her family who ever spoke up to defend Abraham Lincoln. I don't remember ever hearing slavery mentioned, only the unwarranted violation of states' rights and the intrusion of the federal government in the private lives of citizens. Folks never considered that the real tragedy of Reconstruction was its failure to establish social justice for the former slaves. The intense bitterness was mostly confined to our older relatives, who couldn't understand the

desire of some of us younger ones to look more into the future—or at least the present—instead of just the past. (*Hour* 18)

If Carter seized his southern identity in dealing with Vietnam, it was gingerly, less by means of heroic memory than by mirages of a southern liberalism he saw tending "into the future—or at least the present." He identified less with Lee than with the men in Lee's ranks. Carter laid claim to the nonaristocratic, rural, Scots-Irish alternative to cavalier heroism. "It seemed natural," he writes in *An Hour Before Daylight,* "for white folks to cherish our Southern heritage and cling to our way of life, partially because the close ties among many of our local families went back another hundred years before the war, when our Scotch-Irish ancestors had come to Georgia from the British Isles, or moved south and west, mostly from Virginia and the Carolinas" (18). In all of Carter's acts of ancestor memory, he keeps warrior culture at arm's length. Indeed, in 1978, during protracted Camp David talks with Egyptian president Anwar Sadat and Israeli prime minister Menachem Begin, Carter scheduled a field trip to Gettsyburg. Carter was reasonably sure that Sadat got the message that the American president "as a Southerner could understand what it meant to be involved in a terrible war, and also knew how difficult it was to rebuild both material things and the spirit of a people after a recognized defeat" (*Keeping Faith* 389). He wanted to project the image of honest broker and wise heart in the Arab-Israeli strife—a defeated warrior, if warrior at all. About Begin, Carter was not so sure, for the Israeli prime minister seemed more interested in how tactics in the American Civil War lagged behind weapons technology. What Carter did not tell the visitors was that weeks earlier he had called upon Shelby Foote to brief him on the battle, lest he have only his own memory to go on (*Keeping Faith* 371–72). What Carter did not fully appreciate, perhaps, was the extent to which militants on the Egyptian side still identified with the Lost Cause. Sadat was assassinated in 1981; making peace with Israel was his death sentence.

Carter occupies a skewed position in the scheme of cultural memory and political action in the era of Vietnam, juggling southern past(s) and post-Vietnam future. A southerner striving to make his cultural identity relevant in world affairs, Carter was always taxed by the knowledge that one version of his identity (its racism) could be a burden. A second significant part, the memory of warrior heroism, seemed inaccessible to him. Southern cultural memory and identity, eventually, did Carter little good: his presidency was doomed by an Islamist revolution in Iran in 1979.

Jimmy Carter's approach to Vietnam as a cultural condition fraternal to his southern identity varied. As governor of Georgia when Lt. William Calley was convicted of war crimes at My Lai, Carter "declared 'American Fighting Man's Day' and issued a proclamation urging Georgians to display the flag and turn their automobile headlights on during the day" (Drew 133). In his memoir of four years as president, however, Carter uses a less bellicose language. Unlike Gerald Ford's lean in the direction of amnesia, Carter prompted Americans to remember the war in Vietnam as "national defeat," and acknowledged government "lies" in shaping policy in Vietnam (*Keeping Faith* 125, 143). He was also under the impression, probably prematurely if not overpiously, that the "wounds of our war in Vietnam" had been healed by his election (*Keeping Faith* 389–90).

In the summer of 1979, at a particularly low point in a presidency dominated by a permanent ebb, Carter made a speech commemorating Veterans Week. In a White House ceremony he declared, "[T]he nation is ready to change its heart, its mind and its attitude about the men who had fought in the war" (*Time* 11 June 1979, 21). "We love you for what you were and what you stood for," Carter continued, "and we love you for what you are and what you stand for." It is difficult to gauge how presidential language of love and acceptance could, in the pressurized decade of defeat and shame, counter the immense cultural weight of the Vietnam-ized stereotype of the U.S. soldier. Just before John Rambo (Sylvester Stallone) walks away from the camera in the closing frames of *First Blood* (1982), he says he only wants to be loved by his fellow Americans as he has loved America. But, then, he has shot up a lot of America by the end of that movie and the previous film installment of the Rambo saga. One of the veterans in attendance at the Carter speech complained that most Americans still looked upon Vietnam veterans as "Lieut. Calley types, crazed psychos or dummies that couldn't find their way to Canada. That really hurts when you remember the pride we had. We fought hard and we fought well" (*Time* 21). Whether or not Carter's rhetoric of communal and patriotic love reconnected the community with the warriors it had sent forth, the rhetoric itself is a trace of Carter's indebtedness to southern honor in its nostalgia for reintegration of warrior and community.

The year Carter was elected, 1976, was also the year of the publication of Gen. William C. Westmoreland's apologia for U.S. defeat in Vietnam, *A Soldier*

Reports. In *Vietnam and the Southern Imagination* (1992), Owen Gilman reads Westmoreland's memoir in two registers, national and southern:

> Westmoreland comes close to embodying the perfect image of the southern warrior, a stance of honor demonstrated by virtue of service to country, although by the time he completed his military service in 1972, he felt obliged to tell his own story because, in the minds of many Americans, his honor had been severely questioned, most fully in a CBS news documentary concerning his role in managing information about enemy troop strength in the year preceding the 1968 Tet offensive. (25)

By the end of the decade (1979), the release of *Apocalypse Now* had helped to fix in the popular mind the image of the American warrior (southerner included) as a demented killer: in the Francis Ford Coppola film it is not only Kurtz who has lost touch with reality, but "the generals back in Nha Trang" who have lost control of the "insanity and murder" on battlefields they, apparently, barely visit.[8] In *A Soldier Reports,* Westmoreland staked his (southern) warrior honor against this image; if he did not entirely lose his wager, neither did he win.

Since Westmoreland's memoir is given over to his immensely detailed justification of his command in Vietnam (explaining, perhaps, the severe limitation of attention to his childhood and youth in his memoir), readers encounter little of the southern cultural formation in warrior honor that made a military career his destiny. Still, Westmoreland was a South Carolinian, and a particular southern imprint is clear. He claims a great uncle who fought under Lee at Gettysburg (Westmoreland 12). At West Point during Westmoreland's cadet career in the early 1930s, the commandant was Lt. Col. Simon Bolivar Buckner, son of Confederate general Simon Bolivar Buckner, who surrendered Fort Donelson to U. S. Grant in 1862. Buckner *père* was not an unalloyed example of the southern military ideal, although in his memory of West Point Westmoreland never connects the son, Lieutenant Colonel Buckner, to the father. It came to the elder Buckner to surrender to Grant because Confederate commanders of the fort senior to him declined to do so and decamped. Nathan Bedford Forrest, more or less always an independent commander, also led his cavalry out of Fort Donelson rather than surrender. Buckner, an old friend of Grant's who had known the Union general in earlier times, saw no way to break the Union siege without needless loss of life (Ward, *Civil War* 96–7). Grant, relatively new to command himself in 1862, offered the only terms he could recall from the field manual: unconditional surrender. It was because Buckner accepted that Grant acquired the *nom de guerre* "Unconditional Surrender" Grant.

As a warrior, however, Westmoreland was less interested in the ironies of history than he was in monolithic categories of behavior and identity. He could have lived in the Old South Wyatt-Brown describes. One of the foundational beliefs that bound him to West Point and to his identity as an officer is the image of the virtuous warrior. "An officer corps," he writes, "must have a code of ethics that tolerates no lying, no cheating, no stealing, no immorality, no killing other than that recognized under international rules of war and essential for the military victory" (Westmoreland 11). This virtuous "officer corps" is lifted above and beyond the vicissitudes of historical circumstance by the ancient mythology of *le chevalier sans peur et sans reproche.* Gen. Douglas MacArthur, a clear career model for Westmoreland, voiced this mythology during a visit to West Point. Cadet Westmoreland was in the assembly, and he quotes the "old soldier": "The military code that you perpetuate . . . has come down to us from even before the age of knighthood and chivalry. It will stand the test of any code of ethics or philosophy" (11). Westmoreland echoed his hero's belief in a history beyond history when, much later in his *Report,* he explains the meaning of military medals: "The importance of medals is indicated by the tradition of wearing them over the heart, which can be traced to medieval times when the Crusaders wore the Christian cross, symbol of their fight to free the Holy Land from Islam" (305). Perhaps because he held such a long view of his identity and the meaning of his actions as a soldier—a view particularly southern in its leanings toward chivalry and Christian symbolism—Westmoreland could not see the circumstances on the ground in Vietnam through the mythmaking apparatus he used to interpret them. For instance, when it became clear through press reports and widespread images of burning huts that the tactics called "search and destroy" had acquired an undesirable set of associations, Westmoreland did not change the tactics but rather ordered the name changed to "reconnaissance in force" (83).

General Westmoreland was a product of the fully mythologized and conventionalized identity category of American soldier—an officer and a gentleman with a southern pedigree. If Wyatt-Brown's paradigmatic man of warrior honor ever existed in the flesh, it was Westmoreland. And if ever one needed evidence of the anachronism of that type in the twentieth century, that was Westmoreland too. Clearly, his southern formation and history fitted him backward into the continuity of Civil War memory. His identity had been, in other words, aged over time in a certain type of regional, cultural cask. It was possible for him to believe, without irony, that his "code of ethics"—as naïve as it might echo today—was in fact achievable on any field of battle. The war it was Westmoreland's misfortune to walk into in 1967 when he assumed command in Vietnam proved to be a historical event stronger than the myth or set of conventions he deployed to digest it. Westmoreland was trapped in the cultural no-man's-land between an official memory that prescribed and legitimized a certain identity and a historical present that, to echo *Apocalypse Now,* terminated all access to that identity with "extreme prejudice."

Still, the memory of honor in the past summoned by a southern soldier thrust into Vietnam proved to be a powerful plot. James Webb's novel *Fields of Fire* (1978) revises Westmoreland's portrait of warrior officer and corps. Whereas Westmoreland had invested heavily in the ritual and symbolism of the warrior caste—its medals and uniforms, jargon and hierarchy—Webb minimizes the trappings and symbols in favor of direct address to kin communities of memory.[9] Webb's warriors are the Scots-Irish ancestors Carter invoked—less likely to be moved by cultural symbolism pinned to a uniform than they are by deeply felt currents of kin identification.

Some comparisons with James Jones's iconic World War II novel, *From Here to Eternity* (1952), are helpful here because the two novels so strongly mirror each other. Like all novels in the genre (e.g., *The Red Badge of Courage, A Farewell to Arms, The Naked and the Dead*), both *From Here to Eternity* and *Fields of Fire* trigger habits of reading basic to community membership: the American youth or novice comes of age through his initiation into barracks life, which segregates him within an exclusively male, aggressively homosocial version of civilian domesticity. The female (even his mother, in the case of Henry Fleming in *The Red Badge of Courage*) is marginalized, even stigmatized. The novice is blooded in battle. Facing death, he finds that almost none of his civilian vocabulary is relevant. Coming home proves to be almost as wrenching as going away.[10] *Fields of Fire,* like other novels in the genre, conventionalizes its war, Vietnam, with the basic formula distilled from earlier wars. But more important, both *From Here to Eternity* and *Fields of Fire* ask readers to supply an extra, acquired cultural knowledge of "southern" to the basic mix.

Both *Fields of Fire* and *From Here to Eternity* assemble a barracks or company of American men from a range of regions and classes reflecting the conventional social mapping of the warrior brotherhood. In Jones's novel—accurate to its pre–Pearl Harbor setting—no African Americans are present in G Company at Schofield Barracks. The only black American marginally present is the unseen man who plays echo trumpet to Prewitt at Arlington National Cemetery (Jones 36). In both novels the men are subjected to military initiation and training (on duty and off), and take on (or fend off) relationships of friendship, mentorship, hatred, and role modeling with their backs turned to civilian life. The men of *From Here to Eternity* are not subjected to enemy attack until the final pages, when Japanese planes attack Pearl Harbor on December 7, 1941. In many ways not a moment too soon, for Jones's peacetime army is not very successful at molding the "natural" rivalries in a group of Slavs, Italians, Jews, Irish, and one coal-country southerner (Prewitt) into a phalanx of ideal warriors. *Fields of Fire*, on the other hand, is dominated by killing action from the start; the "*Pequod* crew" of the rifle squad in Webb's novel are "buddies" in-country from the outset of the novel.

Southern regional identity shapes both novels, for in both the central character is named for General Robert E. Lee: Robert E. Lee Prewitt (Jones) and Robert E. Lee Hodges (Webb).[11] Webb's Hodges (like Webb himself) is formed by strong ancestral memory of warriors stretching back from World War II (in which the author's father served) to the Revolution and even earlier to the nearly mythic Scots-Irish who fought the British before emigrating to the American South. Hodges's cultural memory almost perfectly duplicates Chick Mallison's in Faulkner's *Intruder in the Dust* (1948). Whereas Chick finds ancestral memory both enabling and confining (and ultimately decides that he must depart from "his people's" racial mores), Webb's Hodges finds (or hopes to find) only enabling energy in memories of his Scots-Irish kin. In quick succession we are informed that Hodges has a "Rebel ancestor," visits kin who live on ground where "Jackson's people fought," and lost three ancestors in Pickett's Charge (Webb 22, 23, 26). All or most of this lore is told to the young man by his grandmother, who remembers family history all the way back to the seizing of the land from the Cherokee (25). Hodges collects these memories on the eve of shipping out to Vietnam—plot timing that suggests, as Wyatt-Brown in fact declares, that assuming the warrior identity means simultaneously assuming the kin-community's collective persona and history. That communal persona, Webb implicitly argues, is more genuine than the one Westmoreland envisioned for the "officer corps" he idealized. For Webb's Hodges, warrior identity or persona is not a vehicle for affirming lofty traditions, transferring identity from the age of knighthood, and preserving social privilege and symbolism from place or region in "the corps." It is rather a ritualized opportunity for shedding blood so as to earn an even more intimate tie to place and people. Glory, for Hodges, is real; it dwells in "whole rows of men . . . felled" at Gettysburg (26). "It was the fight that mattered, not the cause. It was the endurance that was important, the will to face certain loss, unknown danger, unpredictable fate" (28). So vital is this masculinist, regionalized, and thanatopic test that, for Hodges, "If there had been no Vietnam, he would have had to invent one. . . . But there was Vietnam, and so there would be honor" (29). Here, Webb's novel sets a trap. What Hodges expects and needs from battle in Vietnam we (readers) already know (in 1978 and later) he will not get. In *Fields of Fire,* death is more certain than honor.

James Jones's Robert E. Lee Prewitt is a similar southerner in a very different war. Even though Prewitt is a southerner, James Jones (who was not) distances him from the regional warrior tradition. Prewitt's South is the coal country of Kentucky's Appalachia. Webb's Hodges comes from the same general region, but Prewitt's heroes are Harlan County miners, labor-warriors rather than anticolonial rebels. His ancestral hero is an uncle who fought against Philippine insurgents and learned enough about military violence there (or about his real class loyalties?) not to enlist for "the Great War" in 1916 (Jones 14–16). Southern warrior tradition in *From Here to Eternity* is further stripped of content by the way Jones deploys the genteel southerner Lieutenant Culpeper, "a little man, shorter than Prewitt," full of a sense of entitlement to his "2nd Lieutenant's bars" and his West Point privilege (56). "Culpeper," a Virginia place name redolent of engagements in Lee's campaigns, becomes the name of a Westmoreland-like tradition of officer privilege threatening to artificialize the masculine community of warriors. Jones's Culpeper, "son of Brigadier Culpeper, grandson of Lt. General Culpeper, great grandson of Lt. Col. Culpeper, C.S.A.," is more interested in his golf game and parties at the Officers Club than the manly arts of soldiering represented by the novel's hero, and Prewitt's would-be mentor, Sgt. Milt Warden (51). To indict Culpeper and the false tradition he clearly embodies, Jones depicts Culpeper's defense of Prewitt in a legal action as his narcissistic preoccupation with symbols. Adorned with a new yellow leather briefcase and a matching Parker 51 pen and pencil set, Culpeper advises Prewitt to plead guilty, with the explanation that he was drunk and could not control himself. Prewitt refuses; "I aint guilty," he says. "And I aint going to plead guilty. Not even if it would mean a full acquittal" (513–516, 516). Warden admires Prewitt's natural honor; Culpeper sees only the groupthink of the army from the top down.

Webb's Hodges is belched into Vietnam as a marine lieutenant, and meets his squad in a geographically (and historically) ominous region: the An Hoa basin in which the "hamlet" of My Lai is located, a place within a place in the cultural mapping of Vietnam. The squad in *Fields of Fire* functions in the novel similarly to G Company in *From Here to Eternity:* both embrace a cross-section of American male experience and identity, aim to train away regional and class differences to create a new democratic man and effective killer. Even though Webb's novel contains no training scenes (and Jones's is full of the monotony of base routine), *Fields of Fire* "includes" that subject matter by intertextual short-hand: Hodges's favorite movie hero is Sergeant Stryker, played by John Wayne in *The Sands of Iwo Jima.* Stryker weans young men from overbearing mothers and fathers, provides cowards the sacrament of restitution, and hallows all his cultural work by dying of a sniper's bullet after victory has been achieved and the American flag is raised on Mount Suribachi.[12] The plot outline of *The Sands of Iwo Jima* may be hackneyed, but its insertion into *Fields of Fire* is not. Lurking in the dense foliage of southern and Vietnam arrays of reference, the film reference subtly destabilizes Webb's obvious sincerity by adding at least one replica to all of the genuine sources of Hodges's character.

Hodges tries to lead his squad in Vietnam with the honor he assumes he will find in himself no matter the circumstances. Like his namesake, who issued a field order forbidding the Army of Virginia from plundering farms in Pennsylvania on the way to Gettysburg, Robert E. Lee Hodges orders a member of his squad to return a pair of shorts, taken as a souvenir, to the Vietnamese woman who owned them (Webb 85). When a fellow marine officer helicopters in just to touch the "field of fire" and earn combat verification, Hodges lectures him on the responsibilities of true leadership (288).

But Hodges's drive for strength and meaning in southern warrior memory (171) is inevitably defeated by Vietnam. Before he even leaves the fire base, his major tells him: "Nothing in your entire goddamned life will have prepared you for the bush. Not a damn thing. . . . You'll go wild, too. Wild as hell. You spend a month in the bush and you're not a Marine anymore. Hell. You're not even a god-damn person" (58, 59). Honorable warfare does disintegrate. Members of Hodges's squad wound a Vietnamese woman who had crept out of the bunker to which she was ordered during a fire fight. Another shoots a wounded

NVA sapper who is making too much noise and thereby drawing fire on the squad. Still another kills a Vietnamese man riding a bicycle before ascertaining whether he is or is not a combatant.

More generally, there is simply no way to measure whether your side is winning or losing. The ground literally dissolves into paddies and "bush"; the "enemy" wears no uniform or insignia. One member of the squad, nicknamed Senator because he had dropped out of Harvard to serve in Vietnam, confronts the "horror" of the vacuum where honor loses its meaning and its history: "When meaning becomes purely personal, so does glory. No great cause. It makes less and less sense" (100).

Hodges is wounded, heals, and returns to his squad. He is eventually killed in combat. Both Jones and Webb, apparently, can find no comfortable place in a postwar world for their Lee namesakes. Hodges leaves a Japanese wife and a son who never met his father but wants to be a marine and a warrior as he watches American soldiers on Okinawa, where he was conceived and born. Nearly all the other members of Hodges's rifle squad are killed, in one or another meaningless way: one is surprised and killed by an NVA sapper while masturbating; "Snake," an inner-city black man who had found in Vietnam redeeming comradely value for his street smarts, does not make it home. Senator survives, although one of his legs is amputated. He returns home struggling with a fierce moral ambiguity the war has only intensified. When organizers of an antiwar demonstration, very similar to the Dewey Canyon protests of 1971, ask him to speak to the protestors, among whom are many veterans, he cannot come to terms with survivor's dilemma: he wants the killing to stop but feels that aligning himself with the demonstrators would be treason to his buddies (331).[13] Only Forrest Gump, the "idiot" of Winston Groom's novel (1986), can live with the contradictions of Vietnam; he has no cultural memory of belonging to any past.

For Webb's Hodges, though, the only alternative to honor is death. Going into a fight for the first time, Hodges prays not to the Christian God but to his ancestors:

> All my life I've waited for this, he mused. Now I've joined you and your losses are a strength to me. I ache and yet I know that Alec retched with pain on the dust road that went to Corinth [after the Battle of Shiloh, April 1862]. I breathe the dust and yet I know that Grandpa breathed the gas that made a hero out of Pershing. I flinch when bullets tear the air in angry rents and yet I know that

Father, and three farm boys at Pickett's Charge felt a cutting edge that dropped them dead. How can I be bitter? You are my strength, you ghosts. (171)

It was not membership in Westmoreland's chivalric officer corps that gave Hodges honor amid the chaos of Vietnam. Rather it was the memory of (and longing for) suffering and death among ancestors that made honor possible. Webb's predecessor James Jones held no brief for the institutional army either. If there is no automatic honor in the officer corps in *From Here to Eternity*, there is honor, commemorated not by insignia and symbols but by death itself, as Prewitt's death in a sandtrap proves when he tries to return to G Company after sleeping through a hangover and the December 7 attack. He dies "a soldier," turning to face the machine gun rather than be shot in the back, and he passes up the chance to fire back, an ultimate, honorable choice: "They [the sentries who shoot him] were the Army, too. And how could a man kill a soldier for just simply doing a sound competent job?" (Jones 789).

Jones's novel was a model for another Vietnam War novel with a southern accent in 1978: Winston Groom's *Better Times Than These*. Better known for *Forrest Gump* (1986), Groom in his first novel pays outright homage to Jones—he, along with Groom's father, "who served in a different war in different times," is named in the dedication. *Better Times Than These* hews to genre specifications: a numerous, diverse group of American men leave behind civilian lives, hometowns, marriages, and loves to become soldiers, some willingly, some half-willingly, some simply compelled by the draft. The novel follows Bravo Company, part of the semifictitious Fourth Regiment of the U.S. Army's Seventh Cavalry (Custer's doomed regiment), from embarkation in San Francisco in the late summer of 1966 through several months of fighting and dying in the Ia Drang Valley. The novel comes to a sonorous conclusion in February 1967.

The main character is a Jewish southerner from Savannah, Lt. William (Billy) Solomon Kahn, who has interrupted graduate studies in geology at Florida State University to join the army. As a lieutenant in command of a rifle company, Billy Kahn is driven through the paces of the novice soldier. He moves from huddled privacy in his thinking to loving identification with the men under his command; in the last battle the company fights for him, he bonds with them lovingly: "It didn't look good, but they were a tough bunch of boys, these boys of his" (Groom, *Better* 321). Michael Shaara's rendition of Joshua Chamberlain's brotherly bond with his "Maine men" is a similarly sublime gesture toward a war Vietnam never was.

Two of Kahn's "boys" are fellow southerners. One is African American, Private Carruthers, a black man from the low country whose accent is so strange to other officers that Kahn—because he too is a southerner—is called upon to translate. Not only are Carruthers and Kahn brothers in exclusion, as African American and Jew respectively in the white, gentile South, they also come from the same city, although as black and white southerners they do not know each other until they meet in uniform.

Another southerner in the novel is perhaps more redolent of southern stereotype. Pvt. Homer Crump, a lanky, slow-talking Mississippian who recalls his momma's voice in tight situations, foreshadows his more famous successor, Forrest Gump. Crump, however, is not "a idiot" but rather a southern type with a long genealogy, a Deerslayer or Sargeant York. Crump is the first of Bravo Company to kill a Vietnamese (whether the victim is a soldier or not is ambiguous), by calling upon his deer-hunting experience (Groom, *Better* 151). Like Ike McCaslin in Faulkner's *Go Down, Moses,* Crump survives in the Vietnamese rain forest through a combination of woodcraft and native cunning. Crump is socially at home in-country because the peasants he encounters on patrol remind him vividly of the poor whites and blacks he knew in his native Tupelo (121). Homer Crump, however, is no simple bumpkin. Gump's Medal of Honor is undercut by a wound to his buttocks; Crump leads his platoon out of a potential mutiny but dies in a later fight when his position is overrun by the North Vietnamese.

Kahn's gradually developing brotherhood with his Yankee counterpart, Lt. Col. Francis Holden of New York, scion of a long WASP social and military heritage, ironically reprises the intersectional romance of Reconstruction fiction. Kahn feels no southern historical or cultural heritage urging him to the battlefield. Indeed, until he is fired upon he has no answer to the interior question why he feels compelled to go to Vietnam; the interior voices he hears come from his father and uncle, who advise him to keep an eye open for business ventures while he is on the battlefield. Absurdly, he finds one. Holden, on the other hand, has generations of family military service pushing him out of the comfortable life of Princeton graduate and Ivy League tennis star. The two men reflect the lovers of the intersectional romance of Reconstruction.

Holden begins with the relatively safe duty of aide to the lieutenant colonel in command of the sector, and then is "promoted" to the field as Kahn's executive officer. While Kahn is away from the fire base facing court-martial for criminal acts committed by another officer while Kahn was on patrol, the NVA and Viet Cong in a Tet-like offensive kill Holden and most of the company. Kahn returns to find his command all but wiped out. Seething with guilt, rage, and shame, Kahn upbraids his commanding officer, and threatens to bring him before a board of inquiry for persistently refusing to consider tactics that would have prevented the over-running of the American position. The lieutenant colonel buys off Kahn's threats with an offer of early discharge. Kahn accepts, the prospect of more "meaningless" killing being more than he can tolerate (Groom, *Better* 221).

Kahn's rebirth begins with Holden's funeral in a Manhattan church, a scene that uncannily mimics the wedding scene that culminates so many plots of Reconstruction romance.[14] Kahn's attendance symbolically and thematically "weds" Christian (the Holden family is Episcopalian) and Jewish, northern and southern traditions into one American tradition. With apparent effort, Groom aims for the conclusion of his novel to reach a cathartic unity in the wake of the massive disintegration of Vietnam. Pathetic fallacy plays its part. In *A Farewell to Arms*, Hemingway has Frederic Henry walk away in a famous, rainy pathetic fallacy that signifies sorrow, confusion, and the lowering of the horizon of meaning for war and glory and honor. Groom furnishes Holden's funeral service with a more hopefully bright but "cold February sun" (411). The organ music accompanying the service achieves "a huge radiant burst" (410) that is meant perhaps to drown out remembered bursts of M-16s and mortar fire. The soloist's voice is "[c]lear and sweet," and Kahn himself sheds a tear while rising from his pew to salute the coffin of his comrade. Kahn will never forget Vietnam, but he will not be disabled by his memory: "He [Kahn] knew he could go home now to the life that lay in front of him—even though the biggest thing that probably would ever happen was already behind him" (410). *Better Times Than These*, like *From Here to Eternity* and *Fields of Fire*, concludes with a dismembered wedding; only one half of the romantic couple survives, unpartnered, widowed, ambiguous. The procreative future is compromised.

Two novels by southern women, Bobbie Ann Mason's *In Country* (1985) and Jayne Anne Phillips's *Machine Dreams* (1984), take up the crippled romance from the point of view of women excluded from the masculine warrior myth, Vietnam version, but necessary in a patriarchal imagination to the marriage plot. Both novels are cited as texts in which southern memory overrides the boundaries of gender. Richard Gray, in *Web of Words: The Great Dialogue of Southern Literature* (2007), asserts that Mason's main character, Samantha (Sam) Hughes, works through the recovery of the memory of her father in Vietnam by appropriating his experience in a way that organically connects her to the southern past, and to an extent regenders her as male. She reads a diary sent home from Southeast Asia among her father's meager effects, tries to duplicate his experience "in-country" by isolating herself in a local wetland overnight, and finally achieves emotional closure at the Vietnam Veterans Memorial, where she traces his name in the stone with her finger. But my contention throughout this chapter, and the book of which it is a part, is that cultural memory inhabits forms (as well as words, imagery, and symbols) in asymmetrical ways, and the romance is particularly susceptible to intricate meanings. In this frame, then, just as Billy Kahn's attendance at Holden's funeral mobilizes the marriage form as the subtextual conclusion to *Better Times Than These,* Mason's and Phillips's novels conclude more obviously.

Sam's androgynous nickname and her breakthrough to her dead father lead Gray to suspect that gender divisions are abolished by certain formal iterations of cultural memory. "Imitating her father [by isolating herself in the woods all night]," Gray suggests,

> is beginning to teach her—although, of course, she cannot put it in these terms —that male and female are not static absolutes but multiple, fluid construction. The bounds between male and female are so porous, so permeable, Sam discovers, that, on close inspection, they can even begin to disappear. Mason, in effect, rewrites male ritual as a kind of androgynous ceremony or, to be more accurate, as a celebration of the sexually unspecific character of certain primal experiences like the search for the primitive. The ritual becomes a function of a common human need, a shared longing, not one that belongs to either men or women. (*Web* 53–54)

Gray locates the knowledge Sam acquires formally in the "wilderness tale" (56), a narrative form that appears in literary texts as the whole or a part; in southern writing, perhaps the most well known is Ike McCaslin's coming-of-age in

Faulkner's "The Bear" by venturing into the big woods without compass, rifle, or timepiece.

After Sam's long and fearful night in the local wildlife preserve, she is frightened by an intruder, a "Viet Cong," who turns out to be, in fact, her Uncle Emmitt, her mother's brother, the self-described "damaged" Vietnam vet (Mason 225) who has, in ways perhaps both conscious and subconscious, tried to reverse the inevitable habits of masculinity that shoved him into Vietnam in the first place. Sometimes Emmitt wears a skirt, and he spends a lot of time in his kitchen, the traditional domestic space of the woman. But it is not just the suggestion of gender recrimination that mars the "celebration" in *In Country*; it is Emmitt himself. Retrieving Sam from the artificial Vietnam of the local woods, Emmitt tells her a blunt fact: "You can't learn from the past. The main thing you learn from history is that you can't learn from history. That's what history is" (Mason 226).

In *In Country*, what Sam learns from, finally, is culture, and what her southern culture teaches her is that Vietnam has done such deep and perhaps irreparable damage to the masculine hegemony on which that set of ethics and behaviors (the base for Wyatt-Brown's assertion about "the South") was founded, that she must, for her own survival, forge a separate self that has less to do with merging male and female than learning to do without the former. Her boyfriend Lonnie suffers from a particularly low horizon of expectation, and an underwear fetish. When Sam tries to have sex with another vet, he is impotent. Sam concludes that both Emmitt and her impotent lover need penis implants (130). But the problem is beyond the help of prosthetic devices.

Like her avatar, Scarlett O'Hara, Sam paradoxically benefits from a war that wipes out a goodly portion of the male population and exposes the traditional role of women in that culture as the velvet prison that it is. As much as Sam seeks her father in the novel, it is the recognition that she does not want to become her mother—or a woman like her—that defines the success of Sam's quest. She sees her mother feeding her new baby and becomes depressed; she compares her best friend Dawn's pregnancy to seizure by body snatchers (155–56). When she finally gets to the Vietnam Memorial in part three of the novel and finds her father's name on the wall, Sam is not finished. Her finger traces another name on the stone, coincidentally her own and the name of another dead soldier, and in the polished surface she sees her own face. She is not her father's daughter, but herself. Unlike Gray, I see this moment not as embracing a common human need but as rejecting a specific male and southern one: the need to take up a weapon and kill, or die, as the ritual that entitles the apprentice male to memory and privilege only by spilling blood. In other words, a spouse does show up at the culminating "altar" of *In Country,* but it is Sam herself, testing a new formal configuration of the romance.

Jayne Anne Phillips's *Machine Dreams* (1984) is an even harsher indictment of the warrior hegemony in southern memory. *Machine Dreams* is a family saga, covering three generations of the same bloodline in a small West Virginia town. The father's generation fights World War II, the son's fights Vietnam. In the Vietnam generation, Danner (her name just as androgynous as Sam's) and Billy Hampson are sister and brother who come of age during the 1960s. As they watch their parents' marriage crumble, exposing the inherent (but never overtly exercised) violence in their father, they also come to terms with the moral and cultural crises of Vietnam. Danner becomes openly antiwar. Like Sam, she hangs out with Vietnam veterans and takes (and, perhaps more important, disposes of) lovers from time to time from among the organizers of demonstrations. She even borrows money to finance her brother's flight to Canada when, in the lottery of December 1969, he draws a low number.

But Billy won't go to Canada, and enlists instead. His motives, as Phillips outlines them, are far from heroic. In fact, Billy's "motives" barely rise above self-destructive fatalism. "Supposedly they'd [the government that had established the draft lottery] set up the war, too, but Billy wasn't sure. He didn't know histories or politics—he didn't need to know. Knowing wouldn't change what was going to happen. It had no more to do with him than this bus ride . . ." (Phillips 278–79). Ceding his moral conscience to the state, Billy Hampson feels a kind of sublime fulfillment high above the killing fields as the door gunner in a helicopter. If the southern warrior of traditional memory was something of a chivalric hero, then his reincarnation in Billy Hampson as Vietnam warrior is the end of that memory:

Now that I know I'm going to Nam, I would just as soon go, [he writes to his sister] stop thinking and waiting. Probably when I get there the only familiar thing will be the gun and I will be feeling like holding on to it. It's nothing like John Wayne or that show we used to watch after school—what was it?—*12 O'Clock High.* Used to love that show and the bomber jackets. When you get finished firing fourteen rounds on an M-60, you get this vibration in your body that's like the *ack-ack* of the ammo, except it's silent, and a hot flash like a drug hit as you step away. (323–24)

With orgasmic aftershocks from an M-60, who needs a human lover? Who needs any society at all except the "horribly typical" brotherhood of killers? Phillips's invocation of the southern warrior in his Vietnam incarnation is an example of the "intertextuality" that Richard Gray proposes (*Web* 17), but not necessarily the positive one we would like. Phillips calls up the facet of southern warrior memory that Walker Percy's Will Barrett, in *The Last Gentleman* (1966), fends off as one would a deadly toxin: "Southerners have trouble ruling out the possible. What happens to a man to whom all things seem possible and every course of action open? Nothing of course. Except war. If a man lives in the sphere of the possible and waits for something to happen, what he is waiting for is war—or the end of the world. That is why Southerners like to fight and make good soldiers" (Percy 10).

Later in Percy's career, the southern male propensity for death-dealing became apocalyptic in *The Thanatos Syndrome* (1987). What novelists Mason and Phillips point out, writing about southern warrior memory from the margins to which the feminine is banished, is the narcissism and death at its ritualized core. Gray asserts, hopefully, that "[e]ven an event like the Vietnam war can be lived through, risen above," if the novelist imagines "in the long reach of time" (*Web* 21). But I am not so sure that "the long reach" in the southern novel of Vietnam grasps much more than an empty form and a devalued memory. Gray's conclusion about the direction of history and memory in *Machine Dreams*:

The loss of Billy [son and brother, missing in action in Vietnam in 1970] is traumatic and definitive for the family and its individual members. But it is placed in a longer sweep of time, tangible history and intangible memory, that, while in no way extenuating the trauma, sees human destiny in terms of rising and falling, flow and ebb, the impulse to ascend into the sky and the inevitable, often abrupt return to earth. The references, in the several epigraphs in the novel, to the myth of Pegasus . . . . perhaps alert us to this pattern, this structure of significance lying behind a moment, shadowing the present in an apparently immeasurable past. Even without those references, however, any reader of other southern literature will be able to take the measure of what Phillips is doing here and throughout *Machine Dreams*. Vietnam is situated in a longer view, shadowed by the stories of other episodes of rise and fall. A "thick" description [Clifford Geertz had been acknowledged earlier] of Danner, of Billy, and their family would catch the signs of a commemorative, elegiac culture in which people may become empty halls echoing with sonorous, defeated names or destiny. . . . (*Web* 17)

Following my ellipsis, Gray appropriates Faulkner's description of the doomed Quentin Compson, then continues to quote an excerpt from Allen Tate's "Ode to the Confederate Dead" on memory. Gray's sense of "a commemorative, elegiac culture" is that it remembers by distancing disturbances (Vietnam) by means of an ever "longer sweep of time" operating through increasingly general images: "episodes of rise and fall," for example, beginning with Billy Hampson's fall and continuing back to the fall of Icarus. In my reading, this recessional view of literary memory thins rather than "thickens" the text. Thickening results when you recognize the continuity of history-and-memory, the reversibility of "tangible history" and "intangible memory" to become "tangible memory" and "intangible history."

RONALD REAGAN (1980–1988)

Post-traumatic stress disorder was added to the American Psychiatric Association's *Diagnostic and Statistical Manual of Mental Disorders* in 1980, the year Ronald Reagan, a man who occupied a curious space in the history-and-memory continuum, was elected president. Reagan campaigned on the slogan "Morning in America," and one of the fixtures of that new day was auto-absolution from the sins and nightmares of Vietnam. In a speech to the Veterans of Foreign Wars late in the summer of his first campaign, Reagan said:

> Let us tell those who fought in that war that we will never again ask young men to fight and possibly die in a war our government is afraid to win. . . . We dishonor the memory of 50,000 young Americans who died in that cause when we give way to feelings of guilt as if we were doing something shameful, and we have been shabby in our treatment of those who returned. . . . It is time we recognized that ours, in truth, was a noble cause. (Cannon 271)

Although Reagan insisted on Vietnam as a noble cause, he admitted to an interviewer during the campaign that "I was one who never believed we should have gone in" (Drew 175). Reagan's approach to the competing claims of history and memory was both simple and bold: he led a movement to replace history with myth. Whereas Ford used the language of amnesia, and Carter heeded the call of patriotic love, Reagan invoked national myth: Vietnam was not a war but a cause; we did not lose it, "our government" did. This bold disconnect—as if "we" and "our government" were not, in many strategic places, one and the same—characterizes the cultural atmosphere of "Reaganism" in the 1980s. A world of myth coexisted with a world of reality. One could claim Vietnam as a noble cause in one statement, and in another maintain that "we [never] should have gone in."

A book on the "Vietnam Syndrome" published early in the Reagan decade, *Self-Destruction: The Disintegration and Decay of the United States Army During the Vietnam Era* (1981), may serve as the "historical" pole of the chasm Reaganism sought to bridge with myth. *Self-Destruction* follows in the wake of the *Study on Military Professionalism* (1970), known as the Peers Report, ordered by General Westmoreland in response to the shock of self-recognition brought on by the My Lai crimes and trials. As read by Kendrick Oliver, in *The My Lai Massacre in American History and Memory* (2006), the Peers Report must have appalled Westmoreland, the MacArthur acolyte who believed so ardently in the officer corps: "Apparently," Oliver concludes, "many senior officers did not aspire to offer ethical leadership to their men, seeking only to serve the interests of their own careers" (244). *Self-Destruction* also documents the reality of the "broken" armed forces, the keystone of the "Vietnam Syndrome." "Cincinnatus," *nom de guerre* of the author of *Self-Destruction,* found the same flaw in the officer corps a decade later, and noted—with respect to the high level of careerism—that by the first of February 1971, over one million medals had been awarded to American troops for bravery in Vietnam ("Cincinnatus"158). Based on estimates of 2.8 million members of the armed forces serving tours in-country, more than one-third were decorated. This makes a stark contrast with the history of the Confederacy, which granted no medals at all but rather held service in arms in and of itself to be the mark of honor.

"Cincinnatus" was no less blunt about the site of blame for defeat in Vietnam. Defeat, he/she announced, was "brought about by the ineptness of its [the armed forces'] soldier leaders" ("Cincinnatus" 23). Complaints that "our government" interfered and snatched defeat from the embrace of victory are simply dismissed. If the strategy was flawed in the large-scale plans of the leaders, then tactics on the ground were even more mistaken. U.S. forces, "Cincinnatus" argued, had failed to "know the enemy" and persisted in conducting "big-unit" operations against a guerrilla "army" that seldom if ever materialized in the field ("Cincinnatus" [9]).[15] One of the "horrors" embodied in the character of Colonel Kurtz in *Apocalypse Now*—the horror gothically proclaimed in the film—is that Kurtz exposed the "big-unit" fixation of the air-conditioned generals by fielding a savage "army" of Montagnards whose battle "ethics" covered killing but not removing bodies and severed enemy heads from the field.

The ineptness of the U.S. command, "Cincinnatus" argues, preceded our entrance upon the battlefield. It began with a failure to prepare American soldiers for the kind of fighting they would have to perform. Hodges's major gives him similar ominous words of warning at the outset of Webb's *Fields of Fire*. "Cincinnatus" is more thorough: "American boys from cities and farms found themselves halfway around the world, living in an alien culture, fighting and dying in a cause they at best only half-understood. They saw their buddies 'blown away' or 'wasted' or maimed. They were repeatedly told they could trust no one—not the bar girl, nor the sidewalk peddler, nor the farmer. They must be on guard against six-year-old-children, for children of that age had been known to be armed and ready to kill" ("Cincinnatus" 98).

Between one extremity of ineptitude, criminal murder, and dementia and another in which "ours, in truth, was a noble cause" stretches a wide gulf. The period in U.S. cultural history coinciding with the two Reagan terms as president was a period of severe and polarizing cultural tension. Maya Lin's design for the Vietnam Veterans Memorial on the National Mall (dedicated on Veterans Day, 1982), for example, uses architectural design to compel face-to-face confrontation with the war. Yet opponents to the design, James Webb prominent among them, succeeded in erecting a figural countermemorial nearby which attempts to cast the war into the noble, heroic mode of past U.S. wars.

Winston Groom's *Forrest Gump* (1986), a picaresque farce to follow the historical realism of *Better Times Than These*, is a southern novel of the period that attempts to deal with Vietnam from this bipolar point of view. In *Better Times Than These*, Groom's Homer Crump personifies southern simplicity as purity, an Ike McCaslin in the highlands and rain forest of Southeast Asia. Crump, an efficient and even stoical killer, is simultaneously humane. When one of his buddies runs out of cash to show his girlfriend a good time, Crump donates his last dollar (Groom, *Better* 63). He is also innately respectful of authority: when his company hesitates to follow an order to attack, Crump is the first to lead them up to a hilltop they all know will be given back to the enemy in a few days or even hours (231). He goes through battles with a pet "banana cat" safe inside his shirt. The pet survives, Crump does not. Forrest Gump does not revise Homer Crump so much as he alters the frame for understanding what happened in Vietnam between the late 1970s and the late 1980s. Gump is the appropriate southern icon of this latter state of Vietnam memory, a Benjy Compson to succeed Ike McCaslin, because only "a idiot" can or will walk the tightrope between the romance and reality of Vietnam.[16]

As broadly farcical as Groom's Gump is, he is not without nuance. Although Forrest knows he is named for Confederate general Nathan Bedford Forrest, he also knows that he wants no part of Forrest's Klan associations; the guys in sheets are all "no-goods" even a simpleton can spot (Groom, *Gump* 2). Although Forrest is drafted for the first time in the fateful year 1968, his local draft board finds him "unqualified mentally" for military service—but not unqualified to play football for Bear Bryant (15). The joke turns back on the army when Forrest flunks out of the University of Alabama (although he does pass a course in advanced physics) and is sent to Fort Benning for basic training. "The one thing I remember from Fort Benning," Forrest reports, "is that they didn't seem to be nobody much smarter than I was, which was certainly a relief" (42).

In Vietnam, Forrest survives the contradictions that detonate in the minds of his predecessors in southern/Vietnam war fiction (Robert E. Lee Hodges, Billy Kahn, and others) simply because he does not think about them. The absurdity of trying to determine, using traditional means, who is winning fails to horrify Forrest: "It is gettin to be dark an we is tole to go up to a ridge and relieve Charlie Company which is either pinned down by the gooks or has got the gooks pinned down, dependin on whether you get your news from the *Stars and Stripes* or by just lookin aroun at what the hell is goin on" (50). A couple of buddies have their heads blown apart (54, 58); Forrest reports the casualties simply, without exclamation. He performs the heroic, but ultimately futile, rescue of Bubba with the same equanimity. It is the educated Lieutenant Dan who tries to make sense of the war, and for his pains Dan is not only physically maimed but psychologically damaged as well (63).

If war goes by Forrest in a bland blur, so does protest. Pulled into a demonstration modeled on the Dewey Canyon protests of 1971 by his girlfriend Jenny and her friends, Forrest throws away his Medal of Honor reluctantly (104). In *Better Times Than These,* stateside antiwar protest and sexual desire are similarly mixed. In the earlier novel Lt. Frank Holden is jealous of an older university professor from the Northeast who not only sleeps with the woman Holden wants for himself but also tutors her on the deceptions of the Vietnam War (Groom, *Better* 26). This professor turns out to be more sensitive (as Billy Kahn learns at Holden's funeral [*Better* 408]) than the stereotypical, manipulative, cynical propagandist of Webb's *Fields of Fire*, for example. In *Forrest Gump*, Groom returns to the generic situation of conflicted vet in an antiwar demonstration. Jenny and her friends in protest have little if any knowledge of or sensitivity for the ordeal Forrest has suffered (*Gump* 66), and Groom uses farce to evade the warrior's dilemma: Forrest flings his medal so hard it injures a guard, and Forrest is picked up for assault.

Forrest Gump suffers as both a protest and a war novel because Forrest himself seems to have little knowledge of what he has gone through—except insofar as it kills Bubba and maims Lieutenant Dan and keeps him far from Jenny. If Groom ended *Better Times Than These* with a forced and problematic upsurge of hope in the conflation of wedding and funeral, he ends *Forrest Gump* on a similar note of ambivalence. The nuclear family surviving Vietnam at the conclusion of *Forrest Gump* is not the rehabilitated trio of Forrest, Jenny, and little Forrest, but rather Forrest, Lieutenant Dan, and Sue—an orangutan. Lest we suspect anything non-normative in this ménage, Groom informs us that Forrest keeps "a waitress in one of the strip joints" to "ass aroun" with (*Gump* 228).

GEORGE H. W. BUSH (1988–1992)

In his inaugural address, January 20, 1989, George H. W. Bush called for an end to the Vietnam War in American memory: "We need compromise; we've had dissension. We need harmony; we've had a chorus of discordant voices. . . . It's been this way since Vietnam. That war cleaves us still. But, friends, that war began in earnest a quarter of a century ago; and surely the statute of limitations has been reached. This is a fact: The final lesson of Vietnam is that no great nation can long afford to be sundered by a memory" ("Transcript" 10). "Cleave" and "sunder" roll with biblical echoes. The first President Bush presented the Vietnam War as a too-long-remembered crime (what but a crime has a "statute of limitations"?) that the nation, for its own survival, must abjure. Like his predecessor Ronald Reagan, Bush used new wars—in Panama and Iraq—to cauterize wounds and memories of an earlier and ignoble one.

The sense of sundering or cleaving that plagues U.S. character, in its masculine gender, was further reflected in the contemporary popularity of "A Book About Men," *Iron John,* by Robert Bly (1990). Vietnam, as the elder Bush then calculated at least twenty-five years removed from its legitimate claim on national attention, figures in *Iron John* as one of the main traumas triggering a crisis in American masculinity. So does southern warrior memory. "The warriors inside American men," Bly writes, "have become weak in recent years, and their weakness contributes to a lack of boundaries, a condition which . . . we spoke of as naivete" (146).[17] Earlier in *Iron John,* Bly calls the malady, with a certain phallic echo, a kind of softness (2). The "soft male," emerging in the 1970s, Bly suggests, is a direct result of Vietnam trauma: "During the sixties, another sort of man appeared. The waste and violence of the Vietnam War made men question whether they knew what an adult male really was. If manhood meant Vietnam, did they want any part of it?" (2). The character Luke Martin, played by Jon Voight in *Coming Home* (1978), paralyzed from his waist down, is a figure of the hard male wounded (fortunately, in many ways) into "softer" behavior more sympathetic to women, less competitive with other men, and more pacific in his attitude to war. Feminism, Bly admits, accomplished a good bit of such gender revision, but Vietnam had its part to play in men "welcoming their own 'feminine' consciousness and nurturing it" (2). Men of this type are "lovely, valuable people—I like them," Bly admits, signaling—perhaps—just the opposite (2).[18]

Bly's prescription is "to bring the interior warriors back to life" (146). Swerving away from aggressive behavior—perhaps the kind that "encouraged the unbalanced pursuit of the Vietnam war" (2)—Bly calls for an interior warrior dedicated to defending borders. His historical precedent, not surprisingly in this context, comes from the borders of Britain, closely approximating the Scots-Irish fighters remembered by Carter, Webb, Faulkner, and others: "The Fianna, that famous band of warriors who defended Ireland's borders" (147). Closer to U.S. history, Bly recommends George S. Patton and warns us against Oliver North; the former could believe in "the holiness of the battlefield" while the latter served a "corrupt" king and cause (150).

Bly's recovery plan begins with the Civil War: "Some people believe that the conscious warrior and his ideals ended during the American Civil War's final battles, which amounted to slaughter rather than chivalric sacrifice. General Grant saw it and chose to remain drunk. At Ypres in 1915, one hundred thousand young men died in one day, all of whom died without seeing the machine gunners who killed them. . . . Anything left of the warrior vanished with the mass bombings of Dresden, the bombs on Nagasaki and Hiroshima, and the B-52 bombings of rice fields in Vietnam" (155). With so much warrior virtue lost or squandered, even in a "good war" such as World War II, there is little wonder that Bly's diagnosis leaves the Vietnam veteran in a deep hole: "The Vietnam veterans suffered soul damage in that they went into battle imagining they served a warrior god, and came back out of it godless" (156).

Bly's remedy, borrowing freely from mythmaking language, is to return the interior warrior to the service of a "True King," "a purpose greater than himself," even "the joy of a noble death" (151, 150). To a literal mind, Bly's prescription might suggest we start another crusade, one designed to be won, designed to be fought without ambiguity in its purpose to restore warrior masculinity in the long, persistently agonizing wake of Vietnam. The actual foe matters less than the phantom in one's own psyche. But Bly, who had after all strongly and publicly opposed the war in Vietnam, goes no further than recommending more metaphorical warrior behavior in relationships and marriages—arguing more fairly and openly with one's spouse, for example, seems to him a suitable substitute for strafing a column of armored tanks.

If there was a crisis in national manhood, as well as in Vietnam memory, in the early 1990s, revisiting the Civil War can be seen as both symptom and treatment. Ken Burns's highly rated PBS documentary *The Civil War,* like Michael Shaara's *The Killer Angels* fifteen years earlier, reframed the 1861–1865 war in the public mind, complete with musical soundtrack, voiceover, hundreds of still images, and the charismatic presence of novelist-historian Shelby Foote—a living connection by way of accent and rhetoric to the heroic age *The Civil War* conjures. On the eve of Desert Storm, U.S. public memory got a refreshed version of just and noble war, and with a heavy southern accent.

If George H. W. Bush thought in terms of, and called for, a shrunken span of history (twenty-five years being long enough to carry a memory), the years of his presidency coincided with renewed interest in and presentation of the noble war of U.S. memory. This had happened before. The fiftieth anniversary of the Civil War in the second decade of the twentieth century had ignited reunions and reenactments, culturally powerful entertainments such as D. W. Griffith's *Birth of a Nation* (1915), scholarly reassessments of the war and Reconstruction, and biographies of the central actors. The centennial of the war was commemorated by Bruce Catton's trilogy (Shelby Foote's *The Civil War: A Narrative* was continuously in progress, the three volumes published respectively in 1958, 1963, and 1974). Willie Morris, a Mississippian living in Manhattan and editing *Harper's* when the centennial arrived, writes in *North Toward Home* of recruiting fellow southerners C. Vann Woodward and William Styron to join with him in a kind of southern SWAT team to counter what Morris thought would be (in the violent early years of civil rights activism) a Civil War memory skewed to the victors' side (Morris 392–413).

Burns's *The Civil War* came to the public at a similarly crucial moment, though not linked to any official anniversary of the war. *The Civil War* project began in 1985; it was broadcast on PBS in 1990 (Ward, *Civil War* xvii). It is worth noting that Burns and Ward, in their introduction to the illustrated book that accompanies the video, *The Civil War: An Illustrated History* (1990), promote the Civil War as "the most defining and shaping event in American history—so much so that it is now impossible to imagine what we would have been like without it" (xvi). Fifteen years after the fall of Saigon, at least twenty-five since our initial military involvement in Vietnam, the Civil War is presented by Burns and Ward (and PBS) as more significant in the shaping of U.S. national character than a failed war that lacked (and arguably still lacks) the solemn closure of ritualized public remembering. Such a strong mismatch in rhetoric and timing suggests the will *not* to remember the late unpleasantness in Vietnam by remembering all too solemnly (and instead) a war that had ended more than a century earlier.

This is not to claim that the Burns project and Ward's script and book represent the Civil War as an uncomplicated heroic adventure. They do not; although Foote's commentary on screen and in the companion book does tend to plummy heroic ornament of the sort Fussell thought obfuscatory. The Burns/Ward version of "the event" begins with John Brown and slavery, presenting vivid testimony of the physical and psychological cruelty at the heart of the practice of slavery, and arguing that its abolition was the one and only cause for the violence. (The Catton centennial version, by contrast, begins with maneuvering in proslavery and antislavery politics, moving the focus from the suffering of slave bodies to political controversies controlled almost completely by white men.) The Civil War roster of Union officers is speckled, in the Burns/Ward version, with time-servers and incompetents. Their Lee is far from perfect, especially at Gettysburg, and their Grant (if not the morose drunk of many portraits, including Bly's thumbnail) is at minimum a brooding problem drinker. Nor are all

the battles conducted according to chivalric standards. Forrest's attack on Fort
Pillow (1864) is called an outright "massacre" and the general himself labeled a
butcher (Ward, *Civil War* 335). The Union attack on Petersburg (July 1864), after
a massive crater was blown into the landscape by a Federal cache of tunneled
explosives, is depicted as a fatal blend of error, incompetence, and racist murder
(312–15). There is no dearth of battlefield images of rotting and bloated corpses,
no absence of letters from the front describing the stench, the postbattle cries of
the wounded—many if not most of them left to suffer and die in misery because
medical care was not then up to treating the type and number of injuries the
soldiers suffered. And no Whitmanic rhetoric sanctifies the suffering.

It might be asked: why these images of mangled, dead, wounded American
bodies; these allegations of criminal murder in wartime; these confessions of
racism in both Union and Confederate ranks? Why remember our Civil War so
vividly when our Vietnam War still lacked reconciliation in collective memory?
A partial answer may be that remembering the earlier war "remembers" the
more recent one by exchanging a "safer" martial memory for one still dangerous. By means of the substitution we accomplish in the past affirmative what is
not possible in the present conditional.

The front matter to Michael Shaara's *The Killer Angels* partially indicates how
this process works. Shaara insists that the America of the mid-nineteenth century was both us and not us, in that "we" then lived in a naïve, sentimental,
and religious phase of our history not thereafter repeated—except, vicariously,
in memory. In an interview culled from two days of discussions with Shelby
Foote—an on-camera celebrity once the program was broadcast—Foote makes
a similar point: "It [the United States] had a simplicity that we are not able to
comprehend. Many people spent their entire lives not being over fifty or a hundred miles from home" (Ward, *Civil War* 264). A simpler, purer people fights a
simpler, purer war. Perhaps the epitome of our national nostalgia for a purer,
more innocent America is reached in the letter from Maj. Sullivan Ballou, 2nd
Rhode Island, to his wife on the eve of First Bull Run. It is a soulful blend of patriotic belief, earthly love, and religious faith. Too long to quote in full, excerpts
will have to suffice. Those who have seen Burns's program will remember the
impact, enhanced by a musical score:

> I have no misgivings about, or lack of confidence in the cause in which I am
> engaged, and my courage does not halt or falter. I know how strongly Ameri-

can Civilization now leans on the triumph of the Government, and how great a debt we owe to those who went before us through the blood and sufferings of the Revolution. . . . I have, I know, but few and small claims upon Divine Providence, but something whispers to me—perhaps it is the wafted prayer of my little Edgar, that I shall return to my loved ones unharmed. If I do not my dear Sarah, never forget how much I love you, and when my last breath escapes me on the battle field, it will whisper your name. . . . Sarah do not mourn me dead; think I am gone and wait for thee, for we shall meet again. . . . (Ward, *Civil War* 82–83)

Ballou was killed in the ensuing battle. What we can, however, remember about ourselves from this American soldier's moving letter is a way we prefer to believe we were. If, in the present, we are disconnected from religious faith, if "our government" lies to us, if our cause is confused or ignoble or in fact concealed from us—it was not always so. If Vietnam has shown us, by 1990, a U.S. "Civilization" unworthy of the name (or, at least, unworthy of the uppercase "C"), and a U.S. soldier (as Bly might argue) distracted from his "interior warrior"—much less the psychotic misfit of Herr's mantra—the Civil War in refreshed public memory delivers the balm the public craves. Then, death in battle had meaning; then, the citizen-warrior knew and felt a connection to noble predecessors; then, the government was worthy of sacred respect.

Foote became the southern-accented voice and image of these cravings. "Duty, bravery under adversity, very simple virtues, and they had them" is the way he described both sides of, not a war, but a "family argument" (Ward, *Civil War* 264–65). His voice both in text and on camera—as it is also in his three-volume narrative history of the Civil War—humanizes battlefield trauma by posting human-scale anecdote against large-scale historical themes such as abolition and states' rights. He brings down the demigods of the conflict by identifying them with nicknames like "Old Blue Light,"[19] and (as Fussell had outlined) translating battlefield events into the language of epic. Antietam, in Foote's comments, is "a highly dramatic action"; the Confederate ranks were characterized by "valor" and "élan"; Chickamauga was the site of a "glorious southern victory" while in the Battle of Franklin (Tennessee) "the flower of the southern army fell"[20] (Ward, *Civil War* 267, 268, 269). Against the echoes of Vietnam, both textual and visual, Foote's rhetoric wages its own battle on the field of public memory. And he wins, teasing us to unlearn the lessons Paul Fussell had been at pains, more than twenty years earlier, to teach us about the refuge of heroic rhetoric.

President George H. W. Bush was not granted the wish in his inaugural speech: an end to the divisive memory of Vietnam. President George W. Bush reignited the feud between history and memory in 2007, in dark days for the invasion of Iraq, when he called on the nation to remember the withdrawal from Vietnam as the effective cause of mass killings in Laos and Cambodia. "Will today's generations of Americans resist the allure of retreat, and will we do in the Middle East what the veterans in this room [Veterans of Foreign Wars National Convention, August 2007] did in Asia?" ("In Bush's Words" A8). The answer will probably have to wait for the time when his war has become a *lieu de mémoire*.

4

HAITI

Phantom Southern Memory in Faulkner and Madison Smartt Bell

∞

. . . part of childhood which all mothers of children had received in turn from their mothers and from their mothers in turn from that Porto Rico or Haiti or wherever it was we all came from but none of us ever lived in.

—WILLIAM FAULKNER, *Absalom, Absalom!*

I n 1935, a year after the United States terminated its occupation of Haiti (1915–1934), Fred Astaire and Ginger Rogers danced through a version of the sturdy "American in Paris" fable in the RKO movie version of the Broadway musical *Roberta.* One of the numbers has become a classic in the repertoire of the American popular song: "I Won't Dance."[1] One stanza in the Dorothy Fields/ Jimmy McHugh lyric seems uncannily appropriate in this "overture" to a chapter on the "American in Haiti" fantasy. The lyricists bring together dancing as the metaphor for sexual desire in a national fable where the United States woos and wins the "French" Other:

> When you dance, you're charming and you're gentle,
> 'Specially when you do the Continental.
> But this feeling isn't purely mental,
> For, heaven rest us, I'm not asbestos.

Astaire sings the song to woo back Rogers, an old flame from the States who is making her way in Paris swathed in the fake persona of a Russian princess. There is a real deposed Russian princess in the story, played by Irene Dunne, and eventually she too falls in love with an American hero, a famous football player played by Randolph Scott.

Roberta is set in Paris, not Haiti, and the woman who dances so charmingly is not creole or mysteriously octoroon or tragically mulatta, but American. Astaire plays a character who could hardly be more American: Huckleberry Haines, the leader of a stranded dance band called the Wabash Indianians. And his foil, the tough and terse John Kent (Randolph Scott), who eventually falls for the "real" princess, is a direct archetypal descendant of Deerslayer and the Virginian. Transport Americans to Paris, and the allegory of triumphant national identities inevitably asserts itself. Asbestos or not, lovers overcome whatever keeps them apart and live happily ever after: all the feminized Other needs is a couple of red-blooded American guys and the tangles of *haute couture* and the Russian Revolution become as simple as boy-meets-girl.[2]

Haiti is not Paris, and never was. But, as J. Michael Dash argues in *Haiti and the United States: National Stereotypes and the Literary Imagination,* "Haiti is imaginatively and culturally reconstructed as the 'Other,' the negative or feminine and marginalized in a symbolic order devised by the United States" (3). Haiti in the historical order, then, becomes the imaginative equivalent—in the symbolic order—of Paris in a hemisphere dominated by the United States. Haiti, like Paris, anchors a culturally necessary narrative "devised by [and for] the United States." And this narrative contains, or attempts to contain, an "Other" whose existence in fact presents a host of fears, contaminations, and challenges to normative identities. In Haiti, for example, the dead not only walk, they dance.

As Michael O'Brien shows in *Conjectures of Order,* a blood- and fear-soaked Haiti entered the southern imaginary from the hard-edged order of historical fact with "a flood of nervous and angry French refugees [from the uprising of 1791 onward], often bringing their reluctant slaves, the former pointing to the possibility of butchery if Southern vigilance was not maintained, the latter remembering the possibility of freedom" (I, 207). From that historical moment on, O'Brien indicates, Haiti was launched as an image with power in both anti- and proslavery narratives: leaders of slave revolts were often tutored by one or more of those "reluctant [Haitian] slaves" or imagined Haiti as their refuge once they had escaped, and proslavery advocates had to do little more than utter the word "Haiti" in order to conjure gory scenes of sexual violation (otherwise unspeakable) and torture.[3]

Haiti is not Paris, but like Paris in a more contemporary and popular American imagination, Haiti in the southern imagination acts like phantom memory, the once and (perhaps) future place for imagining a romance of (white, male,

American, heterosexual) identity triumphant. A Rogers/Astaire vehicle is an adequate, if shallow, outline of the presence of Haiti as phantom memory: the "real" imprint of a place/time never actually visited. In this narrative, the United States is masculine, the island feminine; the United States is a machine, the island a body; the island is prehistorical timelessness, the United States is modernity. The encounter of these opposites, beginning with Columbus, is ongoing. Just as persistent is the insinuative power of Haiti, in the symbolic order, to lead—if only intermittently—a "dance" in the white Western imagination. Doing the "Continental" is complex choreography.

The recent "turn" in southern literary studies both shapes and is shaped by this choreography in the dual orders of history and image. First, the "turn" stretches the boundaries of the "old" territory staked out by the clique Paul Bové called "professional southerners" (the states of the Confederacy, with parts of the border states added as needed).[4] The New Southern Studies annexes the Caribbean and South and Central America, a move prompting almost as many questions, in what Bové calls "the politics of intellectual culture," as it answers.[5] To many in the field of southern studies, this annexation seems "natural." Since both the U.S. South and the Caribbean were, at the origins of their respective histories in the trans-Atlantic narrative, plantation colonies producing wealth on the backs of enslaved Africans, then our understanding of the one must flow into, and with (like a dance) an understanding of the other. Édouard Glissant, in his *Faulkner, Mississippi,* makes a persuasive argument for the reciprocal flow of understanding from the Caribbean to the American South, and several of the essays in Jon Smith and Deborah Cohn's *Look Away! The U.S. South in New World Studies* engineer the bridge from the mainland outward. Barbara Ladd, in two books, *Nationalism and the Color Line* and *Resisting History,* has feathered in the linkages. In *Nationalism and the Color Line* she reads southern authors William Faulkner and George Washington Cable into "*le discours*" of the islands, and in the latter she picks at the subtle threads Zora Neale Hurston used to weave herself into Haiti.[6]

Connectivity reasoning seems so streamlined that it is difficult to resist or question it, to suspect that the narratives by which we tell ourselves Haiti subliminally tell our own fable as well. In "A New World Poetics of Oblivion," George P. Handley ably states the case pro and con: "The historical patterns that characterize the U.S. South also connect it to a larger region of the Americas. . . . These historical parallels, however, should not become justification for assuming that one can find facile homogeneity in the Americas; social, racial, and cultural similarities in the New World cannot be ignored any more than they can be definitively identified" (25). But in turning to the Caribbean on the strength of these "parallels," do we not also risk reinscribing a colonial relationship between islands and mainland older than the Monroe Doctrine? In place of a definitive answer, Handley proposes a "poetics of oblivion," a temperament rather than a technique for telling, representing "legacies of untold suffering for millions of Africans and their descendants . . . often beyond representation because the lived realities were either initially understated or erased in historical documentation in an attempt to conceal accountability" (26). This "saturated, collective amnesia," Handley suggests, probably will not be broken by history, but "a contextualization of the American South within the literary imagination of greater Plantation America allows one to . . . at least begin to appreciate what is forgotten in the forging of imagined communities" (26, 27).

The contextualization Handley recommends is both necessary and inadequate. Without some measure of contextualization, there is no possibility of reading the Other as other than ourselves. Yet contextualization inevitably layers the narrative of the Other with the narrative of the Self. A poetics of oblivion, paradoxically, calls out a poetics of superfluity; often too much is in the frame, text and con-text interfering with, dancing with, each other. We might not be able to do better than read ourselves reading Haiti.

When John T. Matthews, in "Recalling the West Indies: From Yoknapatawpha to Haiti and Back," expands the field of literary critique to reach the "U.S. South's Caribbean horizon" (239), he suggests that the "imagined community" of "Yoknapatawpha to Haiti and Back" might be founded upon an extant poetics. If our southern boundaries are expanded to the Caribbean horizon, will the same canon of texts and authors that buttress our academized fields, periods, movements, and problems hold up? In general, is "Caribbean" actually a term of necessity, or is it a term of convenience for the literary critic in U.S. southern studies, concealing our own maneuvers from us?[7] Is our expeditionary flotilla of books, essays, and conferences in reality another symptom of what Paul Gilroy calls "modernity and its discontents," that reflex of conflicted-ness in the presence of "nationality, ethnicity, authenticity, and cultural integrity?" (2). We can't let any thing, any place be the sovereign Other, beyond the hegemonic reach of our modes of knowing, of gridding and ordering both factual and symbolic orders. We always send in the marines, or Fred and Ginger, or a company of literary and cultural critics.

There has been no dearth of actual U.S. interventions and occupations of the circum-Caribbean nations: Nicaragua, Panama, Cuba, Grenada, Honduras. For my purposes here, though, our vexed relationship with Haiti, especially as it stretches from the revolution of 1791 to our occupation of 1915–1934 and onward to our vexed relationship with the Duvaliers and Jean-Bertrand Aristide, will stand synecdoche for the Caribbean. The reason for my choice of Haiti is obvious: U.S. southern writers William Faulkner and Madison Smartt Bell have made Haiti central to the imaginative fields of their important work. Although he had never been there, Faulkner made Haiti crucial to the character of Thomas Sutpen in *Absalom, Absalom!* and therefore crucial also to an understanding of the southernness of his work. The Haiti Faulkner might have known, in its historical register, was the Haiti of the long occupation. Bell, a southern writer working in postmodern, post-Faulknerian conditions, suggests an ongoing connection between the U.S. South and Haiti with his trilogy of novels on the Haitian revolution (1791–1804) and, most recently, a biography of its leader, Toussaint Louverture.[8] Bell's Haiti is that of Aristide and the revenants of Duvalier. I am interested in the risks mainland southern writers (and the critics who strive to interpret them) assume when, as in Faulkner's case, they attempt to "remember" a place they have never visited or, as in Bell's case, a place to which they are not native. In fact, Bell, like Faulkner, had not visited Haiti before he wrote the first volume of his trilogy on Toussaint Louverture and the Haitian revolution; the coup that removed Aristide for the first time delayed a planned visit (Carnes 198). I use "memory" and its related vocabulary loosely here to refer to the representation of a place-time in narratives when the author has (as yet) no firsthand experience of being there: no ground, literally, upon which to remember it. I am not interested, however, in correcting errors or filling gaps between actuality and representation, that is, restoring the order of fact to preeminence. What I am interested in is how the errors and gaps that inevitably enter such phantom memory seem to matter less than the substitutions and replacements the authors insert. I propose, by example, a version of how a poetics of oblivion might work.

I propose in this chapter, then, to question the "geopoetics" of New World Studies or New Southern Studies as those field redefinitions annex more "South."

I use Haiti to stand in for Caribbean, and balance the larger literary and cultural issues on the backs of two authors, William Faulkner and Madison Smartt Bell, and their works: *Absalom, Absalom!* (1936) and Bell's trilogy on Toussaint Louverture: *All Souls' Rising* (1995), *The Master of the Crossroads* (2000), and *The Stone That the Builder Refused* (2004). Faulkner is, of course, "Faulkner," the major figure whose surname is synonymous with the South and southern poetics: indisputably with the South in the symbolic order, and to an extent in the factual order as well.[9] Bell, like William Styron, whom he resembles as a writer of fiction, is more reserved about his regional roots. Like Styron, who used his southern memory to leverage an understanding of the Holocaust in *Sophie's Choice,* Bell claims to grasp the revolution in Saint-Domingue by virtue of his southernness. "I was trained from an early age," Bell writes in response to questions about his trilogy, "to recognize the bearing of history on the present" (Carnes 206). That "early age" (Bell was born in 1957) was deeply dyed by growing up in Nashville, Tennessee, socially and intellectually close to latter-day Fugitive and Agrarian circles in which his parents moved.[10]

Inevitably, exploring the South/Caribbean nexus begins with Faulkner. In *Fictions of Labor: William Faulkner and the South's Long Revolution* (1997), Richard Godden hacks a path from Faulkner's fiction to the image of Haiti in the related discourses of labor and southern fiction, corresponding approximately to factual and symbolic orders. In his chapter "*Absalom, Absalom!* Haiti, and Labor History: Reading Unreadable Revolutions," Godden suggests that, yes, the "major figure," Faulkner, is still relevant, and might be taken as a reliable choreographer of the dance between the American South and the Caribbean. The melody Godden hears is Hegelian, even if the lyrics are southern. *Absalom, Absalom!* Godden comments, "outcanons all but the most canonical texts" (3). And even though he drops the disclaimer that "Faulkner commands too much of the wrong kind of attention," and that even his [Godden's] own work might be seen as "still more on someone of whom so much has been written" (3, 1), Godden moves on in the apparent confidence that Faulkner's prestige will bear additional weight. This chapter piles on still more.

Godden's "Haiti" is more cultural image than historical entity. Although much has been written, Godden cautions, about Faulkner's anachronistic use of Haitian history in Thomas Sutpen's memory, "the wrong kind of attention" has been devoted to correcting or justifying the alleged "error" of misdating the revolution. For Godden, the Haiti of *Absalom, Absalom!* is a site where southern community comes face to face with its own "fictions of labor"—postponed, deferred, even dumped into amnesia before Faulkner's work in the 1930s "outed" the southern economy's transition from enforced servitude to free labor and thereby exposed the Old South as a white, master-class fantasy. Godden's "Haiti," then, is to be found on an American cultural map at the point where the South's amnesia about the kind of labor that made it possible was summoned to wakefulness by having to deal with Haiti in the 1930s as it had in the 1790s. If Faulkner got the dates of Toussaint's uprising wrong, Godden argues, the historical error is less significant than what he suggests about "fictions of labor" in southern memory.

I want to follow Godden into his reading of "Haiti," but then veer away from his Hegelian reading of labor in *Absalom, Absalom!* Handley, after all, warns against Hegelian dialectic in thinking Caribbean (31–32). Faulkner and his novel of 1936 are still centrally important to any U.S. (and southern) literary-critical discussion of Haiti and the Caribbean. But I want to tailgate on *Absalom, Absalom!*'s surplus canonicity; its momentum is all to the good. Rather than steer into the Hegelian districts Godden favors, however, I want to try the wide Sargasso of cultural meanings in the term "Haiti" as John T. Matthews begins to navigate them. At issue is what we, in the Northern Hemisphere, the "onshore" United States, know of "Haiti" and how we know it. What might "Haiti" have meant to Faulkner when (in the 1930s) he imagined Sutpen there almost a century earlier? Is Madison Smartt Bell's trilogy of novels on the Haitian revolution a major effort to reimagine, re-remember, and get Haiti appropriately sized in the conscious harness of a modern history?[11]

Since my approach in this essay is literary (i.e., through the symbolic order), I will need a trope or theme to plot a course through a range and variety of texts, most of them written. As Gilroy chose ships in the middle passage as his central trope in *The Black Atlantic* (4), I choose dancing. Antonio Benitez-Rojo, whose *The Repeating Island: The Caribbean and the Postmodern Perspective* is crucial to current thinking about the emergence of Caribbean literature in this age of crosscultural turnings, privileges dancing as a marker of Caribbean-ness too.[12] Benitez-Rojo delivers a clear warning to literary critics who venture toward the Caribbean horizon: "What happens is that postindustrial society—to use a new-fangled term—navigates the Caribbean with judgments and intentions that are like those of Columbus; that is, it lands scientists, investors, and technologists—the new (dis)coverers—who come to apply the dogmas and methods that had served them well where they came from, and who can't see that these refer only to realities back home. So they get into the habit of defining the Caribbean in terms of its resistance to the different methodologies summoned to investigate it" (1–2). The closed loop of the Heisenberg principle is shopworn—those who apply "dogmas and methods" to new phenomena usually see those dogmas and methods only—but in the present context it jolts the conversation at the U.S side of the bridge to the annexed South with creative self-examination.

Here is an example of what I take Benitez-Rojo to be warning us against; it is located in time closer to *Absalom, Absalom!* than it is to the present. In "Skypaths Through Latin America," a team of American "conquistadores" from *National Geographic* fly over Haiti (and the complete curve of the Antilles) in an airplane furnished by (what would soon become) Pan American Airways. Their aim *seems* benign: "We were to study the various races of mankind encountered, observe the wilderness, the farms, industries, and cities; land wherever we wished, make the best pictures ever taken along this route, and bring back an account of our experiences for educational purposes only" (Simpich 1). The assumption of developed-world entitlement to Caribbean landscape and mankind is embedded in such phrases as "land wherever we wish." Nor is it wholly coincidental that the photographic apparatus used to "make the best pictures ever taken" "looked more like a young howitzer than a picture-taking machine" (Simpich 20).[13] The cultural terrain seems firm enough to the *National Geographic* explorers; but from a postmodern perspective—the one recommended by Benitez-Rojo—the same terrain is best read as "aquatic": it appears solid from the air, but is apt to swallow up the first confident footstep (Benitez-Rojo 11). And our confidence that we proceed impartially, "for educational purposes only," must always be reconciled with the rhetoric of entitlement.[14] The *National Geographic* "explorers" reenact in miniature the Columbian intervention. Is there any other narrative poetics for this subject matter? What is to excuse Faulkner and Bell, and all of the rest of us who have come with "dogmas and methods" for understanding Haiti, from the arrogance of the *National Geographic* Indiana Joneses?

"Chaos," rather than rational or machinelike precision, describes Benitez-Rojo's poetics for the Caribbean-as-text (Benitez-Rojo 3). Fluidity, rather than fixed edges, "defines" a Caribbean sense of form: "The Caribbean is the natural and indispensable realm of marine currents, of waves, of folds and double-folds, of fluidity and sinuosity" (11). Feminizing the Caribbean by one remove of metaphor is not new; indeed, it is one of the favorite pastimes of the colonizers. To give Benitez-Rojo due latitude, though, his "feminizing" is deliberate, and part of a larger project to make the region so complex that developed-world thinking cannot regiment it.[15]

Benitez-Rojo's identity, his sense of "being Caribbean" (21), is housed in memory, lodged in a kind of primal moment of woman/sinuosity/motion—a dance. He "can isolate with a frightening exactitude" the genesis of his Caribbean consciousness. As a child in Havana on a "stunning October afternoon," during what was called in the hemisphere to the north the "Cuban Missile Crisis," young Benitez-Rojo, sharing with his brothers and sisters in the north the anxiety Faulkner succinctly phrased in his Nobel acceptance speech as "when will I be blown up," nevertheless did not banish tension by running to a bomb shelter or practicing "duck and cover." He saw, from his balconied window, a pair of older black women walking the otherwise deserted Havana street "in a certain kind of way," a kind of way that said to him, perhaps not in these words at that time in his youth but certainly later in his life: "Here I am, fucked but happy" (Benitez-Rojo 10).

This is the lived moment, with the signature doom of the developed world (The Bomb) hovering in his consciousness, in which the alternative discourse of Caribbeanicity strikes its roots. It is the female body dancing, dancing even in utilitarian locomotion: the rhythm of footsteps flowing out to "neck, back, abdomen, arms, in short all [one's] muscles" (Benitez-Rojo 19). Thus, the Caribbean body flows in a certain kind of way appropriate to "Peoples of the Sea" (17), but not "Sea" exactly, rather "archipelagoes" mixed of land and water, places that make the disciplines of territorial boundaries, distinctions between solid and liquid, only and always provisional.

Sutpen doesn't dance. Many readings of Sutpen's sojourn in Haiti, following Grandfather Compson's grant of "innocence" as ratified by his son and grandson, and his grandson's Canadian roommate, conclude that Sutpen arrived on the island handicapped by the lack of a certain kind of knowledge (and the imaginative grace to pick it up) of the place he had come to. "'He went to the West Indies.' . . . 'That was how he said it.' . . . 'So I went to the West Indies, sitting there on the log with Grandfather.' . . . " (Faulkner, *Absalom* 193). We have often investigated, speculated about, *what* Sutpen said; less frequently perhaps do we ask ourselves why Quentin is so impressed by *how* he said it. Perhaps Quentin (remembering 1820 in a remembered 1910) knows, or thinks he knows, what Faulkner (in the 1930s) might more plausibly have known about Haiti since he put Sutpen there in the immediate wake of U.S. occupation—that Haiti was a loaded choice, that of all the places on earth Sutpen might, in his innocence, have chosen, Haiti was the one destination guaranteed to devour innocence. One does not simply "go" to the West Indies; one from the developed world especially goes to the West Indies with cultural memory, "dogmas and methods." Even the college boys in a Harvard dorm room know that much.

How could the boy Thomas Sutpen have been imprinted with the narrative that "there was a place called the West Indies to which poor men went in ships and became rich"? (*Absalom* 195). If Faulkner imagined the answer to have been accessible in some archive, perhaps he imagined that Sutpen had somehow heard of Christopher Columbus, who was in the American history narratives of Quentin's time a poor man who had gone in ship(s) to the West Indies hoping to become rich. Columbus "discovered" Hispaniola, the island that was to be renamed Haiti by the self-liberated slaves who declared it a republic in 1804; his grave is in Santo Domingo, and there is a statue of him in Port-au-Prince. Sutpen apparently did not hear the part of the Columbus "voyage and riches" narrative that tells other details: that Columbus wasn't looking for the West Indies but the Orient, that he never became rich, that he and his crew went much of the time in mortal fear of "cannibals."[16]

Sutpen could not have heard a plot synopsis of *Jane Eyre* (1847), in which another young man goes to the West Indies, becomes rich, but also acquires a mad wife; Charlotte Brontë hadn't written it yet. If Sutpen could not have heard of Rochester, William Faulkner might have. Joseph Blotner does not chronicle Faulkner reading Charlotte Brontë's novel at all, and Faulkner apparently did not read *Wuthering Heights* until he was writer-in-residence at the University of Virginia in the 1950s (Blotner, *Faulkner*, II, 1658). Maybe Sutpen's incubator had "heard" about the Brontë sisters' novels by some other means. More to the point, whatever the character Sutpen could plausibly have heard about Haiti, Faulkner probably knew a lot without deliberately studying the subject.

Regardless of what the young Sutpen had heard about the West Indies, he only registered the uninflected lexical meaning of the words: the machine aspect of the words, none of the dance, as Benitez-Rojo might have it (Benitez-Rojo 7). Faulkner and his narrators in *Absalom, Absalom!* register this crucial distinction between the phonetic utterance and the signifier "Haiti" with its full complement of associations. Richard Godden, for example, is not the only critic to admire, even to be moved by, the depth to which Faulkner registers the enormous human misery buried in the word "Haiti." Shreve might want to reduce the decades of violence, the hundreds of thousands of deaths by torture and murder to a James Micheneresque romance: "'It's a girl,' Shreve said. 'Don't tell me. Just go on'" (*Absalom* 199).[17] But Faulkner knows that Haiti is more than a swashbuckling diversion, that it is as Grandfather Compson says, "a spot of earth which might have been created and set aside by Heaven itself . . . as a theatre for violence and injustice and bloodshed and all the satanic lusts of human greed and cruelty . . ." (202).[18]

Sutpen's way with language, specifically his way with French and the island patois he had to learn if he was to oversee the slaves on a sugar plantation, concerns Faulkner enough for him to pass it on to Quentin.[19] The multilayered retelling of Sutpen's history in Haiti is strung together as the retellers repeat their wonder at the way such a semiliterate man could survive in a complex and exotic culture so deeply embroiled in languages: French, Spanish, English, Kreyol, and the vestiges of several African tongues. Sutpen, "who knew no tongue but English and not much of that" (199), nevertheless sailed away from Haiti alive. Perhaps it was just that—not ignorance, not innocence, but utter machinelike usage of language—that enabled Sutpen *not* to know (or even to imagine) the meaning of the vodou fetish meant to bring about his death (203). He had learned as much French and local dialect as he needed the same way he had learned to be a sailor (200). There is no nuance to a knot if it is nothing to you but rope. As Melville punned upon Sutpen's precursor, the blissfully literal-minded Amasa Delano: "knot in hand, and knot in head."[20] For Sutpen there was no conversation, only declaration. He "went out and subdued them" (204) is all he can say about his conquest of the rebelling slaves—not because the details are too harrowing to remember, to put into words—but because those few words are literally the only words Sutpen has to name the event. The conundrum of Sutpen is how a man locked in the factual register of language can negotiate two places (Haiti and the South) so layered in the symbolic order. In the end, the mystery is that there is no mystery—the narrative of *Absalom, Absalom!* is the tellers striving to implant it.

Grandfather Compson had detected the language gap in Sutpen's education in humanity, for he suggested to the newcomer to Yoknapatawpha that he should have taken a girl to live with him and thereby learned the local Haitian language the "easy way" (200). In a sense, Grandfather Compson understands the acquisition and usage of language the way Benítez-Rojo does. Language is nothing if not embodied; the best way to learn is also the "easy" way: for pleasure and in pleasure. Grandfather Compson's advice might sound odd—not to mention sexist and exploitative—coming from one of the old white men of unsophisticated, backcountry Mississippi. But, as I wish to read Haiti in *Absalom, Absalom!* (and in Bell's trilogy, to come), it is central to Faulkner's understanding of the image of Haiti, central as well to Quentin's astonishment at Sutpen's ability to survive Haiti without feeling an iota of its sensual meaning. More puzzling than Faulkner's misdating of the revolution in Haiti is his skirting of any explanation of the means by which Grandfather Compson came to know so much about Haiti, and acquired his "poetics of oblivion."

Perhaps no actual college freshman in 1910, but the character of a college freshman in 1910 (Quentin) imagined by an adult American writer in the 1930s, would have been equipped with much more cultural knowledge of Haiti and the West Indies.[21] Edna Taft's *A Puritan in Voodoo-Land* (1938)—a title that so archly sums up Sutpen that Shreve might have coined it—begins with the kind of knowledge that Sutpen fails utterly to acquire: "The few torn pages [of an ancestor's journal of slave trading in the islands], inscribed with faded ink, told of a lovely land of lofty folded green mountains, emerald verdure, brilliant sapphire skies and stately palms swaying at the water's edge, whilst on higher ground grew intensely vermillion trees that could be seen far off at sea. A land of beautiful women of mixed blood" (Taft 12). Clichés of sensuality abound in Taft's prologue to Haiti: mountains "fold" and palms "sway," establishing the conventionally "puritan" knowledge of the island as the place where libido surges to freedom (and chaos). Along with the clichés of landscape is the equally obvious (visible "far off at sea") addendum to riches: "beautiful women of mixed blood." Sutpen, Quentin seems about to ask, was surprised by miscegenation in Haiti? "Riches" are not the only reason young men go there. The tragedy of *Absalom, Absalom!* is not so much the vortex of fratricide, incest, and slavery in the puritan-obsessed U.S. South, but that all of the misery could have been brought about by one man so ignorant, so impervious to the meanings which flowed so thickly in the island air he inhaled.[22]

It is not language in general that needles Faulkner to imagine a certain kind of Sutpen, but French in particular—and the one site in the United States where French might be heard and spoken, a place where Faulkner had spent time:

New Orleans.[23] Mr. Compson, alone among all the characters in the novel, is particularly fascinated with New Orleans, and takes pleasure he cannot wholly conceal in imagining Charles Bon in "that city foreign and paradoxical, with its atmosphere at once fatal and langorous, at once feminine and steel-hard" (*Absalom* 86). Polymorphous sexual libido throbs in Mr. Compson's prurient imaginings of Bon with his mistress; if Sutpen is impervious to the similarly libidinous "atmosphere" around him, Mr. Compson is supersaturated with it. If he could not be an American in Paris, he would be a Mississippian in New Orleans. He is so carried away by fantasies both "feminine and steel-hard" that he represents Henry, Quentin's alter ego, in a way that must have been fatally damaging to his own son: "this grim humorless yokel" whose great embarrassing flaws are a lack of French and a puritanical aversion to sex (*Absalom* 86, 89). With this father (no better than Sutpen for Henry), why would Quentin even need guilt for racism, slavery, and defeat in a civil war to do away with himself?

Thomas Sutpen is not, however, *sui generis,* nor is his "design," so often linked to the innate wrongs of the plantation system of labor and race in the U.S. South, and oriented chiefly toward that southern plantation past. I want to complicate the issue of "anachronism" as we use it in discussing *Absalom, Absalom!* As Faulkner gradually completed his novel, the United States was bringing to a close its two-decade-long military occupation of Haiti (1915–1934), a forced cohabitation that must have left its traces on Faulkner and his contemporary audience. In 1933 and 1934, as negotiations were inexorably reaching an end to military occupation and the withdrawal of U.S. marines was measured in months, newspapers, magazines, books, and films were rife with analyses, arguments, and memoirs crowding Haiti into public attention. One memoir with particular (albeit indirect) resonance in *Absalom, Absalom!* (and in the present) is John H. Craige's *Black Bagdad* (1933).[24]

After leaving service as a captain in the U.S. Marine Corps, Craige (foreshadowing the fictional Sutpen) went to Haiti in 1925 to become an officer in the U.S. occupation force, the Gendarmerie d'Haiti. "This was a force of romance," Craige nostalgically recalls (2). The ranks of the Gendarmerie d'Haiti were black and mulatto Haitians; the officers were all white American military and ex-military. As Craige accents his memoir, it seems to reprise white Western male fantasies like *Gunga Din* and *King Solomon's Mines*.[25] He felt some of the prestige of the French Foreign Legion as an officer in the Gendarmerie (54). Craige reveled in his status as a "sort of white Emir to command the black troops of a province" (2). He employed a "Number One Boy" and household servants. His privileges were not only domestic: "To them I was king, sultan and dictator rolled into one. My word was the Law and the Prophets, the Beginning and the End. It came over me gradually, and sometimes took my breath. To be a divinely appointed autocrat who can do no wrong seemed a heavy responsibility" (15).[26] A fraternal comrade of Sutpen, the persona Craige imagines for himself represents a critical response to the temptations in U.S. imperial aggrandizement. If it may be argued that much of Sutpen's context as a fictional character is contemporary to the occupation (rather than retrospective, dredged up from a southern collective memory of plantation mastering), then the charge that Faulkner erred in dating the Haitian revolution could be reduced. We could say that Faulkner did not have to remember Haiti correctly or not in the historical order; he was saturated in the full paradigm of the Haiti of the symbolic.

Craige is clearly more aware of his cultural power and privilege in Haiti than Sutpen is; he can, for starters, write a book about it. But still, Craige can't, won't dance. He sees, more than once during his stint as pasha in Haiti, the archetypal walking women (*les marchandes*) whom Benitez-Rojo locates at the origins of Caribbean self-consciousness: "Bare of foot, turbaned, with their long blue dresses, *caracos,* they called them, fluttering behind them, they swung along, backs rigid, haunches rolling, some chattering and gesticulating, but for the most part silent" (Craige 5). Almost immediately in Craige's memoir the clamps on bodily motion (no "haunches rolling" here) snap into place as part of colonial discipline. The occupier's prescription for the Haitian troops he commands, not surprisingly, is regimented, machinelike motion; white superiors drill their subaltern ranks (in English, not creole) toward a "faultless precision" on the parade ground that mechanically abolishes the dancing human body (Craige 15, 53).

But, like the scent of burning sugarcane (*Absalom* 200) that becomes for Sutpen—monodimensional though he is in all forms of language—the olfactory metaphor for the ultimately unsubduable chaos of Haiti—rhythms eventually bring Craige, "the white Emir," to the point of exhaustion. Drums are omnipresent in Craige's consciousness. A "big dance every Saturday night," a vodou rite where he witnesses the slaughter of a pig, a funeral dance of mourning (Craige 58, 96, 121) all involve drums and gradually wear his Nordic mental stamina thin. He becomes eerily Conradian toward the end of his tenure on the island: "I was beginning to regard them [Haitians] with a good deal of horror" (230). Like Craige, Edna Taft, finally succumbing to drums as well, pleads spiritual and psychological exhaustion as she prepares to leave (Taft 368). Those who write charmingly of Haiti, Craige warns, have missed the island's more sinister effects on the civilized psyche. The inescapable sites of mass killing and burial, like the omnipresent drums, impose a burden one would have to be a kind of Sutpen not to feel (Craige 248–49).[27]

It is revealing to relocate Sutpen outside his customary context as the archetype of antebellum southern plantation master. In fact, it could be that the "anachronism" for which Faulkner is often faulted—misdating the slave insurrections of 1791–1804 to the 1820s—is less embarrassing if we accept Faulkner's own present moment (the end of the U.S. occupation of Haiti) as the milieu in which Sutpen is mostly imagined and drawn.[28] Seen in the context of U.S. imperialism in the Caribbean in the 1930s, Sutpen's racism—his simultaneous erotic pleasure in naked-to-the-waist wrestling matches with his male slaves (some of whom might be his own sons), witnessed by his white son and daughter, as against his machinelike discarding of his creole wife on the mere hint that there might be some nonwhite blood in her ancestry—seems as contemporary to the first third of the twentieth century as it does to the antebellum South. That is, it might be a form of racism Faulkner could *know* rather than racism he would have to try to *remember*.[29]

Craige is clearly both repulsed by and attracted to the mixed races of Haiti. "Dusky" is an adjective he repeats when he wants to demean Haitian claims to civilized culture. The Haitian legislature is composed of "dusky Ciceros," and the Haitian social elite is the "dusky Four Hundred" (2, 59). And yet he is continually drawn to the physical beauty in Haitian men and, especially, women. A certain courtesan (Craige calls her a "prostitute") is a figure of mingled attraction and revulsion: Chiquita is ". . . a dream of loveliness, with eyes the brown of a butterfly's wing, a wealth of raven hair and a form to set poets raving. Her skin was the clear red-gold of the ripened orange, the heat of the tropics ran in her veins. Her voice was the liquid warble of the Haitian thrush, and she danced divinely" (194). Chiquita, Craige believes, has poisoned a series of husbands, each one wealthier than his predecessor, on her way up from the slums of the Port-au-Prince waterfront. It is worth mentioning, for the sake of this tropological reading, that Craige associates Chiquita's obvious (and conventional) sexual power with her allure as a dancer. Although Sutpen does not manifest such an articulate and conflicted desire, Shreve and Quentin do when they imagine Eulalia Bon, Charles's mother and the jettisoned wife whose sensuous beauty is succeeded by fierce revenge that, in the young men's concocted part of the story, consumes both son and husband.[30] Shreve and Quentin must imagine Eulalia out of something; I argue that they imagine her out of the feminized Haiti of popular lore: what they "know" about Haiti and are flabbergasted that Sutpen doesn't know. If J. Michael Dash's formulation is valid—that the feminized body of Haiti in the symbolic order oscillates from sensuous to demonic—then the boys follow that arc in imagining Bon's mother as the demonic and his mistress as the sensuous (Dash xii–xiii).

Craige is also revealing on the dynastic anxiety that motivates Sutpen's rejection of his first wife and the disowning of his son with her, Charles Bon. Craige tells the story of a Haitian senator's daughters, the eldest blonde and blue-eyed, the second raven haired, the third "jet-black" and "full of haunting melancholy" (136–37). Explaining the situation with the help of Gregor Mendel and his peas, Craige teaches us (his white audience) that race mixing is, by the law of averages, liable to "atavism" in any single offspring. Thus the birth of a Haitian child in the elite classes, *les gens de couleur,* is always fraught with suspense. Striving always for whiteness ("White men exercised an irresistible fascination upon the Haitian female. . . . To have a white baby seemed the heart's ambition of every native woman," Craige boasts [204]), the expectant couple can never be sure that their suppressed African past won't issue from the womb. The overwhelming presence of anxiety about "atavism" seems to have completely escaped Sutpen's notice; even in the 1820s of memory, historical sources establish, Haitian culture was equipped with a finely tuned taxonomy of mixed bloodlines. Moreau de Saint-Méry had finished his mapping of Haitian types, *Description topographique, physique, civile, politique et historique de la partie française de l'Isle Saint Domingue,* in exile in Philadelphia in 1797. Saint-Méry moves Mendel from peas to human beings, dividing human racial identities into 128 categories from pure white to pure black. Edna Taft was aware of the book; she identified Haitians she met according to which of Saint-Méry's categories they represented (Taft 35–36). That this huge scheme seems to have taken Sutpen by surprise is another proof that he can't dance. He can't even hear the music. He is, in his particular way, like the *National Geographic* flyovers, who, seeing the people of Haiti from a thousand feet, inexplicably concluded that "[s]laves from Africa fathered most of the 2,500,000 people who now fill the valleys and hillsides of Haiti" (Simpich 11). That melodramatic and reductive inaccuracy, reducing multiplicity to an oversimplified, Hegelian either/or, erases black mothers and the tangled mix of rape and love and perhaps even indifference that produced Haiti's wide variety of *sang-melés*.

Absalom, Absalom! is, clearly, more than its remembered Haitian episodes. But those episodes require more than the historical record for an adequate understanding. Haiti held a prominent place in the American popular consciousness when Faulkner was struggling with his novel. If Richard Godden is correct in suggesting that coming to terms with labor in Haiti forced southerners and Americans in general to come to terms with brutal labor realities in the Old South (and to come to this awareness in the decade of the strongest dose of denial, *Gone With the Wind*), then Faulkner's concentration on Sutpen as a peculiarly mechanistic mannequin (in yet another addition to several "Sutpens" conjured up in the novel itself) suggests ways that opening southern studies toward the proposed "Caribbean horizon" might profitably circle back. Sutpen's prowess at subduing native insurrection might not be as anachronistic as it is prophetic of the character of U.S. imperialism in future "black Bagdads" unforeseen when Faulkner wrote. And we who seek the "global South" or the hemispheric extension of southern studies might beware that we don't make Sutpen's error: thinking we can "go out and subdue them."

Michel-Rolph Trouillot, appraising Madison Smartt Bell's *All Souls' Rising* (1995), the first novel in Bell's trilogy on the Haitian revolution (it covers the years 1791 to 1794), implies that historical knowledge (in the author and in his/ her readers) must be the criterion of judgment for this and all historical novels. Of course, Trouillot argues, Bell is at a disadvantage since the history of the Haitian revolution has been swathed in a "monumental silence" among historians (Carnes 184). "How does one write a historical novel," Trouillot asks, "minutely based on real events about which your readers are expected to know nothing?" (Carnes 196). Bell, taking up the question, admits that his plans to visit Haiti while he was writing *All Souls' Rising* were blocked by the coup of 1991 in which President Jean-Bertrand Aristide was deposed by the army. Bell wrote most of the first novel of his trilogy in "a sort of vacuum, sealed by books" (Carnes 198). It might be said that Bell, unlike Sutpen, "went to the West Indies" with too much secondhand knowledge rather than none at all.

But, as the previous section of this chapter suggests, the silence or vacuum Bell describes was far from absolute. Haiti found many ways into the popular (American) mind and imagination, only one of which was historical.[31] In *Haiti, History, and the Gods* (1995), Joan Dayan traces many of the paths Haiti has taken into our knowledge as her own life story was superimposed upon the popular narrative of Haiti. Seeing Haiti, where Dayan spent "a vexed and haunted childhood" (xii), as an entity in the historical record of European exploration and colonization, and as the cultural imagination of a place conceived primarily by Haitians themselves but also by others, Dayan finds accumulated knowledges of Haiti (beyond the island) in a wide range of cultural deposits. The problem of Haiti and history first, as Dayan sees it, is that—as is the case in many slave histories—the actual record is not recoverable. "Facing what remains to a large extent an unreconstructible past—the responses of slaves to the terrors of slavery, to colonists, to the New World—I try to imagine what cannot be verified" (xvii).[32] Whereas Bell was "sealed by books" in his first attempt to reconstruct Haiti, Dayan tries to keep books from dominating other forms of cultural expression by remembering her life in Haiti absent her reading.

Books are still a major part of the pattern to our knowledge of Haiti; since Raynal's *Histoire philosophique et politique des établissements des Européens dans les Deux Indes* (1771 in French; 1776 in English; revised through the 1820s), Haiti and the Caribbean have never been "out of print" in the European imagination. Already in Raynal, the history of Haiti (Saint-Domingue before independence) is attached to the myth of Eden, for Raynal reconstructs a precolonial history in which the indigenous peoples left minimal, but significant, traces. These pre-Columbian traces have survived in fiction and memoir as part of the myth of Haiti, as parts of the "dogmas and methods" we (who, unlike Dayan, have never been there) use to make narratives of the place. Raynal's Carib peoples lived in an unspoiled social Eden much like Thomas More's Utopia (a geopoetic space rather than a geopolitical place). "Although the Caribs had no government of any kind, their tranquility was undisturbed," Raynal writes. "They owed the peace they enjoyed to that innate sense of compassion which precedes all reflection, and which is the source of all social virtues. . . . Since their hearts were not depraved by the bad institutions which corrupt us, the deceptions, the betrayals, the perfidy, the murders so common among civilized peoples were unknown to the Caribs. . . . A people to whom self-interest, vanity and ambition were unknown could not have a very complicated way of life" (Raynal 136). Edna Taft, visiting Haiti in the 1930s soon after the end of U.S. occupation, heard a different version of the myth from her hosts. The Carib peoples, the "cannibals" of legend, were not indigenous to pre-Columbian Haiti; the Arawaks were the indigenous people, gentle and peace-loving (Taft 41).[33] The Caribs, Taft was told, were just the first wave of conquistadores brought by the encircling sea.

Slavery was the evil in the New-World, utopian pastoral, and Raynal acknowledged as much when he (or Diderot, who revised his text) wrote this ominous prediction for Saint-Domingue:

> It will always be a noble spectacle to see peoples in revolt against the enslavement of Negroes. In this case [Saint-Domingue], it appears, they fled into inaccessible mountains, where they have multiplied to such an extent that they can now offer a safe asylum to any slaves who can find the means to join them. There, thanks to the cruelty of civilized nations, they have become as free and ferocious as tigers; perhaps they are only awaiting a conquering leader who will restore the violated rights of humanity by seizing an island which nature seems to have destined for the slaves who till the soil, rather than for the tyrants who have stained it with the blood of these victims. (Raynal 184)

Was Toussaint Louverture produced by the Enlightenment imagination before his historical appearance? That is, to borrow a part of Paul Gilroy's thesis in *The Black Atlantic:* had "the intellectual heritage of the West," lurking in the prophecy of Raynal/Diderot, already constructed Louverture? And, by predicting him, appropriated his meaning to history? If so, what burdens were readymade for him because he was, if only in part, predicted by the imagination of the master?[34] If slavery in Haiti, and in the Caribbean generally, occupies the historical text, it also survives in a constellation of tropes exercising strange perturbations in the historical orbit: a gnawing sense of the cruelty of civilization (in the words of the civilized author); the preparation in the wilderness of the messianic avenger; the appearance of this hero; the pastoral, agrarian Eden soaked with slave blood shed by inhuman white masters; a redemption of sorts by violence. Can the "fresh thinking about the importance of Haiti and its revolution" (Gilroy 17) that Gilroy summons actually be achieved in minds so occupied by the Haiti of myth?

Dayan makes one of these related conventions prominent in *Haiti, History, and the Gods:* "the stereotype of the luxurious *mulâtresse*" (xvi). Choosing this trope from a range of possibilities, Dayan provides a link to Benitez-Rojo's overview of the parts played by the Caribbean in postmodern consciousness, and through Benitez-Rojo to Bell's weighty trilogy. "The stereotype of the luxurious *mulâtresse,* a necessary prop in the colonial fantasy of Saint-Domingue," Dayan writes, "operates as a dream of whiteness against the fact of blackness. The obsession with the light-skinned mistress obscured the presence of black women, who, in a few accounts, appear as well-dressed, as beautiful—and, though unsaid, as desirable—as the mulatta with thin lips and aquiline nose" (180). So necessary to the larger romance of colonial domination is this symbol of racial and sexual power and desire that the "fantasy" of Haiti subsumes its history. Shreve, for example, takes over the Haitian narrative of Sutpen at just the point where "the girl" enters. Craige's memoir of occupied Haiti makes prominent mention of one "jet-black" woman who, *pace* Dayan, *does* remain "unsaid," cloistered in her own enforced shame. Novels like Arna Bontemps's *Drums at Dusk* (1939) and James Michener's *Caribbean* (1989) pair the fiery and passionate mulatta with the fair European. Bell, beginning in *All Souls' Rising,* positions the *mulâtresse* at the crux of the meanings of Haiti, the pivotal counterweight in romance to the Louverture of the historical novels in the trilogy. And, by so doing, tacks perilously close to the rocks of a dialectic that the poetics of oblivion counteracts.

Although, in one part of Dayan's scheme, "the luxurious *mulâtresse*" is a construction of Anglo-Saxon, male, erotic indulgence, she is nevertheless central to Haitian-ness. Jules Michelet, in the nineteenth century, Dayan notes, made Haiti "La Femme"; as Michelet was sure that black women desired white men over mates of their own race, he was equally sure that the black republic sought white Europe for its patron and model (Dayan 48–51).[35] In Virgile Valcin's *La Blanche Négresse,* a novel top-heavy with its self-conscious cultural mission to foster a Haitian renaissance, Port-au-Prince salons gather to extol the black Haitian woman (50, 66–67, 73), and the novel's coda is a paean to the Haitian woman as mother—as Africa is mother to Haiti herself (73, 206–09). In the twentieth century, Dayan reads "Fictions of Haiti" predominantly as the process through which Haitian women novelists have fought to deconstruct this mythology since (like the "pedestal" iconology constructed for the southern belle) it controls representation of Haitian woman and, thereby, the meaning of Haiti itself (Dayan 119–26).

What, then, can it mean when Trouillot asks, in defense of the novel of Haitian history, "How does one write a historical novel minutely based on real events about which your readers are expected to know nothing?" In one sense, the sense of the fable of the betrayed *mulâtresse,* we "know" altogether too much about Haiti—and not its history. Trouillot reveals much (and Bell, who acquiesces in the question, also reveals much about his trilogy) by undervaluing the ways in which Haiti already exists as "the cultural imagination of a place" both onshore and off (Dayan xvi). This tension between the official authority of history and the popular life of "romance" gives Bell's trilogy a problematic narrative course, ricocheting from the one register to the other, attempting a unification in the figure of Louverture. On the one hand, the three novels exist in that cultural territory Dayan calls the "Gothic Americas" (Dayan chap. 4), an archive that weaves race and romance in the colonized Americas through the imagination of the colonizers. On the other hand, Bell's three novels potentially constitute, as one admiring reviewer predicted, the standard against which the as-yet-unwritten Haitian novel must and will be measured (Nzengou-Tayo 184).

The first novel in Bell's trilogy is *All Souls' Rising* (1995). In historical terms, *All Souls' Rising* covers the years from the first violent uprising of slaves on Saint-Domingue (August 1791) to the summer of 1793, when Toussaint Louverture's custodianship of the revolution became embroiled in Revolutionary politics in France and attempts by the Spanish and British to exploit the chaos on the island for their own colonial gain. Saint-Domingue was, at the end of the eighteenth century, the richest colony in the European colonial sphere. As Bell's plot works its way through known historical events, flash-forward vignettes of Louverture's imprisonment in France (from 1802 until his death on April 7, 1803) punctuate the major divisions of the three novels, lending the action in which Louverture fights and intrigues for independence a shadow of historical doom. He will be betrayed (more than once), mocked, and executed by inches, left to the chilly mercies of the French climate in a damp, fitfully heated jail cell. Through the structural device of Louverture's fatal imprisonment, filled with his reveries, interrogations by white jailors and "advocates," Bell suggests a parallel with Nat Turner, leader of a U.S. slave uprising in 1831 who was likewise badgered in his jail cell for his "story."[36] From structuring decisions Bell makes at the outset of the trilogy, it is evident that history has authority over the beginning and the end. It is equally evident that Bell leaves the middle open to the Haiti of our cultural imagination—and like the college narrators in *Absalom, Absalom!* that imagination is drawn irresistibly to the feminine.

"The history of slavery," Dayan explains by way of slavery's representation in and through Haiti, "is given substance through time by a spirit that originated in an experience of domination. That domination was most often experienced by women under another name, something called 'love'" (56). Bell follows this track, for once the historical record is established in the prologue (Louverture aboard ship, bound for prison in France), part 1 of *All Souls' Rising* opens with the gruesome image of a slave woman crucified by her *grand blanc* master, Michel Arnaud. The woman, Mouche, had killed her child, doubtlessly Arnaud's and therefore worth money to him in an economy where slaves were capital and birth rates low. She had driven a nail through its forehead (Bell, *Souls* 19). Childbirth, and its antitheses infanticide and abortion, start early and run through the entire trilogy as tropes establishing women characters in possession of a counterforce to colonial history: their reproductive bodies, the network of desire and property they embody as luxurious *mulâtresses,* and their knowledge of—and willingness to use—methods of killing along with generation. A white French doctor, Antoine Hébert, who has come to Saint-Domingue to search for his sister (the wife of a French planter, Elise Hébert had disappeared after her husband's death), comes upon the crucified woman at the beginning of the novel:

> A foot or eighteen inches below the mark of the chain [with which the woman had been dragged to the site], the woman's hands had been affixed to the wood by means of a large, square-cut nail. The left hand was nailed over the right, palms forward. There had been some bleeding from the punctures and the runnels of blood along her inner forearms had hardened and cracked in the dry heat, from which the doctor concluded that she must have been there for several hours at the least. Surprising, then, that she was still alive.
>
> Pulling against the vertex of the nail, her pectoral musculature had lifted her breasts, which were taut, with large aureoles, nipples distended. Although her weight must have pulled her diaphragm tight, the skin around her abdomen hung comparatively slack. At her pudenda appeared a membranous extrusion from which Doctor Hébert averted his eye. (*Souls* 11)

The description of the dying slave's body continues in this deliberate "gothic" vocabulary, couching erotic description in the blandly anatomical language of an autopsy. Through the white, scientific Enlightenment eyes of Hébert (as yet able to hold horror at bay with objectivity), Bell signals that, in *All Souls' Rising,* the presumptive narrative of history/fact will indeed be challenged (and offset?) by a narrative of/in the female body. "Love, promiscuity, pleasure, and abandon are words that recur throughout French accounts of the colony of Saint-Domingue," Dayan attests (56). And in Bell's gruesome opening scene this Haiti appears, first, as the tortured black woman, her body transformed into a gothic topography of the island by the doctor's meticulous, scientific, and "aerial" survey.

Nor is this scene the fulfillment of the design to locate Haiti in the cultural space bounded by "love, promiscuity, pleasure, and abandon." Arnaud, the vindictive planter, has a wife, Claudine, in addition to the slave mistress he is in the process of butchering. Haiti has deranged Claudine, as it has (to differing degrees, as the trilogy progresses) all the white women who have come there as planters' wives or marriage prospects. Claudine cannot sit for dinner with Arnaud and Doctor Hébert, his guest, for she is the worse for "*un coup de tafia*"— a shot of rum (*Souls* 15). As Hébert undresses for bed, he takes part in a scene familiar in the cultural melodrama and B-movie of the tropics: "A woman stood between him and the candle, which glittered through the loose weave of her clothing and outlined every detail of her body in black. The doctor had not yet got used to the degree of undress Creole women affected. . . . The woman hooked her hands into the waistband of his breeches and sat down backward on the *paillasse,* drawing him down after her" (20–21). For the character of Claudine Arnaud (at least in the first volume of his trilogy) Bell seems to draw on C. L. R. James. In *The Black Jacobins* (1963), James had diagnosed white women in Saint-Domingue as inescapably nymphomaniac: "Passion was their chief occupation, stimulated by over-feeding, idleness, and an undying jealousy of the black and mulatto women who competed so successfully for the favours of their husbands and lovers" (C. James 30). James was only making overt the latent erotic fantasy that both titillates and frightens Shreve and Quentin as they imagine Bon's mother and mistress.

Demure, Claudine Arnaud is not; in the familiar cultural romance of the vampire (here: zombie) fable perennially mapped upon Haiti, Madame Arnaud is infected with the blood she both loathes and desires. Raynal is not the first, just a very early, European observer to locate enhanced sensuality in the tropics; "the passionate temperament" of the black woman, asserted scientifically as a function of climate, becomes a basis of self-absolution for the white man, who cannot but turn his lust free upon her (Raynal 157–58). Where this sexual economy leaves the white woman is clear: as the officially desired object, she is shunted into position as symbol, and European mores prevent her from declaring her own desire—or, like Claudine, she must become an alcoholic and nymphomaniac. Hébert resists the kiss of this spider woman.

Bell's white women characters basically march to C. L. R. James's tune. Claudine Arnaud is driven to sexual (and alcoholic) desperation by the grunts and giggles of her husband and his black mistress copulating in the next room, yet she cannot remember her own pleasure in the same acts, and she is barren (*Souls* 83–84). She sits before her vanity mirror, tormented by the free sensuality in her husband's mistress and her own neuroses, like a modern woman exported to eighteenth-century colonial Saint-Domingue by way of *The Waste Land* (*Souls* 82). She is not alone in *All Souls' Rising*. The wife of another *grand blanc*, Isabelle Cigny, quite literally sleeps with the officer corps of the French garrison to satisfy a sexual appetite broadened by the island (96). More promiscuous than Claudine (and therefore more apt to survive?), Madame Cigny straddles the roles of symbolic colonial Madonna and erotic woman liberated by the tropics when, as cities and plantations burn around her, she "laid him [Capt. Maillart, at the moment serving under Louverture] stiff and bare on a soft mound of carpets in the middle of the floor. Her skirts swung up and over him like a bell and then she settled, nestling, almost like a hen. He smiled at the thought. Then they were joined" (*Souls* 406). Isabelle Cigny survives through the trilogy, never ceases her "promiscuity," and bears a child by a black lover, thereby charting a sexualized feminine course through the chaos of revolution and counterrevolution. If diplomacy cannot (and does not) achieve an alliance of races and classes, sexual desire does. Or, it might; the romance of the symbolic order is always provisional.

Bell's concentration on heterosexual desire, the many forms of its fulfillment from the pleasurable to the brutal, overwhelms the historical register of his novel, putting *All Souls' Rising* into a destabilized dance between history and romance. That is to say, if readers know "nothing" of the actual course of events from 1791 through 1803 in the French colony of Saint-Domingue (in fact, Bell distributes many of these facts in the narrative—and adds a glossary of creole terms and a chronology of historical events to the third volume, *The Stone That the Builder Refused*),[37] we know much more about the Haiti of the symbolic order and from many and diverse elements of romance in *All Souls' Rising*.

The character through whose consciousness we witness the crucifixion of Mouche at the outset of the novel is a doctor of medicine conspicuously lacking the racist preconceptions of the white colonials whom he visits. Not long after he reaches the island Hébert is swept up into "history," the beginnings of the slave revolution, and not long after that into romance. His immersion in the latter is the more interesting node of Bell's contrapuntal plot. That is, once we learn that both Louverture and Hébert are physicians, that the former practices with herbs and the latter with science, it is foregone that they will meet, and even that the Enlightenment-trained physician will be converted to the homeopathic practice of the colonial subject.[38]

The complementarity of Louverture and Hébert is only one of the convergences in the plot. Another concerns Hébert's re-education in the body—a telling irony for a physician who has, presumably, studied all there is to know of anatomy. "The luxurious *mulâtresse*" is of course represented in *All Souls' Rising* as his tutor. She is Nanon, a stunningly beautiful mulatto woman desired by every man she meets. Bell sees her role in the novel as central: "The colored woman Nanon [is] a wholly positive figure, but because she was a prostitute, most Haitian readers don't [see her that way]" (Carnes 206). Nanon's sexual power is a double-edged fate, for most of the men who desire her also desire to humiliate her. Hébert sees her first in a typical street scene; Nanon jumps into his awareness in a way that contrasts sharply with the anatomical coolness with which the dying body of Mouche registers on his scientific mind. "The woman . . . was more than striking, though simply dressed in a single wrap of flower-printed cotton that dropped sheer from its binding to her calves, leaving her handsome shoulders bare. She wore a necklace of gold links and a dozen or so thin gold bracelets on one arm, jingling them as she gestured and swung her hips" (*Souls* 102). Nanon is the sexual, Haitian sublime, the female moving in what Benitez-Rojo (as a boy registering an erotic power he might recall decades later as the central figure in an entire cultural identity) called "a certain kind of way," a way that pivots through the hips—a move both public and intimate. Edna Taft, the puritan lady in voodoo-land, was clearly embarrassed by a similar call-out encounter: she deflected the "peculiar wiggling motion" of the women she saw in the market with a mechanistic metaphor: "Ball-bearing hips!" (Taft 19).

Of course, Nanon and Hébert become lovers; it is a staple of the romance that opposites (like the pairs of racially and culturally crossed lovers in *South Pacific* Emile and Nellie, Joe and Liat)[39] attract, and that sexual attraction collides with social taboo. Louverture schools the doctor in Haiti's herbal cures, while Nanon schools him in sex. Arguably Hébert learns more about Haiti from

Nanon than he does from Louverture—confirming the sagacity of Grandfather Compson's advice to Sutpen on language acquisition. "The doctor turned in time to see her touch herself cunningly just above the breastbone. The cotton wrap came undone spontaneously and whispered to the floor. The necklace winked at him, her bare skin changed its surface like a leopard's coat as she moved forward under the white-hot dots and bars of light that leaked through the weave of the blind. Her bracelets softly belled together as she reached out, and wherever she touched him a piece of his clothing fell away as though cut with a hot knife" (*Souls* 105). How much sharper is the doctor's sexual ecstasy for being mixed with bondage: the gold "links" winking to him in complicity for Nanon's enslavement, the hot sunlight making prison bars of the window blinds, bracelets belling like surveillance devices. Yet, as Bell deploys the sexual meaning of Nanon-Haiti, Nanon is more crucial to the Anglo-Saxon colonizer's survival in the narrative of Haiti than Louverture is. As Bell marches through the trilogy, he must inevitably acknowledge Louverture's political and physical extinction: it is an established fact of the historical record. The gist of his verdict on Louverture would seem in accord with C. L. R. James's: Louverture's "fatal sincerity" led him to underestimate the brutal power of race hatred across the whole spectrum (C. James 364). Nanon and her children survive, however, as a domestic microcosm of the racial harmony that fails in the narrative of history. Bell can manipulate (or try to) the romance narrative as he cannot the historical.

Bell imagines Haiti as hell on white European women sent there to shoulder the roles of wife, mother, social icon. Claudine Arnaud is deranged by the unregulated sexual economy enjoyed by white men. She continues the butchering of her husband's slave mistress, slicing open her womb when she finds her dying on the timbers to which her husband has nailed her (*Souls* 91). She knows she is mad, seeks help from Hébert after her thwarted attempt to seduce him, and eventually uses her status as a madwoman to escape a band of marauding blacks who have freed themselves from slavery. She cuts off her own finger when the leader of the marauders takes a fancy to her ring (167). The marauders take her to be a vodou and give her and the survivors she is protecting a wide berth. Claudine Arnaud, perhaps because the white, European role of woman is traumatized out of her, survives, even confesses the murder of Mouche (to a whiskey-priest, another familiar figure in the romance of the tropics [337]),[40] repenting in almost the same breath the entire colonial enterprise, on behalf of a society for which, because of her sex, she cannot speak. In the subsequent volumes of the trilogy, Claudine is converted from madness to sainthood. She establishes a school in which she teaches slave children to read and fulfills the intuition of the man who takes her ring (and finger) by becoming a human (female) habitation for vodou spirits.

All is not so well, on the other hand, with another European woman, Marguerite, an orphaned cousin of the Lamberts, *grand blanc* plantation owners. Marguerite is a "flaxen blonde with large liquid blue eyes that seemed to show intelligence" (151). Marguerite had been sent to the colonies to find a husband, and was on the brink of success when the Lambert plantation is swept up in the 1791 revolt. Her fiancé is killed with a spike to the forehead (158); the white women are raped, some killed outright, others taken away for further torture. Marguerite is among the latter; her severed head is seen later lashed to the saddle of a rebel slave (220).

If Bell uses European women as indices of his critique of colonization, he uses Nanon to imagine an outcome that comes tantalizingly close to absolution from the sins of history. As much as Bell tries to pull some hope for the future out of the historical narrative, that much does he elevate Nanon among the women in his long narrative to symbolic ideal in a romance narrative. That the doctor and Nanon become lovers does not mean that Nanon can or even wants to shed her former, white benefactors. Chief among her colonial liaisons is one with Maltrot, a *grand blanc* representing the most repressive and cynical royalist (and racist) regime of Saint-Domingue. Maltrot is one of the characters to whom Bell attributes the royalist plot to foment a slave uprising (the one which Louverture then commandeers in 1791), which the plantation masters had orchestrated in order to cow the mixed-race population (*les gens de couleur*), who had been encouraged to think of their own elevation to equality with whites by talk of the "Rights of Man" thousands of miles away in France.[41] Maltrot is himself the father of a mulatto son, Choufleur, whose hatred for him turns to patricide: Choufleur flays the body of his father, Maltrot, and makes Nanon (who rejects him) a gift of his father's, her lover's, mummified penis. (235). The racial and sexual indications of overwhelming white patriarchy are thick and obvious in such episodes where the symbolic order overwhelms history.

The relationship of Hébert and Nanon, however, survives the abattoir in the historical strands of the plot. Nanon conceives a child with the doctor, a son who at birth appears to be "very white" (345). Isabelle Cigny, inured to the creole experience of procreation in which avatars of the racially repressed seem always about to issue from the womb, tells the doctor that all babies are white at birth; she can already see the marks of mixed blood in the doctor's son. Atavism is no shock to her—at least when the child belongs to someone else. But Hébert is un-fazed; in fact, Bell takes a huge risk in imagining the doctor's outlook as utterly unconcerned about his son's racial identity. There is, on the margins of the birth scene, a rain shower that douses the burning city (the baby is born in the midst of a battle), a turn toward pathetic fallacy that pulls overtly against the histori-cal narrative. More central to the scene is Hébert's first close look into the face of his son, a look that continues the series of self-regardful looks made possible by the shard of mirror the doctor keeps throughout the events of the narrative as a kind of fetish: "Already his small face was changing. When the doctor had first seen it emerge, the face had been without a doubt his own grandfather's. There were still the odd dog-shaped, crumpled ears, a Hébert family trait, but the other features were settling into something that belonged to this one child alone. Not himself, not Nanon, but a mingling—something new. This, the doc-tor realized, was what all the trouble was about" (345). "This" is both powerfully signifying and ambiguous. With "this" Bell intends to shift the weight of history (the designs of France, Spain, and England to create great wealth from colo-nial soil and black bodies, entire national appetites for sugar) with a mixed-race baby born both inside the taxonomy of race ratios and outside the grid of preju-dicial classification: "something [rather, someone] new." What makes this scene profoundly counterhistorical is that Bell must "know" that texts like Craige's and Taft's (among many others) testify that, were Hébert a person in history, his hopefulness at the birth of his *sang-melé* son would founder in time. The son would become Charles Bon, and the father Thomas Sutpen. It is in scenes like this one in *All Souls' Rising* where Bell's twining of factual and symbolic orders foregrounds the story or Haiti over Haiti-in-history, and undermines his own hopeful intentions: as if he could "unwrite" *Absalom, Absalom!*

Mixed-race children born and then folded into familial community func-tion as a linking trope in the Haiti trilogy. As the blended families mothered by Isabelle Cigny, Elise Tocquet (Hébert's venturesome sister marries a *bucca-neer,* arms dealer, a mixed-race man whose bloodlines disappear into the Carib-Arawak past), and Nanon grow, we see them at play with the children of freed plantation slaves in a series of scenes, across the volumes of the trilogy, that con-front the historical record with a brave hopefulness. In the second volume, *Mas-ter of the Crossroads* (2000), Nanon gives birth to a second son, this one most

certainly the son of Choufleur, the mulatto patricide, who had seized Nanon
while Hébert was serving as medical officer to Louverture's troops. Choufleur
kept Nanon in racial and sexual bondage to which, troublingly, she had submit-
ted. There is still, Bell seems to say, a residual sexual heat that draws "blood"
to "blood." When Choufleur comes to the plantation to kidnap Nanon, Elise
Tocquet sees him in the dark: "That limberness, the fluidity of his movement,
Elise thought, set him apart from a white man even in the dark" (*Master* 200).
Choufleur's island sensuality bonds Nanon to him: "Then too, there were the
pleasures of love. The release of Choufleur's long-bottled passions excited her;
he had convinced her with his body that they had truly been waiting all their
lives to be joined. He was a fiercer lover than the doctor, and if he sometimes
frightened her a little, the fear was no more than the shivering edge of the thrill"
(348).[42] Soon, though, Choufleur gives evidence of the fantasized "weakness"
inherent in the mulatto male, for he extends his hatred for his father, Maltrot
(whom he has already killed), by humiliating Nanon, his father's mistress. He
keeps her in iron, not gold, chains and shackles, and rapes her into traumatized
passivity. She conceives a child in bondage to Choufleur. The boy (named François) is clearly not Hébert's, but the doctor accepts him nevertheless.

In the same act of adoption Hébert accepts as his son a boy born at almost
the same time to Isabelle Cigny. This child is quite dark; his father was a black
officer in Louverture's army with whom Madame Cigny had had an affair (con-
travening Louverture's orders, Bell points out). Nor is this boy (Gabriel) an "accident." Isabelle Cigny has had one husband and many lovers, but children only
when she intends them. In the second volume of the trilogy, *Master of the Crossroads,* she feels the threat of banishment that befalls a white woman who gives
birth to a mixed-race child, but maintains her love for Gabriel's father (Louverture had him, and several other officers, executed for alleged treason) even
as she takes other lovers from the cohort of French expeditionary officers. She
agrees to Nanon's scheme to have the two boys, François and Gabriel, presented
to the world as twins—even though it is evident to any observer that they are
not related. Hébert agrees to acknowledge them both, and in the climactic scene
of *Master of the Crossroads* he marries Nanon, thus creating a microcosmic republic of romance in which the racial distinctions that cleave the macrocosm of
history are simply ignored. François and Gabriel are then pushed forward as the
Romulus and Remus of this symbolic New World nation.

This design is completed in the third volume, *The Stone That the Builder*

Refused (2004), when Elise Tocquet seeks and finds an abortion to terminate her pregnancy. Like Isabelle Cigny, Elise had had an affair with a black officer in Louverture's corps. Elise first asks her brother, Hébert, to perform the abortion, but he pleads that he has neither the skill as a European physician nor the herbs of the local practitioners to perform the procedure. Elise finds a local woman to terminate her pregnancy, and comes close to death before she recovers from internal bleeding. In what seem to be her final moments she confesses to her brother that the father was a black man, but not Louverture (it was Hébert's question), although she had been with the General just "the one time" (*Stone* 612).

What comes of these recurring scenes of copulation, conception, pregnancy, childbirth, and incorporation of the mixed-race children into a harmonious family, spread over three volumes and nearly 1,500 pages, is a counternarrative to the overwhelming historical record. Bell knows, as do his readers, that democratic self-governance has never achieved permanence in Haiti. James Anthony Froude was not the first white European to demean "this paradise of negro liberty" (181). Visiting in the 1880s, he found a failed experiment less than a century after the high hopes of independence:

> They were equipped when they started on their career of freedom with the Catholic religion, a civilised language, European laws and manners, and the knowledge of various arts and occupations which they had learnt while they were slaves. They speak French still; they are nominally Catholic still; and the tags and rags of the gold lace of French civilisation continue to cling about their institutions. But in the heart of them has revived the old idolatry of the Gold Coast, and in the villages of the interior, where they are out of sight and can follow their instincts, they sacrifice children in the serpent's honour after the manner of their forefathers. (Froude 183)

Back aboard the ship that will take him to comfortable British Jamaica, Froude delays his breakfast so that he might "strip and plunge into a bath and wash away the odor of the great negro republic of the West" (188).

Nor have twentieth-century European and American opinions been kinder. General Smedley Butler, commandant of the U.S. Marine occupation force, viewed Haitian formal dress and the society it signified as no better than minstrelsy (Thomas 219). John Craige, a mercenary in that same force, concluded that "men with primitive, Stone Age craniums cannot compete with men who inherit their brains from the able white races of Western Europe" (Craige 132). "In all their history," Craige wrote, "they had never produced a government that developed beyond the stage of military despotism" (133). Edna Taft chips in as well, citing climate and "lustful relations" between races as the causes for "a race of half-castes, in whom noble sentiments of honor and delicacy warred constantly with arrant cruelty and abject superstition" (370).

It is this deep vein of Western, white contempt, fear, and weirdly prurient superiority that necessitates, in Gilroy's schema, "fresh thinking about the importance of Haiti and its revolution" (17). But it is not clear that the erotic and reproductive "fresh thinking" Bell offers in his trilogy does not in crucial ways derive from, and map itself on, the old thinking. Against this surplus of historical "knowledge" conscripted to a nationalist project of European superiority, Bell imagines a different Haiti, one issuing from the womb of the sensuous but eventually domesticated Haitian woman. And yet, as Joan Dayan vigorously argues, that woman is a construct produced by interests other than Haitian women themselves. The risky business of using the stereotype to rid oneself of it is Bell's way to imagine Haiti out of the "problem" status described by what Noam Chomsky, thinking of Haiti among all developed-world colonies, labels "the standard accompaniment of conquest": "the wondrous capacity for self-adulation" in any and all romances of conquest we might tell ourselves, and "an intellectual armory to ensure that nothing is learned from what they [we] have done" (Farmer 17).

If Bell might be located on the Chomsky side of the many-faceted problem of writing about colonial conquest from within the mind of the conqueror in the first volume of his trilogy, by the third he has cooled his "wondrous capacity for self-adulation" in a wash of post-9/11 geopolitics. In *The Stone That the Builder Refused,* completed and published in 2004, a quartet of young French captains in Leclerc's doomed expeditionary force ship out from France to Saint-Domingue consciously spurred on by the "image of that raghead Negro" (157). The phrase recurs several times in the novel, along with other seemingly anachronistic phrases such as "kill zone" and "killing fields" (70, 480). Like Faulkner, Bell might be faulted for tripping on anachronism, suggesting through speech idioms deriving from ongoing wars in Iraq and Afghanistan that Haiti continues in the U.S. cultural imagination as one in a series of "black Baghdads."

Bell's response to the implicit challenge in writing as a conqueror is carried by the women among his characters. The men, with few exceptions, are locked into the mechanical calculus of sugar equals money equals guns (*Stone* 44). In the final volume, one of the young French captains who have come to (inevitably) reverse Louverture's revolution and take him prisoner insults Nanon by calling her a whore (576). Hébert challenges the captain to a duel, and bloodshed is averted only when the captain's fellow officers pressure the offender to apologize. Even then, Hébert is disinclined to accept an apology. It is Nanon herself, eavesdropping on the coerced apology, who accepts in her own name, and then, when the same captain falls ill with (and eventually dies of) yellow fever, it is also she who nurses him. The way out of the record of historical failure, Bell seems to say, is not led by warrior males, but by the women, who have suffered the longest and have the most to forgive.

5

PARODY, MEMORY, AND COPYRIGHT
The Southern Memory Market

∞

Whose mother is Mammy?
—EVE KOSOFSKY SEDGWICK, *Between Men*

The spring of 2001 seems like a barely remembrable past, almost a year of "magical thinking" pushed beyond recovery by the history-transforming events of the following September 11: the trauma that "changed everything."[1] In March of that obliterated spring a controversy arose, swelled, and had largely evaporated by early summer. However short its burn, the controversy over Alice Randall's parody of *Gone With the Wind, The Wind Done Gone* (2001), should have become a signature event in the ongoing creative evolution of *Gone With the Wind,* one of the most long lived contests between memory and history in southern identity turning on a literary text. Controversy blossomed not because of questions of literary quality that Randall's novel raised, although the aesthetic merits of Mitchell's and Randall's texts will continue to concern some readers. Adam Gopnik, reviving the hauteur with which some cosmopolitan reviewers greeted Margaret Mitchell's *Gone With the Wind* in 1936, missed the point of Randall's parody: "Why not show up the hollowness of a bad book by writing a good book, rather than a new version of the bad book?" (Gopnik 37). Readers like Gopnik still are not persuaded that whether or not Mitchell's novel is "good" or "bad" has nothing to do with its importance to literature in general or to the formation of southern memory-and-history in particular.[2] Professional historians continue to add to shelves of works on the South and slavery; this does not mean that most people, American and otherwise, do not trace what they "know" about both to *Gone With the Wind.*[3]

The impending publication of Randall's parodic novel initially triggered alarms, not at first among literary critics, but in the financial vaults where *Gone*

With the Wind functions as a commercial dynamo for investments descended from the original trust established by the childless Margaret Mitchell for the benefit of her nephews, Eugene Muse Mitchell and Joseph Reynolds Mitchell. Having obtained advance copies of *The Wind Done Gone,* scheduled for publication by Houghton Mifflin in spring 2001, attorneys for the Stephens Mitchell Trusts (named for the novelist's brother, an attorney, who inherited her property when she died in 1949) filed for a temporary restraining order in the Atlanta Division of the U.S. District Court, Northern District of Georgia. This was not the first time Mitchell's lawyers had risen to defend the commercial interests of the *GWTW* property—for property the novel had become, certainly as early as the release of the Selznick film in 1939. In 1979 attorneys for the Trusts had effectively shut down a musical, "Scarlett Fever," satirizing the novel and movie, between dress rehearsal and opening night.[4]

In court filings seeking a temporary restraining order to block the publication of Randall's novel, the Mitchell trustees, citing the Copyright Act of 1976 (Title 17 U.S.C., Section 106), claimed infringement of their exclusive right "to prepare derivative works based upon the copyrighted work." Such an unauthorized sequel as *The Wind Done Gone,* the plaintiffs argued, would inflict irreparable market damage to the *Gone With the Wind* franchise and interfere with demand for the original, and for any official sequels the copyright owners might license in the future.[5] This was the same commercial argument they had made against the musical in 1979, although in that case plaintiffs stressed the damage any dramatic performance might inflict on demand for the film. Houghton Mifflin argued in defense that Randall's novel was a parody, not a sequel, authorized or not, and therefore entitled to protection under the copyright exception for "fair use" as outlined in Section 107 of the 1976 legislation. Section 107, the "fair use" exception to copyright protection, lists four factors that may be considered in such disputes. Houghton Mifflin and Randall claimed exemption under the first of the four: *The Wind Done Gone* was not a sequel but a parody, and therefore Randall's acknowledged use of the original was "educational" and "transformative" rather than "commercial" and "reproductive." There was no intent to replace the original in the marketplace, just to make "transformative" use of it.

A hearing on the injunction was held on March 29, 2001, with Judge Charles A. Panell, Jr., presiding. Judge Pannell, a native of northwest Georgia, found in favor of the plaintiff, the Mitchell Trusts, and on April 19, 2001, the court "enjoined [Houghton Mifflin] from further production, display, distribution, advertising, sale, or offer for sale of the book *The Wind Done Gone*" (*SunTrust v. Houghton Mifflin*).[6]

Judge Pannell's order immediately triggered Houghton Mifflin's appeal to the Eleventh Circuit Court, and that appeal in turn elicited letters of support (on behalf of both defendant and plaintiff) from fiction writers, literary scholars, literary and media organizations, and publishing professionals. With the appeal, *SunTrust v. Houghton Mifflin* (SunTrust Bank administers the Mitchell Trusts investments) was transformed from one of several legal skirmishes to turn back threats to the *GWTW* property (beginning even before publication of the novel in 1936) into a firefight in the ongoing memory-and-history border war, with race and gender added to the mix. At stake for the plaintiff was the copyright holder's commercial interest in maintaining high popular demand for *Gone With the Wind*'s characters, scenes, and storylines so that sequels and authorized merchandise "derivatives" might remain viable commodities in the southern memory market. At stake for the defendant (never ignoring Houghton Mifflin's financial investment in *The Wind Done Gone*) was the felt (by the author and most of her supporters) obligation to repossess the cultural and racial memory appropriated by *Gone With the Wind* novel-and-film; to take back some degree of identity from decades-old clichés about race and sexuality, voice and cultural power; to take control of (and answer) such questions as Eve Kosofsky Sedgwick had asked in *Between Men: English Literature and Male Homosocial Desire*: "Whose mother is Mammy?" (9). If there ever was a case of modern capitalism "parasitically" climbing, like kudzu, on southern memory—even the fake one Romine analyzes in *The Real South* (6)—*SunTrust v. Houghton Mifflin* is it.

Richard Harwell, more than three decades ago in his introduction to a selection of Mitchell's letters, anticipated most of the issues in the copyright contest as they entangle literature and history, private ownership and the popular domain, in his adulation for *Gone With the Wind*: "Forty years after its publication [his selection of letters was published in 1976], Margaret Mitchell and her book are indelible parts of America. She furnished our past with a Scarlett O'Hara, a Melanie Wilkes, a Rhett Butler, and an Ashley Wilkes. They are as American as Jefferson Davis and Robert E. Lee, Abraham Lincoln and Ulysses S. Grant, Tom Sawyer and Huckleberry Finn. Why, in a large way they—book and author— belong to all of us" (xxxvi).

Harwell is comfortable with, even celebratory of, the power of *Gone With the Wind* to occupy the historical (and literary) record of the nineteenth century with memories of characters and events made up in the twentieth. Harwell did not, however, specify *which* past or *which* "our" was the focus of his ebullience. Judging from his examples, it seems clear he was thinking of a white past, and that that "past" encompassed both the historical record—where one might run across Davis, Lee, Lincoln, and Grant—and the fictional past—where Scarlett and Melanie, Rhett and Ashley, Tom and Huck (but not Jim)—are so familiar we may address them by their first names.

The Mitchell Trusts, however, insisted that the book in its whole and in its parts belonged to them, not to "all of us." *SunTrust v. Houghton Mifflin* turned on two issues raised by the Copyright Act of 1976. One was a hybrid of legal and literary discourse in which intellectual property and parody jousted for primacy. This was the battle over the status of parody within the "fair use" exemption. The literary community of writers and readers in which parody is a frequent rite assumed the sharability of texts; indeed, the word "community" would have little or no meaning without that assumption. Individuals of this persuasion generally contributed affidavits to the defendant's side. The market in texts-as-things, however, depends on exclusive possession and ownership: nobody owns the river, but I own the ferry. Several publishing professionals, seeing books as merchandise, supplied affidavits for the plaintiff. A third group, disapproving of Randall's explicitness in treating racial and sexual mores on the plantation (and therefore in southern memory-and-history), sent statements faulting the author's taste and literary skill. What was significant in many of the affidavits supporting Randall, and in those denigrating her literary merit, was the issue of cultural memory and its relationship to identity. Can one person claim ownership of an engine of that memory and pass it on, like real estate or silverware, to her heirs and assigns? Do those excluded from the power to alter the memory in which they appear have no redress—except to write their own books?

Parody is protected under U.S. copyright law; cultural memory is not. The boundaries of parody exist somewhere near the farthest reaches of "fair use"; courts determine that line. "Fair use," as defined in the 1976 copyright legislation, is not simply an issue of word count (the third of the four factors for adjudication: amount and substantiality of original used), of how much of an original a "second-comer" may use without formally obtaining permission. "[N]o official mathematical rules exist for determining how much may be safely used under fair use," writes Donald F. Johnston in the *Copyright Handbook* (2nd ed., 1982). "It all depends on the context and the circumstances" (133). In other words, the boundaries of the original and of the parody are always already in flux. Courts must weigh the "character" and "purpose" of parody's incursion upon the original work. Different courts may be more or less inclined to see business interests rather than literary and cultural interests as pivotal in setting boundaries; that is, a court might weigh the fourth factor (effect of the use on the market for the original) more heavily than one or more of the others. Has the second-comer appropriated so much of her predecessor that the new work superimposes itself on the older work in the marketplace, leading potential consumers to mistake the one for the other and to buy the parody thinking they have purchased the "real" thing? Judge Pannell detected such "irreparable harm" (*SunTrust v. Houghton Mifflin* 16).

The concept of the literary text as a thing that might be replaced in a marketplace by a similar thing loomed large in the Trusts' argument. Kevin J. Anderson, an experienced author of commissioned prequels, sequels, and derivatives for such franchisers as Lucasfilm (i.e., *Star Wars*), described Scarlett O'Hara as "undoubtedly one of the most famous *assets* of Ms. Mitchell's 'Gone With the Wind' universe," and further warned the court that "misappropriation of the Mitchell characters and character relationships would seriously taint the original *property* for further legitimate *development* by the rightful copyright holders."[7] Anderson's rhetoric suggests that any published parody would push *Gone With the Wind* in all of its manifestations into a kind of receivership where "assets" and "property" would cease to hold value. Alex Holtz, a literary agent, described the deleterious effect of a rogue sequel on the "sales performance" of the original product and warned of "reduced distribution and representation for subsequent titles" (Holtz affidavit 2). Putting the financial stakes into sharper focus, a representative of St. Martin's Press, purchasers of the rights to an official sequel (St. Martin's published *Rhett Butler's People* by Donald McCaig in 2007), claimed to have paid "well into seven figures" for the chance to reap even more. Being worth a lot of money shifted the language for defining *Gone With the Wind*. As an "asset" or "property" ripe for "development," the literary text was ushered into the same class of objects as a prime tract of land or a patented pharmaceutical formula. Parody thus became the wild card in a high-stakes financial game, a dimension to its meaning seldom discussed in dictionaries of literary terms.

Copyright law grants that a new work claiming to be a parody may appropriate *some* of the original; otherwise, the object of parody would never be known and no social good or change (transformative use) could ever arise from lampooning it. Too much appropriation invites the legal judgment that the work claimed as parody is (like its imagined author) passive or lazy, a "lite" substitute for the would-be parodist's own imaginative effort ("reproductive" rather than "transformative"). Some supporters of the Trusts made this argument, counting characters both major and minor, settings, situations, and turns of phrase from the original that could be identified in *The Wind Done Gone*. One affidavit for the plaintiff contains more than twenty pages of parallel citations (Beeber affidavit 1–23). These supporters urged the court to conclude that Randall could not produce her own original, "good" book, and so she merely reproduced material from her predecessor.

Since Randall (an African American woman living in Nashville) freely admitted that, as a devout southern girl and woman, she had read Mitchell's novel more than once, the similarities charted in the affidavits were never contested by Houghton Mifflin. The judge listed among his "findings of fact" that "Ms. Randall had access to *Gone With the Wind* when she wrote *The Wind Done Gone*," and that "[t]here are substantial similarities, objectively and subjectively, between the two books; that an average lay observer or a reasonable juror would find the works substantially similar in expression; and that those similarities involve copyrighted material" (*SunTrust v. Houghton Mifflin* 17). These "facts" being uncontested, the argument turned to their potential for "transformative" effect on the "average lay observer," the average consumer of the *GWTW* commodity.

Related to the quantitative question is the qualitative one: how "transformative" is the new work? "Transformative," that is, of both the "original" work itself and of the reading audience's understanding of that work and what they had taken to be its meanings. Here, the localized legal case opened out into the sea of memory-and-history. If the parody changes cultural perception of the original deeply enough, then the memory-and-history "normal" would have to change. If the presumptive parody leaves "the average lay reader" thinking she or he has read merely another version of the original—not a different version with its own dynamics—then the legal finding is very likely to be "piracy," not parody. In the often-cited copyright case *Campbell v. Acuff-Rose Music* (1994), in which Acuff-Rose Music, copyright holders in Roy Orbison's rock classic "Pretty Woman," brought suit against 2 Live Crew for its rap version of the song, with rewritten lyrics (and lost on appeal to the Supreme Court), the Court found, among other things, that the rap version "transformed" the original by naming what Orbison's hit had silenced. Orbison's version, a majority of the Justices decided, condones casual and opportunistic sex, with all the risks to public health and morals omitted from the lyrics, while 2 Live Crew's version exposes these evasions. The rap therefore "transforms" the original and the public by repositioning the meanings of the original, even providing a kind of public service admonition.

The law's definition of "parody" was crucial to the initial finding in favor of the plaintiffs, the Mitchell Trusts. The definition Judge Pannell relied upon, as I will argue momentarily, is particularly dated, applying as it does a one-dimensional test: does the alleged parody elicit laughter?[8] Judge Pannell made his finding against *The Wind Done Gone* as parody because he could not imagine the ubiquitous "lay reader" laughing at Randall's novel in a sufficient number of places. He did allow that certain episodes might achieve "comic effect," and thereby approached the parody exception, but without necessarily eliciting the continuous laughter that characterized, for example (an example the court did not invoke), the Carol Burnett spoof in which Scarlett has Mammy make her a dress out of Miss Ellen's "po'teers," and emerges with a curtain rod stretching across her shoulders.[9] When Judge Pannell did find humor, he did not find enough of the proper kind to establish legal parody:

> For example, the defendant argues that Garlic, instead of being portrayed as the loyal and obedient slave Pork in *Gone With the Wind*, controls his "master so thoroughly that, when Garlic pulls the strings, the master dance[s] like a bandy-legged Irish marionette.". . . Whether this achieves "comic effect" is not the only question. While the scene may be funny, it does not receive the benefit of the fair use doctrine simply by being so. The key issue is whether its purpose, when written, was to create a comedic scene that demonstrates the irony of the slave controlling his master or was created to further elaborate upon an extant character from *Gone With the Wind* in a sequel which only happens to be funny or comic. (*SunTrust v. Houghton Mifflin* 8)

The either/or test proposed by Judge Pannell, clouded by authorial "purpose," is an ambiguous standard at best. So thoroughly does comic effect define Panell's thinking on parody at this level that other effects do not influence his judicial thinking at all. In *Campbell v. Acuff-Rose Music,* the Supreme Court, reversing a lower court's decision that 2 Live Crew's rap version of Roy Orbison's "Pretty Woman" was not entitled to the parody exception under U.S. copyright law, applied the concept of parody as "transformative" rather than simply funny. Justice David Souter, writing for the majority, found sufficient "transformative" use other than comedy, hearing 2 Live Crew's additional rap lyrics as bringing to the fore what Orbison's lyrics keep behind a veil:

> While we might not assign a high rank to the parodic element here, we think it fair to say that 2 Live Crew's song reasonably could be perceived as commenting on the original or criticizing it, to some degree. 2 Live Crew juxtaposes the romantic musings of a man whose fantasy comes true, with degrading taunts, a bawdy demand for sex, and a sign of relief from paternal responsibility. The later words can be taken as a comment on the naiveté of the original of an earlier day, as a rejection of its sentiment that ignores the ugliness of street life and the debasement that it signifies. It is this joinder of reference and ridicule that marks off the author's choice of parody from the other types of comment and criticism that traditionally have had a claim to fair use protection as transformative works. (*Campbell v. Acuff-Rose Music*)[10]

The Supreme Court had already thought beyond Judge Pannell in this respect: a parody, to merit legal protection, need not achieve solely "comic effect"; it might indeed "comment on the naiveté of the original of an earlier day." Judge Pannell was eventually reversed on similar grounds. The Eleventh Circuit found that he had granted too much weight to "commercialism," too little to the new work's "transformative" value, and sent the case back. The two parties, reading between the lines, settled out of court.

Alice Randall's novel turns upon large and fundamental transformation of an "original of an earlier day" by revoking any defense of "naïvete." What made *The Wind Done Gone* so alarming to the defenders of "the original," perhaps, was not that it usurped market share but rather that it made pleasure in the original a guilty pleasure.

Randall begins her transformation by reimagining the white plantation master as the father of a mulatto daughter (Cynara) whose mother is Mammy, thereby answering the question Sedgwick had posed fifteen years earlier, and removing Tara from the cocoon of naïve memory and plunging it into history. When Randall "invents" an interracial sexual affair between Gerald O'Hara and Mammy, she knowingly uncovers an omission in the willfully naïve memory of the South. Near Macon, Georgia, about the time the fictional Gerald O'Hara was assembling the acres of Tara, another Irish immigrant to Georgia, Michael Morris Healy (1796–1850), was assembling his land holdings too, first from free land won in a state lottery, and later by purchase. Indeed, the mystique of land possession (O'Hara's mantra in Mitchell's novel) is powerful enough in the historian's world to color the description of Healy's Georgia soil written by the researcher who recovered his story: "This is not loose, dull-gray soil that sifts easily through the fingers, but a wet, hard-packed clay of startling red, indelibly staining anything it touches. A place like any other, Jones County is just different enough to seem at once familiar and exotic" (O'Toole 5). This description, the historian more or less acknowledges a page and a half later in his evocation of Michael Healy in Georgia, has been governed by Mitchell's version of Gerald O'Hara's awe and greed: "a savagely red land, blood-colored after rains, brick dust in droughts, the best cotton land in the world" (O'Toole 7; Mitchell 10). That the place is "at once familiar and exotic" is attributable to its dual existence in both history and cultural memory, geography and printed text/cinema screen. The historian has already "seen" what he sees for the first time because memory supplies the image.

The historical Georgian Michael Healy fathered ten children, nine of whom survived into adulthood, with Eliza Clark, "a woman who was at once his wife and his slave" (O'Toole 14). It is not the interracial sexual contact that is notable in this relationship between historical persons, but rather the steadfast and, apparently, monogamous nature of Healy's "marriage" to Eliza Clark. Mitchell's fictional plantation is, of course, a haven of proper sexual segregation and behaviors —supervised in many ways by Scarlett's mother, Ellen Robillard O'Hara. The miscegenation and sexual exploitation of the slave that characterized the actual historical record are everywhere omitted in *Gone With the Wind.* When lines of sexual propriety are crossed, they are crossed by whites of the lower classes. Ellen O'Hara is killed by an illness she contracts in nursing the illegitimate child fathered on a poor white girl by Tara's (Yankee) overseer: a bit of sexual misconduct that sparks in Gerald O'Hara a kind of glee. Randall's "transformative use" of Mitchell's novel exposes Mitchell's omission of a prevalent sexual practice (one very similar to the omissions Justice Souter found in the Roy Orbison original), restores interracial sexual exploitation to the center of the plot, and—coincidentally—echoes the proximate historical record written by the Healy family a few counties adjacent to fictional Tara, the actual site of much that was crucial to Margaret Mitchell's memory and identity (Pyron 47–48).

Louis D. Rubin, Jr., in his affidavit in support of the plaintiff's motion for a temporary restraining order and preliminary injunction, registers a similar objection to Randall's amendment to the record of master-slave sexual mores. In his objection to the explicitness of certain passages describing Rhett and Cynara in bed, Rubin inadvertently focuses on one omission Randall seeks to restore to the naïve original: the subjectivity of the African American characters. Digressing from his charge that Randall "has not emphasized the burlesque or undercutting of racial stereotypes" (Rubin affidavit 5), Rubin comes close to calling *The Wind Done Gone* pornography:

> As for the supposed sexual realism, it is absurd to claim that the author's intention was to show the elements of miscegenation that "really" went on in "Gone With the Wind." Instead the author has used the broader acceptance of sexual activity in contemporary fiction, and which was not the case in popular fiction when "Gone With the Wind" was published, to draw upon the reading public's interest in sexual description by depicting certain of Margaret Mitchell's characters engaging in vividly described sexual relationships. (Cf. Rhett Butler making love to Cinnamon [Cynara], pp. 28–29.) This goes far beyond any need to show the existence of black-white sex: it is an effort to appeal to the reader's prurient interests. (Rubin affidavit 6)

The problem is not "the broader acceptance of sexual activity in contemporary fiction," but rather the enforced silence on the subject that *Gone With the Wind* as a cultural project imposes on the public conversation about the South, history, and the character of the African American as slave. *The Wind Done Gone* gives the stereotyped and silenced their proper voices and subjectivities. In the case of black women on the white plantation, black female subjectivity faced being closed down by sexual exploitation. Randall explores what Margaret Mitchell would not even touch, and what the Mitchell Trusts, authorizers of sequels and derivative works for profit, would never allow: sexual relations between white and black, and subjectivity for the black characters involved in that nexus of power and violence. And that subjectivity is not only expressed in Cynara's erotic pleasures, but also in Randall's reimagining of Mammy. Notoriously compared, by Mitchell, to an elephant in the original, Mammy is portrayed by Randall as a slender and sensitive young woman when she first becomes Planter's (Gerald O'Hara's counter figure) mistress, bearing him Cynara. When Planter marries Lady (Ellen Robillard's counter figure), Mammy is hurt, and that is the beginning of her deliberate weight gain. Psychological plausibility aside, for the moment: Randall's design is clearly to loosen the totalitarian hold of stereotype on black and female identities.

What Randall's text acknowledges, albeit not always overtly, is that the purposely naïve memory narrative in *Gone With the Wind* drowns out a history narrative—and not the history narrative of the Battle of Atlanta and Reconstruction. Cynara narrates a life parallel to the one orbiting her half-sister (Other in *The Wind Done Gone;* Scarlett in *Gone With the Wind*). In this parallel life, Cynara sees the domestic life of Mitchell's Tara from the point of view of the slaves, who have alternative explanations for events canonized in *Gone With the Wind*. This general structural premise—that the work we are reading takes place offstage of a much more famous text we might be able to quote verbatim—has been used before. Tom Stoppard's *Rosencrantz and Guildenstern are Dead* is perhaps the most well known. But, whereas Stoppard's play *plays* with the language of a text (Shakespeare's *Hamlet*) far gone into the public domain, Randall's novel transforms its precursor text by insisting we pay attention to the former's omissions, specifically the racial and sexual omissions with which *Gone With the Wind* evades history and lays claim to blurbs announcing it as one of the greatest love stories of all time.[11]

Randall's complex point is that without *Gone With the Wind*'s omissions and willful naïvete, the myth of the plantation South would never have survived in cultural memory; its survival constitutes a silencing of other memories; and that the readings of *Gone With the Wind* clueless to these evasions need to be smartened up. In Judge Pannell, a native Georgian himself, the defendants were initially unlucky, for in the final lines of his opinion granting the restraining order he shows that he is inclined to believe in the myth rather than the omissions, inclined as a reader of fiction to be naïve rather than realistic: "When the reader of *Gone With the Wind* turns over the last page, he may well wonder what becomes of Ms. Mitchell's beloved characters and their romantic, but tragic, world. Ms. Randall has offered her vision of how to answer those unanswered questions, albeit with a partially parodic purpose in mind. The right to answer those questions and to write a sequel or another derivative work, however, belongs to Ms. Mitchell's heirs, not Ms. Randall" (*SunTrust v. Houghton Mifflin* 16). Anyone willing, even eager, to believe that characters in a "romantic, even tragic" fiction possess lives that continue, albeit unwritten, after the final page of the text in which they exist, is probably not ready to believe that conscious and subconscious selections and omissions went into the writing in the first place. This reader is, on the other hand, the ideal champion of a sequel in which he may find answers to his longings—the ideal consumer, in fact, of the derivative works the Trusts were hoping to produce in a future protected by copyright.

Although the plaintiffs eventually lost on appeal in the Eleventh Circuit Court, their cause summoned an entourage of professional literary critics and a host of lay readers who wanted to protect their investments in, as Louis Rubin wrote, "elements of historical myth that have made Margaret Mitchell's fiction memorable" (Rubin affidavit 3). Rubin was confident that "it would be difficult to imagine many contemporary readers who believe that the depictions of black-white, slave-master relationships in 'Gone With the Wind' are historically realistic" (Rubin affidavit 4), so he could therefore see no constructive reason to make a parody of the novel on those themes. Randall's premise, however, assumes that it is scary to see how much contemporary conflation there actually is between "historical myth" and the "historically realistic." Privatized memory, like privatized property, can produce redoubts where the construction of history by social memory, bypassing the check-and-balance system of fantasy and "proof," supplies only one master narrative. To disentangle, if only partially, historical myth and historical reality is the work of postmodern parody.

The legal arguments in *SunTrust v. Houghton Mifflin* seem to have been shaped by an outmoded and less flexible model of parody as a corrective to unbalanced power, one based solely on the production of demonstrable comic effects. If the new work elicits laughter at the original, parody should be deemed successful and fair use protection extended. The purpose of parody, as it most often appears in legal discourse, is conflated with this effect: if the "average lay observer" laughs at the parodic work, then the second author's purpose must have been to induce that laughter. No laughter, no parodic purpose; no purpose, no protection.

In adjudicating Houghton Mifflin's claim that Randall's novel is a parody of *Gone With the Wind,* and therefore protected, Judge Pannell imagined a single and inflexible lay reader: one who could respond to *The Wind Done Gone* with laughter alone. The author of one affidavit for the plaintiff invokes this older definition of parody, a definition derived from the works of eighteenth-century English satirists (Swift, Dryden, Pope) that seek to ridicule extant works then high in public esteem (Motola affidavit 2). J. A. Cuddon's formulation in his *Dictionary of Literary Terms* is as familiar as it is petrified: "The imitative use of words, style, attitude, tone and ideas of an author in such a way as to make them ridiculous. This is usually achieved by exaggerating certain traits, using more or less the same technique as the cartoon caricaturist. In fact, a kind of satirical mimicry" (483). Basing his affidavit on Cuddon's definition, a supporter of the Mitchell Trusts concludes that "while parody may allude to another work or figure, it does so briefly while securing its own imaginative plot and language so that the parodied work is ultimately put aside in the reader's imagination, replaced by the work being read" (Motola affidavit 3). In fact, although Cuddon's reading of parody is traditional, he does admit Henry Fielding's *Shamela* (1741) as an example of an entire parodic work in which the original is never "put aside," but parodied as a work entire rather than in its parts (Cuddon 484). The court, however, was apparently uninterested in such literary distinctions: ridicule, cartooning, and caricature—the broader and briefer the better—encompass the definition of parody the court applied to *The Wind Done Gone.*

The court's version of parody took no notice of recent revisions, especially those by critics working on postmodern and postcolonial texts, for whom parody goes beyond stylistic imitation (between factions within a single hegemonic group—Fielding ripping Richardson, for example) and instead serves as a textual strategy for recouping cultural memory and identity by groups excluded from the making and distribution of that memory. Linda Hutcheon, for example, retheorizing parody within a postmodern poetics, draws a distinction between the old and new practices: "The definition of parody as ridicule that developed in tandem with the art of Pope, Swift, and Hogarth doesn't necessarily feel right today. . . . [Parody] has come to refer less to the short, occasional, satiric jibes of the eighteenth century and, instead, to those familiar extended ironic structures that replay and recontextualize previous works of art" (xii). Replaying and recontextualizing previous works of art, however, involves the contemporary parodist in an almost-certain trespass on prevailing copyright law since the difference between ridiculing parts of texts from *within* the reigning ideology and "recontextualizing" whole works from the outside requires the appropriation of more "extended ironic structures." The Supreme Court seemed to be thinking in that direction when it decided the "Pretty Woman" case; but that precedent did not trickle down in *The Wind Done Gone* dispute.

Hutcheon admits that parody has ever been, and in contemporary times is even more, "suspect": "It is clear, then, that parody can be deemed suspect for all kinds of reasons: for being too ideologically shifty or, on the contrary, for being too direct a threat, either through its formal collusion with satire or because it is seen as a menace to the ownership of intellectual or creative property. . . . Not only can parody destroy the Benjaminian 'aura' of an original work through reproduction but it can actually undermine that work's monetary value" (xiv). Here, of course, is where legal and literary claims collide in the case of the Trusts versus the novelist. U.S. copyright law (applying Hutcheon's language further) shows signs of "[r]omantic rejection of parodic forms as parasitic" and "reflect[s] a growing capitalist ethic that made literature into a commodity to be owned by an individual" (Hutcheon 4). It is a small, semantic step from commodity to "asset." And if that asset is an incubator of cultural memory shaping and enabling hegemonic (and monopolistic) racial and gendered stereotypes, how can access fairly be denied to those who have been thus stereotyped and now seek redress?

Beyond the individual, however, in a more distant textual-cultural space where literary forms are seen as vital to group expression and identity, an extended form of parody replaces both the hit-and-run style of traditional parody *and* the assumption of texts as wholly owned properties. Henry Louis Gates, Jr., in a "declaration" supporting the defendant, claims that "parody is at the heart of African American expression, because it is a creative mechanism for the exercise of political speech and commentary on the part of people who feel themselves oppressed or maligned and wish to protest that condition of oppression or misrepresentation." In Gates's view, parody is entitled to "extensive evocation of the original" when it restores to an oppressed group the power to represent itself (Gates declaration 1–2). Gates does not invoke the "cake walk" as an example of African American use of parody, but he surely could have done so.[12]

In the court's thinking, however, "extensive evocation" amounts to literary kleptomania. Parody reaches the threshold of legal protection only when it claims a limited selection of parts from an original work, willfully and wittily distorted to shower the original with ridicule. In such cases the "commentary" or parodic work displays its own work ethic—making fun of the original through ingenuity rather than mere repetition. But parody is piracy when that same selection is not distorted but rather amplified, extended with the same tone or temperament shaping the original work, but with ideological assumptions inverted. If this type of postmodern parody is successful, it is exactly the "average lay reader," she or he invested in the prevalent ideological memory, who *won't* get it. While this kind of parody comes off in court as mere duplication, it is in Hutcheon's and Gates's views closer to the function of parody under postmodern conditions. Perhaps Hutcheon is too triumphant to call our present moment one of a few rare "periods of cultural sophistication" (19) that makes a special skill and virtue out of decoding parody. Nevertheless, her understanding of parody's place in the contemporary literary topography responds to contemporary reconfigurations of authorship, audience, and literary power.

Gates's argument, asserting that the African American tradition has long relied on a sophisticated recognition of parody to recover some of the identity suppressed by slavery and racism, is a particular rendition of Hutcheon's general view. The defendants in *SunTrust v. Houghton Mifflin* did not, in hindsight, make the Gates-Hutcheon postmodern argument as affirmatively as I attempt here; they strove, instead, to defend themselves against the obsolete one. The senior editor at Houghton Mifflin who acquired and edited *The Wind Done Gone* admits in his affidavit that the publisher "attempted to be careful not to use 'parody' in the sense that it is often used, a comic broadside" (Mueller affidavit 9). But "comic broadside" apparently was the only definition the court recognized. At the district court level, the novel lost.

Another issue raised in the months of legal arguments is, perhaps, clearer, even though it flows over the dikes of jurisprudence into cultural studies. Although lawyers for the Mitchell Trusts consistently argued commercial damage to their property as the central issue, most of the supporting affidavits and letters collected by both sides argued history and cultural identity. Toni Morrison's declaration puts the questions succinctly: "'Who controls how history is imagined?' 'Who gets to say what slavery was like for the slaves?' The implication of the claims suggests a kind of 'ownership' of its slaves unto all future generations and keeps in place the racial structures Gone With the Wind [*sic*] describes, depends upon, and about which a war was fought" (Morrison affidavit 3). By eliding history and imagination in her first question, Morrison marks the location of this controversy as a contested border where the traditional "facts" of history are plotted on the freer contours of cultural memory. Does invoking "the South" put one in possession of the real thing, or is that real thing always already a derivation, or—more confounding to someone seeking a firm hold on terminology—a derivation of a derivation? It is difficult to imagine jurisprudence surviving in such a multiplication of realities.

One pillar of the Mitchell Trusts' argument was that in writing *Gone With the Wind* Margaret Mitchell had created wholly original scenes, characters, and events which she could bequeath to her heirs as property since these entities had not existed before her novel. The defendants did not counter this claim. Houghton Mifflin never disputed the other side's claim that *Gone With the Wind* was an original work—that as an original work it somehow stood outside and free from the historical and cultural contexts Morrison identified in her affidavit. A case could have been made that both sides underestimated the pull of collective memory on narrative and history, even on such an immense gravitational source as *Gone With the Wind* itself. If contestants on both sides, Rubin and Morrison, use concepts like myth and history, history and imagination, as if they were interchangeable in the orbit of *Gone With the Wind,* what do we remember when we remember the past through it?

In the section of his order subtitled "Likelihood of Success on the Merits," Judge Pannell seeks to draw a fine distinction between fiction and history. The latter, of course, is common property; no individual can "own" Lee's surrender at Appomattox simply because it is an event in history, and no individual can lay claim to having made it up. Copyright law specifically excludes historical fact from protection. And even in fiction, the judge continues in his written opinion, there are certain "sequences of events which necessarily follow a common theme.... Incidents, characters, or settings that are indispensable or standard in the treatment of a given topic are not copyrightable" (*SunTrust v. Houghton Mifflin* 3). In literary discourse, these "indispensable or standard" elements might be classified as "tropes." The tropological outskirts, however, is as near to the muddled frontier of cultural memory and history as the judge is willing to venture.

At some point in the narrative of property, the "indispensable or standard" "sequences" and "incidents" (things that happen *and* the ways they are represented in memorial narrative) become "original." Therefore, the court, in determining whether infringement has occurred, must decide where the textual moment of *Gone With the Wind* begins; that is, at what point it becomes original by detaching itself from the elements of "a common theme" and the way these are expressed in texts. Fixing this point is crucial. The "sequences of events" at issue in this case are both historical and literary. Actually, the court's thinking collapses distinctions between history and literature: once a "fact" enters textual discourse, it becomes someone's property to some actionable degree. The entry point is arbitrary, for the court can decide at what point shared context ends and originality begins. On the one hand, there are facts such as Civil War and Reconstruction, sequences of events no one can hope to copyright since they are part of the narrative of U.S. history. On the other, there is—in the court's formulation—"the wholly original work *Gone with the Wind,* with its tone, plot, characters, theme, setting, mood, and pace," which, the court eventually holds, are copyrightable (*SunTrust v. Houghton Mifflin* 4).

But how "original" is Mitchell's novel? Tone, mood, and pace are inert concepts detached from a text. Plot, characters, theme, and setting seem far more convertible into literary property. But who gets to own the conversion? For example, is "Bovarisme" a tone or mood, a plot or theme? Could Flaubert have copyrighted Emma Bovary's yearning under the provisions of the Copyright Act of 1976? Where (and when) do the parts of a narrative become detached from storytelling conventions? If the answer is "never" and "nowhere," then legal distinctions vanish. Quoting from Justice Learned Hand, Judge Pannell's ruling verges on a "gold rush" theory—the first one to stake a claim owns the site (*SunTrust v. Houghton Mifflin* 4).

It might take more than jurisprudence to disentangle plot, characters, theme, and setting from southern plantation narrative. Thomas Nelson Page's "Marse Chan" features a plot in which romantic lovers (the male a paragon of southern aristocratic honor—kind to his slaves and skeptical of the politics of secession; the belle a heroine of self-sacrifice) are separated by the Civil War, like Ashley and Melanie. In Page's story the hero comes home a corpse, and the belle spends the rest of her life cherishing his memory—spouse to a cause, not a living human being. "Pageism" as a "brand" of Civil War and Reconstruction myth was a precursor Mitchell was careful to avoid; she, like Randall after her, had read her precursor's work. Mitchell showed respect for Page and avoided disdain in a letter to fellow book reviewer Julia Collier Harris of the *Chattanooga Times:* she set out, Mitchell said, to write a smart novel of the Jazz Age, avoiding both the phrase "son of a bitch" and "a sweet, sentimental novel of the Thomas Nelson Page type" (Harwell 5). Is this an indication that Scarlett and Rhett (whom no one can accuse of sweet sentimentality) are to a certain degree parodic of a tradition Mitchell inherited? Stark Young's *So Red the Rose* (1934) was another matter; Mitchell did not read it when it was published, she said, fearing a kind of anxiety of influence (Harwell 31). Mitchell, then, was clearly aware that she toiled in a busy field, and that that field was thick with characters and episodes and moods and tones. With such a densely populated set of precedent texts, is it safe to claim that *Gone With the Wind* is "wholly original"?

Who is to say that Margaret Mitchell, who honed her novel in order to deflect imagined charges that she had not got the history right, did not absorb or appropriate material precursors in the particular field of discourse she cultivated: prose texts, fiction or nonfiction, written by women and men who were directly involved in the Civil War and Reconstruction in the South, and specifically in Georgia? Mitchell had in fact confessed to a childhood act of literary piracy when she wrote a play consisting mostly of characters and scenes lifted from Thomas Dixon's *The Clansman*.[13] Her father "gave [her] a long lecture on infringement of copy-rights" (Pyron 56). Maybe Mr. Mitchell, an attorney, came down too heavily on the side of law and too lightly for literary freedom. Whether he did or not, his daughter, in her letters to fans after publication, freely "confessed" to a host of sources to her "wholly original" book. There were others she did not mention.

Eliza Frances Andrews, for example, published *The War-Time Journal of a Georgia Girl, 1864–1865* in 1908. Among the plot elements of Andrews's journal are incidents that foreshadow similar ones in *Gone With the Wind*. Andrews writes of arduous work in Washington, Georgia, cooking for and feeding paroled Confederate soldiers straggling back from Appomattox. During similar work Scarlett sees Ashley limping back to Melanie, and Mammy tries to keep the designing woman from interfering with the reunion of husband and wife. Washington, Georgia, Andrews informs us, is the county seat of Wilkes County (Andrews 182). Is this merely a coincidence, or does Mitchell pay private tribute to a precursor text by making the county name the family name of her obsolete chivalric hero? The historical Eliza Andrews, like the fictional Scarlett, had a fierce contempt for Yankees and a devotion to her father, although Andrews's father was "a strong Union man" (188). And Andrews was once blocked on a town street by a group of ill-mannered Union soldiers and freed slaves (251)—a scene that takes place in *Gone With the Wind* and, as well, in Thomas W. Dixon's *The Clansman*. If such "similarities" in Mitchell's work are not outright piracy, then perhaps the repetition of the scene in separate texts suggests that the genre possesses certain perennial (and therefore uncopyrightable) elements—like three wishes or talking mirrors in folktales—that are parts of narrative morphology and not unique to an individual imagination.

Myrta Lockett Avary, in her *Dixie After the War: An Exposition of Social Conditions Existing in the South, During the Twelve Years Succeeding the Fall of Richmond* (1906), might be the source, or corroboration, for the scene in Mitchell's novel when Ashley, Rhett, Frank Kennedy, and unnumbered other white males band together one night to clean out a squatters' camp, whence it is believed came the would-be rapists who had accosted Scarlett and insulted southern womanhood. Avary's scene is far from exact in its parallelism to *Gone With the Wind*. In her "exposition," the heroic male of a proud southern house is absent all night, returning on a lathered horse. He reveals to his betrothed and his sister that he is a member of the Ku Klux Klan, retrieves his regalia from a hiding place in the hearth, and bids the two women to sew a copy of it. The parallel to the similar scene in Mitchell's novel is loose, at best; in fact, a similar scene in *The Clansman*, which Mitchell had known since childhood, seems closer.[14] In this case, a charge of plagiarism against Mitchell seems irrelevant, but the repetition of nearly similar plot events in distinct texts destabilizes the claim that *Gone With the Wind* is "wholly original."

Mary Ann Harris Gay's *Life in Dixie During the War,* published in Mitchell's hometown in 1894, is perhaps a more convincing exhibit in counterargument to Mitchell and her Trusts. Gay labored in the Confederate field hospital in Atlanta, performing the kind of humanitarian work that Scarlett could not stomach (Gay 97ff.). Scarlett's lively contempt for Yankee occupiers is foreshadowed in Mary Gay's forthright verbal criticism of her oppressors. As women, the historical Gay and fictional O'Hara provoke admiration rather than fear: "I glory in your spunk . . .," one charmed Federal officer tells Gay (119). If not a full parallel, then Gay's characterization qualifies as essential for the southern belle during Reconstruction—and might describe Scarlett when she visits Rhett in a Yankee jail. Of more curious concern, however, is the close parallel between a refugee trip Gay describes and the arduous journey Scarlett makes from Atlanta to Tara with the weakened Melanie and her baby. Mary Gay also flees the scorched earth of Sherman's army—but from Jonesboro to Augusta. She moves a refugee mother and her children in a scavenged and makeshift wagon pulled by a superannuated horse too worn out for use by Federal soldiers or fleeing Confederates. Mary walks, rather than ride the horse, so that the mother can "hum a sweet little lullaby to her children" (202). At one point the horse collapses, but unlike Scarlett's steed, Gay's does not die (211). Like Scarlett, Mary Gay is accompanied by a female slave (Telitha to Scarlett's Prissy). Prissy is a problematical character in *Gone With the Wind,* an overly charged stereotype of white racist contempt for the African American. Scarlett's slap of Prissy is still a flashpoint of controversy.[15] Telitha is, similarly, of little help to Mary Gay on the women's odyssey, but chiefly because she is deaf (Gay 216).

Mary Gay and Scarlett rise to a similar apotheosis. Mary Gay, finally arriving home and finding it, as Scarlett finds Tara, a place of looming starvation, seizes the moment as Scarlett does in the novel and, more memorably, just before intermission in Selznick's movie. Mitchell's version of the apotheosis is clearly one of the most vivid moments in American popular culture: who cannot answer the question, "What character in fiction, holding a barely edible root vegetable up to heaven, cries out: 'As God is my witness, I'll never be hungry again. Nor none of mine.'" Here is what Mary Gay says in her similar moment: "What was I to do? Sit down and wait for the inevitable starvation? No; I was not made of such stuff" (Gay 245). Did Mitchell "wholly" invent her characters and situations and effects, or did she have a better ear for dialogue than her predecessors? Does copyright protect original creation, or rather the most successful rewrite?

The defendants in *The Wind Done Gone* case did not make this counterargument either, but it is doubtful an even more thorough argument along these lines would have carried much weight in the courtroom. Granting copyright seems to stop one clock, the continuum in which literary works absorb, change, and remix their cultural sources, while it starts another, the life span of the work as commercial property.[16] In its new condition as a commercial property, *Gone With the Wind* undergoes a mysterious transformation. With the legal imprimatur of copyright, it is lifted out of historical context and flow—the same context and flow that gave it content and shape. The granting of copyright seems also to confer legal amnesia; only works coming after the (so-called) original enter the discussion; predecessors are irrelevant.

Judge Pannell's court goes further in its eliding of history and literature when it states that "the new work [*The Wind Done Gone*]" tells *Gone With the Wind's* story (not its own), using "the original's" characters, settings, and plot.

Moreover, the new work does not simply make use of noncopyrightable stock scenes or historical events, like the antebellum South, Reconstruction, the mistreatment of slaves, or the relationship between master and slave. Reaching for a metaphor, Judge Pannell grasps painting. *The Wind Done Gone* uses *Gone With the Wind* as a "canvas . . . backdrop . . . exploiting its copyrighted characters, story lines, and settings as the palette for the new story" (*SunTrust v. Houghton Mifflin* 5). What is curious here is the court's insistence on an absolute distinction between new and old; nothing like a continuum shapes legal thinking on literary production. Mitchell's text is (legally) forever "the original," Randall's "the new"—even though it may be argued that Mitchell's was once "new" to now-obscure "originals." Clearly the court is not prepared (nor perhaps should it be) to accept a wide-ranging formulation like Gérard Genette's "hypertextuality," in which each and every text is always already generated by and generating another (Genette 7–9). But the distinction the court does use **bolds** the distinction between literature-as-cultural-property and literature-as-personal-property. Commonly received historical events do in fact exist in a common account; but the court grants them such generalized significance as to make them almost unusable: "the antebellum South" and "Reconstruction" and "the mistreatment of slaves" are always already paraphrases of the single test of memory-and-history. The court takes no interest in exploring the question of how readers, writers, citizens realize a "fact" such as "mistreatment of slaves" without something like Scarlett's slap of Prissy to give actuality to the general phrase.

One thing, at least, is clear: *Gone With the Wind* is an unfinished project. How would we know what to remember and what to forget about the South without *Scarlett* (1991) and *Rhett Butler's People* (2007)? What do these authorized derivatives do? In the realm of property, the answer is relatively straightforward: they serve to extend the time period during which the copyright owners may enjoy "exclusive rights" to their assets. According to the Copyright Act of 1909, under which *Gone With the Wind* had one twenty-eight-year span of protection from date of publication plus one additional twenty-eight-year renewal, the original copyright would have expired in 1992, fifty-six years after publication. The copyright act of 1976 extended the period of protection to fifty years. Sound business practice called for producing a sequel (work-for-hire) that would gain the *Gone With the Wind* property an additional fifty years of commercial protection. Alexandra Ripley's *Scarlett* was published in 1991, gaining the Mitchell Trusts protection until 2041. An extension to copyright legislation passed in 1998 extended that protection to ninety-five years for work-for-hire. With the publication of *Rhett Butler's People* in 2007, for which the trust commissioned Donald McCaig, the franchise is, presumably, safe through the twenty-first century.

If the commercial function of the sequel is clear, the cultural work of the sequel is more complicated, for it has to do with refinishing flaws in the memory created by the original, and re-fitting that "naïve" original to a subsequent public living in a "new normal." *Scarlett,* for example, might not be a "good" book by the standards of certain literary critics and reviewers, but it is significant because of the ways it glosses imperfections in the "original," subtly adjusting coordinates of cultural memory that, over time, might push the original into the bin of anachronism. That is to say, the purposes of sequels are not that divergent from the purposes of postmodern parody; indeed, both *Scarlett* and *Rhett Butler's People* might just as easily qualify as parodies as *The Wind Done Gone*. Copyright might protect Scarlett and Rhett as commercial products, but something more will be needed to uphold the claim that they are "two of the most famous lovers in the English-speaking world since Romeo and Juliet."

Leaving aside, for the moment, arguments against *The Wind Done Gone* by publishing professionals, the literary scholars and critics on both sides generally divided over treatments of (or silence on) slavery and sexuality. The problems of defending (or evading) slavery in *Gone With the Wind* are obvious, as are Mitchell's paradoxical maneuvers to, on the one hand, defend it as humane and, on the other, to link it with convict labor as just another form of economic exploitation. Early in the novel, in a part of the plot excised from the screenplay, Gerald O'Hara, perhaps without his full knowledge, purchases the slave Dilcey from John Wilkes, and thereby unites a family. Dilcey and Pork, the first slave Gerald had ever owned, had been married and produced a daughter, the Prissy whom Scarlett famously abuses. Dilcey's effusive gratitude stands, in the original novel, synecdoche for all slave gratitude to white masters. The unification of the slave family affirms one of the chief points in proslavery literature and propaganda, at least since *Uncle Tom's Cabin* made public rejoinders necessary: if slaves could not maintain family solidarity on the plantation, it was not because white masters deliberately worked against them. There was nothing, *Gone With the Wind* argues, in slavery as it was practiced at Tara or Twelve Oaks (or in the South), that fundamentally misunderstood or demeaned the African American. Late in the novel Big Sam, leader of the field crew at Tara, returns from the North during Reconstruction, complaining of homesickness for his former bondage. Such is "proof" that bondage was preferable to freedom. In parts of *The Wind Done Gone* virtually unmentioned in the legal wrangling, Randall imagines a post-plantation (and post-Rhett) life for Cynara in the free black community of Washington, D.C., where she participates fully in the evolution of an elite, educated, and culturally sophisticated African American middle class. Such an outcome is, of course, beyond the "memory capacity" of the naïve original, *Gone With the Wind*.

Mitchell's representation of slavery is not completely forgiving, however. In a still later scene, Ashley Wilkes complains to Scarlett about her decision to lease convicts to work (and probably to die) in her lumber mill. Ashley cannot stomach the naked equation linking working bodies and money, and he delivers (for him) a passionate protest against enforced labor. "But you owned slaves," Scarlett rebuts him (Mitchell 967), and Ashley falls mute. *Gone With the Wind*, then, has ambivalent moments on the issue of slavery, opting for the genteel memory of paternalistic kindness until Reconstruction, when national economic invasions reveal a form of labor (convict leasing) just as bad.

In *Scarlett*, though, we might read Scarlett's career as a progressive landlord in Ireland as an attempt to use the sequel to reshape our collective memory of the ambivalence in the original. Scarlett, in the process of a divorce from Rhett but pregnant with his child (a fact of which he is unaware), arrives in Ireland after giving up (temporarily) on a reconciliation. She is in possession of a half-million-dollar settlement from Rhett, and seeing potential in Irish farmland mismanaged by English landlords, Scarlett purchases the ancestral O'Hara holdings. She is on track to repeat her father's history, but without the burden of slavery that made the otherwise lovable Irish blowhard vulnerable to Randall's parody.

Scarlett, now "The O'Hara," owns the acres but not the people, and invents on the estate of Ballyhara a kind of utopian cooperative farm to compete in *GWTW* memory with the plantation. The first sequelized Scarlett recreates Tara, and our memory of it, *not* out of her experience of the plantation as it was in history, but out of an image of what it aspired to be in myth: "The farmers really did know more about farming than she did, and she could learn from them. She needed to. Three hundred acres of Ballyhara land were set aside as her own farm. The farmers worked it and paid only half the usual rent for the land they leased from her. Scarlett understood share-cropping; it was the way things were done in the South. Being an estate landlord was still new to her. She was determined to be the best landlord in all Ireland" (Ripley 597). And she succeeds. With the aid of several fine growing seasons in succession, wheat, potatoes, and dairy products fetch high prices on the market (imagined in the sequel along the lines of the European Common Market), and her tenants are happy. "And she was going to make a fortune" on her agricultural products and commercial properties in the local village (Ripley 623).

Scarlett's success in Ireland enables consumers of the *GWTW* brand to "remember" the slaveholding South in a kinder, gentler light. On a return trip to Georgia (planned to bring Wade and Ella Lorena to Ireland—a plan Scarlett surrenders quickly), she watches a party of northern tourists aboard a Charleston excursion cruise: "Look at all those fat-faced Yankees, she thought with hatred, they're just lapping this up. Cruel slave owners, indeed! Sold down the river, my foot! We loved our darkies just like family, and some of them owned us more than we owned them. *Uncle Tom's Cabin.* Fiddle-dee-dee! No decent person would read that kind of trash" (Ripley 632). Scarlett the character, here as in Mitchell's original text, might be a shallow, self-centered ego, but the first sequel, by layering her progressive labor utopia upon the memory of slavery (the character's memory and the literary memory invoked and reshaped by the sequel), works to mitigate, or partially address, objections to the representation of slavery in *Gone With the Wind*. At its most severe, the sequel has Scarlett wholeheartedly endorse an armed slave rebellion (the Fenian resistance headed up by her priest-cousin Colum O'Hara [Ripley 611–13]). Sequels, then, exercise a measure of the freedom of the counterfactual or science-fiction genres (subjects of the next chapter) which are by rule exempt from responsibility for historical fact. A sequel may add to or refashion an original text and our memory of it by virtue of the illusion of continuity with the original.

The proprietors of the Mitchell copyright might have learned something from the legal battles in 2001 over *The Wind Done Gone*. Although as the financial beneficiaries and legal trustees of Mitchell's work, they have an interest in preserving its commercial viability, they seem belatedly to have realized that the franchise must adapt to a present continually stretching the cultural memory in which the original was born over new consuming publics who might not be subject to branding by the unchanged product. As Ripley's saga of Scarlett in Ireland manipulates in distant retrospect the representation of slavery in the original, Donald McCaig's *Rhett Butler's People: The Authorized Novel Based on Margaret Mitchell's "Gone With the Wind"* (2007) addresses, discretely, some of the criticisms incited by Randall's parody. Years in incubation, according to the publisher's website, McCaig's official replica of the iconic southern novel is, arguably, aimed at expunging the memory of Alice Randall's *The Wind Done Gone* without ever mentioning it, and at "correcting" Mitchell's characters and situations without ever admitting that they need correcting. If Rhett is suspected of fathering Belle Watling's son out of wedlock in the original, in *Rhett Butler's People* he is exonerated—but he is still the best foster father the boy could ever have. If he is reported to have killed a Negro in the original, McCaig twists Rhett into existentialist moral knots to explain his actions: the dead man actually pleaded with Rhett to kill him before a lynch mob could torture him. If Joel Williamson hints that Rhett, as drawn by Mitchell, exhibits some of the conventions commonly used to code fictional characters as black or mulatto (and if Ripley has her Scarlett greet her second daughter by Rhett as "[m]y beautiful dark baby" [Ripley 577]), McCaig is quick to aver that if there is nonwhite blood in the hero, it is probably Native American, not black (McCaig 15).[17] There is no explanation of how Rhett might have acquired this alleged Native American heritage, except that Rhett's "blood memory" might account for his naming his horse "Tecumseh."

Updating in the "Authorized Novel" goes beyond untying potentially embarrassing knots that Mitchell had left in the original. Some of McCaig's innovations take into account a contemporary women's audience less inclined, perhaps, to be sold on Scarlett's simplistic coquetry and sexual ignorance. Alexandra Ripley had rather harshly solved Scarlett's distaste for pregnancy (and her banishing of Rhett from her bed in the original) with a gruesome hysterectomy in *Scarlett*. But McCaig is more temperate. Did Melanie Hamilton Wilkes accept the pregnancy that eventually killed her because she had no knowledge of any way to manage her reproductive biology? Read her exchange of confidential letters with Rhett's sister Rosemary in *Rhett Butler's People:* it was not only Belle Watling and her professional sex workers who were cognizant of, and discussed, techniques of reproductive regulation; southern ladies did as well.

Beyond settling individual scores and updating narrative infrastructure, though, *Rhett Butler's People* molds the Old South and most of Reconstruction to an early twenty-first-century reader's memory-and-history in which the Bay of Pigs and the Iraq wars compete with the Civil War as the actual historical events memory transforms into knowledge (McCaig 499). Moreover, Rhett as a capitalist with a genius for generating profits (a trait Mitchell admired in her character, and one that Ripley continued in Scarlett) is amplified in the second sequel. Rhett Butler's "people" are modern venture capitalists. The updated Rhett has a flair for making money in diverse ways, none of which ties him to an office or a boss: brothels and blockade running are not forgotten, but McCaig's Rhett makes yet another fortune supplying general merchandise to miners during the California gold rush, and makes so much money that he lunches with Collis P. Huntington, who had also made a fortune in general merchandise before he went into railroads. Rhett is too smart to bet the long odds on making a strike himself. Mitchell had placed him in the gold fields, but divulged scant detail (Mitchell 223). The original might well be, as jacket copy claims, one of the greatest love stories of all time; but McCaig's sequel is one of the greatest odes to entrepreneurial capitalism ever chanted.

If McCaig tries diligently and overtly to trace Rhett's money to actual and honest sources, he is just as intent on refashioning him as a "romantic" environmentalist in love with low-country landscape and wildlife, and appalled by his father's and his father's overseer's (Belle Watling's brother) harsh treatment of the land and the black people enslaved to work on it. In a very early episode, twelve-year-old Rhett, already at odds with his father and the overseer over their torture of slaves, runs away rather than witness Watling whip to death one of the Butler slaves who had given offense (McCaig 18–20). It happens that young Rhett's flight coincides with the arrival of a fierce hurricane that devastates the plantation and keeps Rhett away from home long enough for his family to presume him dead.[18] Rhett, fortunately, had been rescued from the storm by a family of free blacks—the class of African Americans Rhett's father has vowed to re-enslave if he should be elected to state office in South Carolina. Inevitably, Rhett and his father part on the issue of white supremacy—a foundational moment in McCaig's reinvention of Rhett—and the range of southern racial practices the sequel sets out to launder.

The Rhett of the second sequel is an upscale southerner of the present. In racial attitudes he is liberal, taking as friend and business partner Tunis Bonneau, son of the free black family who had harbored him from the hurricane in their coastal wetlands home. Although Bonneau is the black man Rhett kills, he does so at Bonneau's urging—to spare him an ugly death at the hands of a "cracker" lynch mob.[19] Which is to say: in class and caste politics, Rhett is an aristocrat.

The racist hatred and violence that stain the South occur several class strata beneath Rhett, at a depth where he cannot control outcomes. This article of faith runs consistently so from Mitchell's original.

When the subject is nature, Rhett is an environmentalist who knows the names of local flora and fauna (3). When it comes to love, he is not the rake (or husband-rapist) of the original but an incurable romantic who believes in star-crossed matches (115). In short, the new Rhett is a likely candidate for a feature in *Garden & Gun,* the glossy and well-funded magazine published by a media conglomerate based in Charleston, South Carolina, and headed by Pierre Manigault, hardly the first of his name to hold a prominent place in South Carolina. *Garden & Gun* touts the high end of the southern lifestyle. Chefs from Mississippi shoot quail in Argentina and upscale southerners of the twenty-first century are advised, in advertisements and feature stories, how and where to dispose of their considerable incomes by investing in property and objects with the potential to become heirlooms. This is the hyperconsumerist South Tom Wolfe lampoons in the character of Charlie Croker in *A Man in Full.*[20] And the South where both *Rhett Butler's People* and *A Man in Full* take place is what Scott Romine, in *The Real South,* calls the "deterritorialized" South, fluffed up, marketed, and fake (Romine 15). The sequelized South is a kind of "South in Full," parody triumphant.

6

NOSTALGIA, ALTERNATE HISTORY, AND THE FUTURE OF SOUTHERN MEMORY

∞

It was breathtaking—*breath*taking! Charlie felt a catch in his throat.
—TOM WOLFE, *A Man in Full*

Charlie is Charlie Croker, the Atlanta developer and "man in full" of Tom Wolfe's brazenly satirical novel of the simulated post-South where nothing is genuine and everything can be bought. What takes Charlie's breath away is the view of *his* plantation from *his* G-5 as *his* pilot brings it in for a landing on *his* private landing strip. The gist of *A Man in Full* is that Charlie is made to walk the plank by a ship of fools: trophy wives, an arrogant black athlete, bankers with excess testosterone, and cynical politicians. In a glimmer at the end of the novel, it appears Charlie has salvaged a thimbleful of stoical honor; then Wolfe dispatches him into the netherworld of TV evangelism. But the moment of banking in the airspace over his plantation remains genuine. Charlie might be looking down on simulacra, but what he feels is real. That far, at least, *A Man in Full* locates the paradox of postsouthern memory: the thrill is there, but the South is gone.

Tony Horwitz maps the condition more consistently in *Confederates in the Attic* (1998). A character/person named "Mary Ann," interviewed during Horwitz's hunt for Scarlett, gently breaks the news to a tourist in Atlanta that there was no actual Tara, and if there were, it would not be in Atlanta but somewhere far outside of town, and that the one imprinted on our memories was "actually" in California, on a movie location in the San Fernando Valley where the pale soil was painted red to look like Georgia clay and where the Hollywood subspecies of *Quercus virginiana* were made out of telephone poles. "'Honey,' Mary Ann soothed, 'you know it's a movie, don't you?'" (Horwitz 295).

Resistance to the myth is futile, Horwitz admits: *Gone With the Wind* had done more to keep the Civil War alive, and to mold its memory, than any history book or event since Appomattox" (296). Maybe a fair paraphrase of Horwitz would be: More people remember the South, but each one of us remembers less of the real thing so that the net result for southern memory is a wide spread but a meager depth.

In a particularly aching moment in *Confederates in the Attic,* when the inevitable emptying of historical memory seems actually to have arrived, Horwitz talks with a young African American man sentenced to life in prison for the killing of a young white man (both live in the same Kentucky town in Todd County where Robert Penn Warren was born) who had taunted him by flying the Rebel flag in the bed of his pickup. Cultural pundits hovering around the case of the killing of Michael Westerman found in its entrails omens of great ills in store for Western civilization. Most of those pundits had overlooked the fact that the sentenced man thought the flag Westerman was flying was "the *Dukes of Hazzard* sign" (Horwitz 116). One man dead, another going to prison, and the cause was a television series the most enduring character of which is a muscle car named after the commanding general of the Army of Northern Virginia. With due respect for Scott Romine's sanguine acceptance of the always-deferred demise of the South in *The Real South,* and the infinite series of sim-Souths in which the play of cultural formation continues, someone did kill, and someone did die, in/for a South some of us might have thought was not even there (Romine 16).

The South That Wasn't There has tried to identify and explore the ways simulation never quite jettisons the real thing, and vice versa. Tony Horwitz is as nuanced a reader of this reciprocal South as anyone. The fine grain of his language in *Confederates in the Attic* mirrors his wider narrative of the replacement of history by culturally shaped memory: "*its* memory" seems to claim that events themselves (the Civil War in particular) possess a kind of autonomous existence that survives the original participants and may be claimed—as a cultural heritage and identity—by any of the belated who feel, as many of the discontented he encounters do, in need of anchoring among a play of simulations. Clearly, Horwitz does not fully intend the meaning I am squeezing out of one possessive pronoun: human beings harbor memory, individually and socially, and if we did not generation by generation transmit one version or another of the recalled original, the past would go away. That loss we could not survive—or, if by some fate we did survive with a memory function but no content, we might become the actors in and audience for something like Lars Von Trier's *Manderlay*

(2005), a "sim-South" film based on the premise that there is memory but not necessarily a South to host it. That is, there was a South of plantation slavery, but that South was also a place where dust storms, presumably wandering from the Great Plains to Alabama, could ruin cotton crops. As if the boll weevil were not scourge enough.

The accuracy and faithfulness of human memory are a necessary fiction cherished by those who think the past *we* remember is the past that actually occurred, and that the past lies inert until summoned for human use, and in each summoning the same past appears. *Gone With the Wind* is the reviser-in-chief of memory of the Civil War, operating most faithfully to Pierre Nora's definition, outlined in the second chapter, of *lieux de mémoire*. In the wide orbit of southern memory, Horwitz asserts and few would dispute him, *Gone With the Wind* (Horwitz elides Mitchell's novel and Selznick's movie; he could have known only one of the sequels when he wrote *Confederates in the Attic*— Alexandra Ripley's *Scarlett* [1991]) is present in any act of memory conjuring the Civil War. It is Romine's contention that the relative distribution of real and fake in any marketplace of southern cultural memory is always bullish on the side of the fake. This may be inevitable, but is not always benign. One person's emblem of honorable defeat is another's fast car. It may be that the past remembers us.[1]

Horwitz discovered this nostalgia among the Civil War reenactors he gets to know in *Confederates in the Attic*. They are bound by shared refuge in southern, Civil War memory. Wives and girlfriends are obstacles to be overcome by willfully induced, historically authentic ("hard core") hardship: bad diet, sleep deprivation, physical injury (Horwitz 13–14, 14, 11). In fact, a kind of intimate male homosocial brotherhood replaces the "norm" of heterosexual domesticity: on the march, the men "spoon," sleep together front-to-back, and chat about weight loss and fashion (13). Reversals of social performance seem to go unregistered; what excuses them, arguably, is nostalgia for more meaningful identity in a remembered, reenacted southern past. One weekend Rebel from Long Island tells Horwitz: "This is escapism. For forty-eight hours you eat and sleep and march when someone else tells you to. There's no responsibility. . . . I think there's a lot of people like me who want to get back to a simpler time. Sandlot baseball, cowboys and Indians, the Civil War" (16). The reenactors are mostly white, middle-class, youngish men with jobs and debts and relationships who yet feel unrooted in an American present in which sandlot baseball is complicated by sluggers on steroids and wars resist the cowboy-and-Indian dichotomy.

In the yearning for simplicity, denied in "real" life, the Civil War, especially the Confederate side, is reduced to the level of a Boy Scout jamboree. "There's no responsibility," echoing Tony Judt, for the history we have actually made.

It is unfair to discount these longings; they are part of a much larger cultural climate system. Insofar as the feelings attach to white, heterosexual men, they suggest that the South of memory is not only historical but psychosexual as well. Ross McElwee's autobiographical documentary film *Sherman's March* (1986) tracks the film maker's own drifting love life along the route of General William Tecumseh Sherman's incendiary march through Georgia and the Carolinas at the close of the Civil War. McElwee doesn't set fire to anything—hearts or sheets. But his deftly mocking pairing of Sherman and himself suggests that for the contemporary southern male (and for the women in *Sherman's March* too) narcissism is overtaking region and history.

Horwitz's reenactors seem to flee to the southern past because it makes a kind of masculinity, more or less tabooed in the postmodern present, permissible in the simplified past. Grown men can pee on uniform buttons without shame, and tell fart jokes that escalate into off-color jokes about wives and girlfriends (Horwitz 7, 13). Walt, a cultural secessionist Horwitz meets in South Carolina, rejects every form of state control and confidently repeats the moldy propaganda of Nazi anti-Semitism as if it were newly minted. Horwitz, to whom Walt is talking at the time, is only the second Jew he has met in his life (80–83). When Horwitz later participates in the reenactment of the Battle of the Wilderness, he encounters a milder form of the impulse to secede from the present. Among the Virginia reenactors, men and women, the malaise of ordinariness seems to outweigh a feeling of racial grudge; although the reenactors are "blindingly white," they seem to see themselves as pinned under the heel of "black-hearted businessmen" bent on downsizing them out of their lives (137). "Despite the weekend's discomforts and phony moments," Horwitz concludes, "it had provided a pleasant taste of the enforced leisure and sociability of nineteenth-century life: chatting with the women as we peeled carrots, lazing beside Rob as he slow-cooked his breakfast, ambling down the mile-long country lane between the Union and Confederate camps, a distance that a car would have covered in a minute. Modern life rarely allowed for these simple, unhurried pleasures" (144).

Across the South, Horwitz finds the same nostalgia for a simpler time, a simpler history, and underlying the nostalgia a drive for political power. "But time-travel and nostalgia, and what Robert Penn Warren called 'armchair blood-lust,' explained only so much. For many Southerners I'd met, remembrance of the War had become a talisman against modernity, an emotional lever for their reactionary politics. . . . The issues at stake in the Civil War—race in particular—remained raw and unresolved, as did the broad question the conflict posed: Would America remain one nation?" (386).[2]

Anticipating many postmodern notions, the notion that we are productions rather than producers of memory runs through Faulkner's *Absalom, Absalom!* Earlier in this study of the chemistry of southern memory, I tried to analyze the actions and reactions surrounding "Haiti": a compound of geography and desire, source of being but threat to identity. As one of Faulkner's many narrators in the novel put it: ". . . that Porto Rico or Haiti or wherever it was we all came from but none of us ever lived in . . ." (*Absalom* 239). Faulkner's "Haiti" works like Horwitz's *Gone With the Wind;* both are sets of moveable pieces or icons that stand in for immovable yet unrecoverable fact—the whatever or wherever we came from, the wish for origin being paramount.

When Shreve hijacks Quentin Compson's (southern) memory in *Absalom, Absalom!* he of course pulls it out to the "new" geographic southern horizon of William Faulkner's 1930s, which is less place than fantasy; "that Porto Rico or Haiti" corresponds less clearly to the entities named on maps of the Caribbean than (in this context) to the fields of dreams of late-developing white, male adolescents—reenactors of a kind who should probably get real jobs and let their sisters live their own lives. But invoking place while erasing the stipulations of fact that tend to limit us to one here and now pulls us back, as it does Quentin and Shreve, entirely through memory to a primordial condition anticipating even the past we claim to want to remember. Shreve and Quentin have broken through a barrier and are not even (not yet) Canadian or Mississippian. In the Faulknerian ante-past, all human beings are "actual living articulate meat" (*Absalom* 240), undifferentiated cellular matter to which a flag or a Dodge Charger with that flag painted on it would be, at most, shape and color and sound and fury but not meaning. To Faulkner, our primordial status as meat is a harbor of barely thinkable nostalgia; preceding history, it precedes the misery of being conscious.

Shreve may in Faulknerian time become a cynical Canadian, but most readers have believed him when he names what is at stake in the memory rite: a regional identity laced up with history, and that history with race, and both with misery and apprehension. We have come *not* to believe Shreve when he seems to think he is immune to what tortures his southern roommate. The South (to Shreve) might be a theatrical knock-off of *Ben Hur* (*Absalom* 176), but even if it is, there is still a vestigial South that clamors somewhere behind and prior to the painted set to be understood "[b]ecause it's something my people haven't got. Or if we have got it, it all happened long ago across the water and so now there aint anything to look at every day to remind us of it" (*Absalom* 289). Shreve might deliberately taunt Quentin by placing Pickett's Charge at Manassas (he surely knows better), but the taunting only works because memory works differently in Quentin's consciousness than it does in Shreve's. For Shreve, memory is a movie, to be cut, scored, and edited one way and then another and another: memory without a real South to set its limits. But for Quentin, memory locates the southerner in time and place; it *is* the thing to look at everyday, the thing that makes one and makes one responsible for one life only—even if, for Quentin, it withholds the moment and the circumstances to live (back) up to it. For Quentin, as for Eric Kandel (discussed in the opening chapter), the thingness of memory never goes away. Of course, there is the down side to inevitable southern memory: race and class and gender conventions that indict even as they identify. The "one life only" has to be (as far as Quentin can see) a life of guilt. The correct address is "Miss Rosa" when referring to Rosa Coldfield, for "Aunt Rosa" would mark the woman as black (*Absalom* 289). Shreve knows race and history are inseparable in southern memory, and he likes to prick Quentin with that shiny electrode. Keeping lines between the races makes Quentin southern, and makes him psychotic.

Shreve's final words in the novel entangle race and memory in multiple registers:

> I think that in time the Jim Bonds are going to conquer the western hemisphere. Of course it wont quite be in our time and of course as they spread toward the poles they will bleach out again like the rabbits and the birds do, so they wont show up so sharp against the snow. But it will still be Jim Bond; and so in a few thousand years, I who regard you will also have sprung from the loins of African kings. (302)

In place and time, history's conquest of "the western hemisphere" by the proxy of race has already showed itself—Sutpen, having gone to Haiti, has taken Quentin there and shown him the future he already lives in. But Shreve's prediction also changes that past, for the whiteness he claims in the present of his utterance will have become African in a future time. Memory will reverse its own current and flow into the future.

Positing racial "amalgamation" (the unthinkable taboo of the present to Shreve as well as to Quentin) as the redemption of the South in the future indicts the racial separatism of the South in the past and the present. That *Absalom, Absalom!* gnaws at the guilt this causes, and by its gnawing diffuses race and guilt into southern literature at large, is charted territory. I want to stay in the layer of memory, though, for race identity (in Faulkner's formula) seems to work only if and when a certain memory works. If memory stops working (as, for example, it stops working in a certain kind of way in Benjy Compson in *The Sound and the Fury*), then race socially and historically constructed stops working too. The blacks in the Compson compound are, to Benjy, just that, black bodies. Their blackness is just an optical sensation; they are equally likely to be kind or cruel unless and until they act. What would happen if memory lapsed for a cultural order generally, not just for one damaged individual?

Playing with the flow of memory is a respite from the inevitability of history: things happened a certain way and here we are, responsible for that history but shut out of any choice. A lot of human imagination, restless with the dealt hand, has been invested in building history "otherwise." Horwitz was attracted to the folly of the sincere but displaced persons of memory who tried to build another *now;* Faulkner (in Quentin) was drawn to the tragedy of one who could not imagine things other than the way they were.

Simulation as the habit of an age is, arguably, inundated by the power of "otherwise": the way things are lacks the inevitability of tragedy because it is easy (technologically, at least) to rearrange parts into other outcomes. In architecture (claiming to be the art form in which postmodernism was first practiced and theorized)[3], replicas or parts of replicas of historically distant styles could be, and were, produced in the present. Postmodernism prevailed, for a time, as technologies (especially visual) became available for the creation of the illusion of historicity. This condition is not the same, for example, as the one out of which the Selznick studio produced the movie version of *Gone With the Wind* in 1939; that Tara, that fake Georgia clay, those fake live oaks were never meant to be taken as replicas. In a postmodern condition, the illusion of the original and its repetition can be simultaneous, as in Alice Randall's *The Wind Done Gone.* Her characters are meant to be palimpsests, both illusion and original.

Take another late example of southern memory in an age of simulation, the faux documentary film *C.S.A.: The Confederate States of America* (2005). The premise of Kevin Willmott's film is familiar to the audience for alternate history: If the South had won the Civil War, what sort of "united" United States would have been the outcome? Usually this question is posed so that the answer can be: not as racist and brutal as the victor's version of the defeated has become in official history. As I have tried to show in discussing the authorized derivatives of *Gone With the Wind,* successor texts more often than not exist to silently re-arrange our memory of the original. In Willmott's mockumentary, however, the flow is toward "correction" by outing the "forgotten" pretext; in Willmott's work (as in Alice Randall's), the theme is that the racism latent in U.S. culture at large would have spread easily to fill the "otherwise" national space created by a Con-federate victory. The buying and selling of black human slaves would have been adapted seamlessly to the burgeoning, twentieth-century consumerist culture of television shopping and lifestyle channels. Willmott creates faux commer-cial spots for products that are historically verifiable: "Darky" toothpaste and "Sambo" motor oil (in a television commercial that takes off *The Dukes of Haz-zard* and NASCAR) run seamlessly with come-ons for career advancement at the "Cartwright Institute" for the study of freedom illnesses.[4] What makes Will-mott's presentation disturbing is that the marketing of Aunt Jemima and Uncle Ben, stereotypes laundered and reformulated over decades, testifies to a very high threshold for the tolerance of racism even as these images are revised to-ward an imagined future in which they, as stereotypes, and the public in which they are circulated come to be indistinguishable. Shreve's prophecy echoes in the arena of corporate branding: Jim Bond bleached in the extrapolated future anticipates the new Aunt Jemima and Uncle Ben.[5]

Willmott's script is knitted together by a running narrative surrounding the presidential campaign of a white supremacist, a fictional character named John Ambrose Fauntroy IV, whose platform in a faux 2002 presidential campaign is unabashed Jim Crow. The same ideology, as Willmott sees it, stretches from the antebellum past to the twenty-first-century present in the candidate's promi-nent family and the "C.S.A." Willmott "otherwise" imagines as the present. The candidate's fate, ultimately, is settled when the news leaks that his "pure" bloodline is in fact mixed. What Fauntroy had remembered, like Quentin, as a pure Caucasian identity was after all a fiction, and the confession of it brings down the design he had for the C.S.A. White House.[6]

Willmott's question, "What if the South had won the War?" is partially answered by the persistence of the question itself. If we continue to ask it, then the South did win the war because something about Union victory still feels incomplete. Alternate histories of the South, like the reenactments Horwitz visited, are roped-off spaces for cultural therapy where this lack can be probed and for a time assuaged. It is important to national and regional memory that the southern past be construed as malleable, pushed to its actual outcome not so much by an inherently flawed structure (white racial supremacy) but rather by an event or personality quirk here or there that can plausibly be "remembered" differently in an alternate narrative—for the time being.

Harry Turtledove, author of several series of novels of alternate history and fantasy, creates such a different Civil War outcome in *The Guns of the South* (1992): Turtledove's concocted victory for the South re-presents the South of history as victim as much as perpetrator. Lee's Army of Northern Virginia, in Turtledove's revisioning, is visited by a group of mysterious men who time-travel from the future bringing crates of AK-47 semiautomatic rifles, with which the Confederate troops quickly outgun the Union. These future men also bring nitroglycerin tablets to treat Lee's heart condition, thereby coercing him to accept their gift of firepower even though Lee would prefer to follow his chivalric instincts into a fair fight with equally deadly weaponry on both sides.

The time-travelers, known as "Rivington men" after the fictional North Carolina town in which Turtledove imagines them, also bring with them racial practices and attitudes harsher than those characterizing most of the men in the ranks of the Army of Northern Virginia. One of the Rivington men, Benny Lang, is particularly violent. As slaves unload a shipment of the AK-47s, taking their time with the crates:

> Benny Lang leaped down from his wagon and started shouting like a man possessed: "Come on, get those crates off! This isn't a bloody picnic, so move it, you lazy kaffirs!" The slaves started unloading the wagons at the same steady but leisurely pace they usually used. It was not fast enough to suit Lang. "Move, damn you," he shouted again.
>
> The blacks were used to letting such shouts roll off their backs, secure in

the knowledge that the work would eventually get done, and the yelling white man would shut up and leave them alone. (Turtledove 44)

Lang, however, begins to beat them. White southerners from the historical southern past see the miscalculation in the newcomer's behavior: "'If he treats 'em like that all the time, though, he'd better grow eyes in the back of his head, or else he'll have an accident one fine day . . .'" (44). Slavery in the American past was, in Turtledove's revisionist alternative, less about the infliction of physical pain than it was about having forged (or lived into) a kind of humane social understanding between master and slave. This "alternate history" view does not render African Americans equal—that is, it does not accommodate Du Bois's insistence on social as well as legal equality, and in that sense it merely remembers southern slavery as a humane instance of a worldwide evil. Violence was not, in this alternate view, inherent in slavery, but rather a sign of the failure to humanize it.

It is quickly apparent that Turtledove has imported a squadron of Afrikaners into the ranks of Lee's army in order to argue, via an imagined alternative to the actual record, that however evil slavery in the U.S. South might have been, it was not as evil as South African apartheid. The early 1990s (the season of *The Guns of the South*'s appearance) were fertile years for the re-remembering of U.S. slavery. Nelson Mandela's release from Robben Island prison in 1990 began a process that resulted, a few years later, in the Truth and Reconciliation Commission, an institutional approach to healing the wounds inflicted by the apartheid regime in South Africa much different from the Allies' approach to war crimes committed by the Third Reich in World War II—the Nuremberg Trials. Mandela's liberation followed intense criticism, during Ronald Reagan's two administrations, of U.S. policy toward the apartheid regime in South Africa. Comparisons of U.S. slavery and segregation to South African apartheid were rife, and Turtledove's alternate history takes the clear position that there are, in "fact," no grounds for comparison: his southerners do not recognize the Rivington men as fellow masters.[7]

Lee's army wins the war before Gettysburg can be fought (as, coincidentally, it does in Willmott's *C.S.A.*), and the two nations separate. Jefferson Davis anoints Lee to become his successor as president, but the new Confederacy is a democracy and Lee must campaign against Nathan Bedford Forrest (the villain here, as he is in *C.S.A.*) in the first presidential election in the alternate history of the Confederate States of America. Turtledove exposes the limits of alternate history as a genre in this plot turn, for his rendition of the campaign of 1866 seems much more derivative of the twentieth century than the nineteenth. The Rivington men function as Forrest's political action committee, and even threaten to withhold Lee's nitroglycerin medication if he does not reverse his position on (gradual) political rights for the black population. Rallies, press conferences, and debates blur the historical line between past and present. Turtledove's Robert E. Lee comes across in alternate history as a moderate southern politician resisting the conservative shift identified almost a century after the actual Civil War as Nixon's "Southern Strategy." Lee wins, but not by much.

Since Lee had refused to follow the Rivington agenda, the Afrikaners attempt to assassinate him at his inauguration. Here alternate history speeds up recklessly, for Lee becomes an avatar of Jack Bauer, the hero of Fox's *24*. The Rivington men fail to kill the new president, but Lee's wife is killed in the attack at the inauguration.[8] In his counterinsurgency moves, Lee roots out the Afrikaners and finds among their books a stash of white supremacy literature. Most of it is in German, a language Lee cannot read. There is, however, in Richmond a Jewish merchant who can translate, and he reads enough to indicate that a man named Hitler will appear in the future to lead a campaign for Aryan racial purity, a campaign that will ultimately fail in the middle of the twentieth century but will be taken up again by the Rivington men a few decades later. This prevision of genocide appalls Lee, and he has the reading and translation stopped and the texts destroyed (464). Turtledove's point, surreptitious as it is, is that there was no holocaust in the slave-owning South because, like his alternate-history Lee, no southerner would have condoned it.[9]

Imagining an alternate South inoculated against charges of racism (and taken out of play as a surrogate Holocaust) enables Turtledove and his readers to "remember" the South as part of a possible solution rather than as the root of an ongoing problem inherent in the historical record of slavery. *The Guns of the South* ends when Lee, victorious over Forrest and safe from attack after the Rivington men are rounded up or killed, pushes through the Confederate Congress a program to free slaves gradually.[10] Readers are invited to imagine what might have been, in the history of U.S. racial practice and legislation, if official gradualism had predated, as policy, the actual history of Reconstruction, Jim Crow, and civil rights. In the late years of the twentieth century, Turtledove's invented past serves as an imaginary refuge from the actual problems of race in

U.S. society. The *real* racism of the southern past, Turtledove's alternate history argues, was not rooted in actual southerners (at least not in a majority of them) but rather in "outside agitators" who tried to manipulate a minority of white supremacists to create a regime like South African apartheid. Turtledove's argument is that there were sufficient numbers of humane southerners, especially at the top of the caste system, to carry the gradualist agenda and frustrate Forrest and the Rivington men. The attractiveness of this "memory" is that it instantly transfers the origin of a gradualist agenda into a past distant enough so that its wished-for outcome can be thought of as already achieved, its moral ambiguity mooted by the passage of time—not leveraged for change in the movement for civil rights. Gradualism magically becomes foresight rather than delay. In other words, there would have been no rhetorical space or inspiration for using "Justice delayed is justice denied" as a rallying cry. Morally weak it might have been, but the sin would have been committed in another country. Alternate histories like *The Guns of the South* preserve nostalgia for a permissible southern memory relatively free from the taint of racism and slavery; it is possible to remember the South and southern identity without, in the same act, expressing even covertly a preference for white superiority.

Alternate histories of the South can work in other directions, away from absolution. If the southern past can be re-remembered to take the shape of a "progressive," albeit gradualist, and humane order, it can just as readily be used to build the bridge of memory that the largely unrecoverable historical record of slavery leaves blank. Octavia Butler's *Kindred* (1979) is vividly illustrative on this point. Usually classified as science fiction, Butler's novel can also be seen as a shrewd comment on the interdependencies tangling history and memory in the record of slavery in the United States. Like Charles Johnson's *Middle Passage, Kindred* is an involved companion text to Morrison's canonical *Beloved*.

Kindred is set in serial historical moments in the antebellum past from 1815 to 1834. The central character, an African American woman named Dana who supports her ambitions to become a writer by doing temp work, lives in Los Angeles in the year of the Bicentennial, 1976. Dana can trace her ancestors back to slavery on the Eastern Shore of Maryland, territory closely associated with Frederick Douglass and Sojourner Truth. She holds some palpable symbols of her heritage; a family bible includes a genealogy (with some gaps) back to an ancestor named Hagar, the daughter of a slave woman and a white man. But in the Los Angeles of 1976, these physical objects do not add up to a felt identity.

Dana is an African American character defined by her need for the uninterrupted and bodily provenance of slavery, the sort of direct, traumatic evidence that Morrison examines in *Beloved.*

As it turns out, Hagar's mother's master is the boy Dana is wrenched into the past to rescue several times before Hagar's birth in 1831. Dana's time-travel, though traumatic, is inescapable: the white boy will grow up to be the white man who will impregnate Dana's direct female ancestor. Each one of Dana's time travels is progressively longer and more dangerous; she can only be brought back to the "present" by suffering life-endangering fear in the "past." Cumulatively, Dana experiences slavery fully enough to, finally, "remember" it in 1976 as part of herself on the centenary, not coincidentally, of the year in which Reconstruction was officially ended as U.S. policy and Jim Crow slipped into the void. Indeed, Dana's final return to the present results in the loss of her left arm: Butler thereby links her to the avatar of the rebel slave, Bras-Coupé.[11]

Butler's interweaving of time-travel and slave narratives is complicated by Dana's life in the twentieth-century present. She falls in love with and then marries a white man somewhat older than herself, and beginning with the third transport to the past Kevin, her white husband, is transported with her to the Weylin plantation where Dana's pre-past is lived, and where, like the cyborg of the *Terminator* series of movies, she must do just enough but not too much to protect individuals crucial to a certain historical outcome in their future and her present. Between the second-to-last and last transport, Kevin is marooned in the antebellum past, and Dana's ultimate mission becomes the double rescue of two white men, her distant white ancestor (who must live to impregnate his slave mistress so that Dana herself might be born) and her marooned white husband—whose temporary exile in the historical past brings him face to face with his racialized assumptions about his personal and national identity.

Clearly, Butler uses the possibilities of the time-travel narrative to examine issues current in the 1970s, most prominently feminist issues of gender equality in society at large and marriage in the personal realm. Butler, like Morrison in *Beloved,* sees African American racial memory as centrally female; that is, one rhetoric serves both sets of experience: slavery and marriage. At one moment in her relationship in the present with Kevin, for example, he asks her, only half in jest, to type one of his manuscripts and in return promises to marry her. Not the least in jest, Dana declines; she has her own work to do, and her work as a modern American woman is hers to control, as is her sexuality. Dana had "seen" enough of slavery at this point in *Kindred* to know that autonomy had never been available to women of color on the plantation. Kevin and Dana part in some anger; Dana comes back the next day, however, amenable to marriage but unwilling to type (Butler 109). In the past/present oscillation of the plot, Butler sets up a strong echo between the history of sexual enslavement of African American women in the southern past and its continuation by other and more surreptitious means in the sexual politics of the 1970s, heightened at the time by the politics flaring around the failure to ratify the Equal Rights Amendment. In the episode of the marriage proposal and Dana's incensed rejection of even the suggestion of enforced labor, Butler does not so much substitute an alternate history for the record as try to link past and present in the continuum of a narrative of power seated in both race and gender. Slavery, in *Kindred,* did not "end" in history by an act of legislation or by any other means; it continues in the genealogies of women of color into the present. Toni Morrison does nothing less in *Beloved.*

Elsewhere in *Kindred* Butler uses her contemporary moment to understand conditions of slavery absent or underrepresented in the historical record. Dana is transported to the past with all of her 1970s temperament, originally at least, intact. She assumes the independent agency of a woman of her century and decade, wears pants (a habit she does not modify for antebellum customs on the Weylin plantation), and carries back her assumptions about time and work formed in the late twentieth century. Time in slavery, therefore, depresses Dana as monotonous and boring; she begins to understand one psychological facet of slave bondage resistant to representation (its monotony) by contrasting it with the pace and variety of her own modern life. The torpor of merely passing time and the lack of variety in physical sensation under slavery seem to Dana close to unbearable, altered only by violent suffering, exhaustion after hard work, and fear.

What distinguishes *Kindred* in the discourse of alternate history is the degree to which Butler uses Dana's layered consciousness to enliven the pastness of the past, to repair gaps in the historical record—to enable memory to win out over history. Dana feels, for example, both the terrible fear of intervening in the whipping of slaves and the moral obligation (grounded in her sense of twentieth-century agency) to do so. That is, she can imagine what is largely unrepresented in the past of 1819—a slave not cowed by slavery, but morally offended rather than only physically fearful. Butler, however, keeps Dana a spectator. Kevin, transported back with Dana to one such episode, argues for historical absolutism rather than moral action: anything he and Dana might do could alter the history that produced them before the fact of their existence. Dana understands, but still questions:

> "You might be able to go through this whole experience as an observer," I said. "I can understand that because most of the time, I'm still an observer. It's protection. It's nineteen seventy-six shielding and cushioning eighteen nineteen for me. But now and then, like with the kids' game [they had seen some slave children rehearsing their own bondage in a role-playing game], I can't maintain the distance. I'm drawn all the way into eighteen nineteen, and I don't know what to do. I ought to be doing something though. I know that." (101)

The character Dana's moral sense, groomed in a historical present familiar with activism, is represented as powerfully, but not absolutely, ahistorical. Paradoxically, in the episode of nonintervention in the past, Butler imagines remembering the present as a way of realizing the past. Reversing memory, Butler is able to enter the "unrecoverable" territory of the mind and temper of the plantation slave, even though she stops carefully short of acting in it like a comic-book superhero. *Kindred* can, in these ways, construct a "memory" to replace the one erased over generations of unrecorded and unvoiced slave lives.

Butler makes the interpenetration of memorial and historical knowledges gained through experience and the historical record most explicit in the conclusion to *Kindred*. Kevin and Dana have definitively left the past (Dana's ancestor is successfully born and out of danger to her survival), but they travel to the Eastern Shore of Maryland in the present in search of archival records of what they had both "experienced" in their time travel. To strengthen her theme of different modes of knowing for memory and history, Butler has the couple find no records confirming their experience. Kevin, to whom the experience of slavery means less in terms of personal identity, seems resigned that they will never actually document the fates of slaves sold south, families split. Dana, though, touching the scar on her forehead inflicted by her master's boot, disagrees (264). She had read books about slavery, seen photographs of scarred bodies (113, 117), but the intellect does not automatically know what the body knows, and slavery is carried in the body's memory. Dana's scarred forehead and amputated arm become her "documents," her "data" (answering Orlando Patterson's lament for the missing tangible record).

If *Kindred* argues that some felt connection to the past is attainable, and that memory might recover real experience even if the palpable evidence (symbolized by a severed arm) is missing, Lars Von Trier's film *Manderlay* (2005) restates Shreve's mocking assumption that southern memory is open to any gamer with more dexterity in the manipulation of cultural images than understanding for those who might live in its system. Only the means are left, more or less void of everything but ludic value, *Manderlay* suggests; the ends are beyond everything but nostalgia, and that is a ruse. Von Trier's film, financed by Danish, British, German, and Dutch investors, is a bludgeoning example of a deterritorialized South (its fantasies of being indigenous held up to global ridicule) financed by euro-capital and dispatched back to a nation Melanie R. Benson, in *Disturbing Calculations,* takes to be afflicted with the narcissism of the colonizer (4–5). *Manderlay* is the cinematic companion to other euro-capital "invasions" of the U.S. South: BMW went to South Carolina and Mercedes-Benz to Alabama in 1993, and Volkswagen announced Tennessee as its choice for a manufacturing plant in 2008. Being in the subject position in a burgeoning capitalistic world order is not new to southern cultural experience (as Duck, Benson, Bone, and others have shown). What might be new is having one's cultural memory, along with one's job, delivered by the invader.

The credit sequence at the end of *Manderlay* is, in this sense, the best place to start: the soundtrack rocking with David Bowie's 1970s' anthem "Young Americans," Von Trier runs a series of nonrepeating still images (visually tracking the rapid litany of Bowie's lyric), opening with black and white shots of the KKK and images from the civil rights demonstrations of the 1960s. An approximate chronology of race, region, and violence seems to be the pattern, then stills from the videotape of Los Angeles police officers beating Rodney King appear, followed by scenes from the Vietnam and Gulf wars, the Twin Towers (still standing in the historical past but of course ever on fire in post-9/11 memory), then back to close-ups of the corpses of Martin Luther King, Jr., and Malcolm X, a random selection of street crime in which African Americans are depicted as the victims, and on and on. Von Trier's design is clear: the United States is a dysfunctional civilization, race and violence are at the heart of that dysfunction, and the South, once at the center of racist-haunted memory, is now part of a national repressed memory *Manderlay* has exposed. This formula could stand as a fair condensation of a wide swath of southern studies new and old. For Von Trier, however, the South, now an infinitely repeatable cultural narrative, is a memory that has outlived its historical placed-ness.

Manderlay follows Von Trier's earlier film *Dogville* (2003) and brings his young, white, female, idealistic, and spoiled heroine, Grace, out of Colorado (the setting of *Dogville*) with her gangster father, Daddy, and his henchmen into the South in 1933. The dating is redolent of U.S. economic failure. The gangster motorcade stops for rest near a plantation called Manderlay, where they find that slavery is still in force seventy years after the Emancipation Proclamation.[12] One of the slave women comes out from the fenced compound and appeals to Grace for help, for the masters are about to whip a slave named Timothy on a trumped-up charge. Grace, partly to frustrate Daddy and partly to coddle her own naïve idealism, decides to intervene. Daddy only makes her more determined by arguing that racial issues are a "local matter" in which they should not get involved. Free the blacks, Daddy cynically argues, and they will just be re-enslaved by way of the exploitative economic arrangement of sharecropping and their own victim pathology. But Grace makes up her mind to bring liberal democracy to Manderlay and twists several of Daddy's best "associates" out of his posse to help her enforce reform on the plantation. The gangster-liberators burn the sharecropping agreements with the white owners, replace them with deeds-of-gift that make the ex-slaves the owners and the white overseer and his family indentured servants, then wait confidently for the dawn of a brave new world.

No new days ensue. The slaves simply do nothing. The shock of being thwarted in her power kills the mistress of Manderlay, leaving a vacuum. The leaderless ex-slaves fail to plant a cotton crop, expecting someone else (white) to tell them what to do and when to do it. It is not that they do not know how to run a plantation, Will'm, the senior house slave, explains; it is rather that they have all become accustomed to operating according to "Mam's Law," a system that classifies the slaves by type and prescribes times and places for almost all of life's activities. Grace is appalled both by the rules and by the slaves' submission to them, and sets about to hold classes on how to live as liberal democratic individuals within a progressive community.

After a little hesitation, the Manderlay ex-slaves begin to operate like a democratic, agrarian community. There is one holdout, the "proudy" slave Timothy (whom Grace had initially saved from a lashing). Timothy refuses to thank Grace for any of her innovations, and continually reminds her that for all her altruism she still cannot tell one black face from another. And he flaunts his sexual dominion over the black women where and when Grace cannot ignore it, igniting her own furtive desire and the cliché of the irresistible sexual power of black men over white women in the bargain.

Hard times fall upon Manderlay when a dust storm—rare in the Alabama of fact—damages the cotton plants. One of Grace's progressive reforms, cutting the timber on the plantation to use in repairing the leaky and drafty cabins, removed the windbreak that had protected Manderlay in windy seasons past. But the community that starves together stays together, and from the reduced number of plants the workers had been able to rescue from the dunes of incoming dust they harvest a fine crop of higher-quality cotton. Ginned and sold, the cotton brings in a fistful of cash, and the integrated community (the white overseer and hands have been accepted, after a few rough encounters) celebrates with a harvest meal. Capitalism is no great leap, just an easy step—as long as the white lady shows the way. Grace, though, still longs for fulfillment. Von Trier writes a Grace for whom social progress is hardly enough to satisfy an obsession with the Other. She spends an increasing amount of time imagining the black male bodies on the other side of the washhouse walls (given that the set is transparently minimalist, her imagining is easy), and excusing herself from the harvest supper, she responds to Timothy's magnetic powers of seduction.

From this point in the plot onward, there is little but a series of bitterly reversed assumptions calculated to make Grace look like a neoimperial fool. Timothy is not the noble African prince she had feverishly imagined but a con man who has stolen the cotton proceeds as well as her sexual self-esteem. "Mam's Law" was not imposed upon the slaves by an overwhelming, racist economic order but rather was written by Will'm to provide "the lesser of two evils"—a means of protection for the blacks in an American world that professed belief in equality but actually was not ready to accept free people with black skin. Her self-image turned inside-out in public, Grace becomes Ma'am; in the closing scene, she whips Timothy out of her combined sexual and racial rage and flees across a map of the United States to the North.

Manderlay treats the South as a board game. It is not filmed on location (a place), but rather in a hangarlike space of lighted zones surrounded by an enveloping darkness. Chapters or acts (there are eight) close with towering overhead camera shots that remind us of the flatness on which the southern memory game is played: sites are demarcated with broad dotted lines and identified with runway-sized lettering; much of the action (opening doors and hoeing in imaginary fields) is pantomimed (the sex is more realistic); and a voiceover commentary (read by actor John Hurt in a ripe British accent that renders "Alabama" a near-rhyme with "Yokohama") undercuts respect for all of the characters except the cynic Daddy.

If *Manderlay* represents the extended field of play for the cultural marker "South," then perhaps all but the gaming is over. Von Trier reproduces a "fake South" that, unlike most of those Romine handles in *The Real South,* leaves a toxic mark. *Manderlay,* unlike, say, sequels to *Gone With the Wind* or "living history" tours of restored plantations, is not kitsch. It is memory-and-history from which, Von Trier seems to tell us, we Americans do not even know we cannot awaken ourselves—a continuous present running from roadside lynchings to our mean urban streets, our prisons and death rows, and our neocolonial wars. Maybe you can't get to the South from here-and-now ever again, "here" being the postsouthern position of infinite (or almost infinite) simulacra. If Von Trier reads us accurately, then the U.S. South is a memory without a place to have it.

If southern memory has a future, it would seem to be among the simulacra that crowd in upon the omnimediated experience of the present. Another moment in Tom Wolfe's *A Man in Full* illustrates the brazen face of illusion among the ranks of the so-called real.[13] One of Charlie Croker's many jealous nemeses has traveled to Nassau, capital of shell corporations and illusory headquarters offices, to recruit a fellow conspirator in the looting of Croker Global assets. Wolfe can't resist the opportunity to fill us in on the meaning of Nassau, Bahamas, as readers of the *Wall Street Journal* might require. But he mixes his orders, conflating facsimile and history, geopoetics and geopolitics: "Not for nothing did Nassau call itself Little Switzerland. Ever since the Civil War, when blockade runners—such as Rhett Butler in *Gone With the Wind*—used the Bahamas as a safe harbor from which to do business with the Confederacy, Americans had been using the Bahamas to get around American laws" (Wolfe 536). When one of the most ironic of postmodern authors doesn't "know it's a movie," it might be safe to say that the absorption of history by memory is more or less complete—that the South is gone but the memory survives.

NOTES

Introduction: Memory, Culture, Identity

1. *Brown v. Board of Education:* "A sense of inferiority affects the motivation of a child to learn."

2. I'm borrowing "disturbances" from Benson. Benson locates disturbances in scenes of calculation; I find disturbances in various textual sites.

3. I'm not the first. See Crouch.

4. See Hobson, *But Now I See.*

5. See Nora's note, p. 25, explaining the relationship of this piece to his entire seven-volume work on the national memory of France. Halbwachs (1877–1945) did the greater part of his work on the collective memory in France between the world wars; he died in Buchenwald.

6. The project of *Look Away!* is not summed up between its covers. See Smith, McKee, and Romine.

7. See Houston A. Baker, Jr., and Dana Nelson, eds., *American Literature* 73 (June 2001). Both the University of Georgia Press and the University of North Carolina Press have series in the New Southern Studies.

8. See Jon Smith's objection and Ladd's response in "Forum," *PMLA* 121.2 (2006), 549–52.

9. Ladd identifies race and gender as continuing constants in new directions for southern studies ("Literary South" 1630).

10. See *The Real South* (17), where Romine links faking and sampling as equally plausible ways of enacting culture. Romine also alludes to the passage on forgetting in Renan; see *The Real South* (15). He is, unlike Judt, satisfied that forgetting the real in favor of the fake is what cultures do.

1. "Something of an Obstacle": Remembering Slavery in Morrison's *Beloved*

1. See, for example, Goodheart or Yoder. Yoder's article advertises "Travel and Adventure for the Southern Soul"—refurbished sharecropper cabins in the Mississippi Delta for blues tourists.

2. See chapter 7 for a discussion of works in this genre.

3. See Elkins, third ed. The third edition is identical to the first except for additions consisting of responses by Elkins to the critique his work had raised. See particularly III, 4: "Adjustment to Absolute Power in the Concentration Camp." For another discussion of Elkins and the representation of the South and slavery, see Brinkmeyer 321–24.

4. See Szabo.

NOTES TO PAGES 29-55

5. The Underground Railroad Freedom Center contains a contemporary example: the coop or pen vies with restored lists kept by white masters of named slaves and purchase prices.

6. Perhaps the less deliberate designs on place are implemented, the more the aura remains: visit the minimally preserved house of Medgar Evers in Jackson, Mississippi.

7. See, for example, James Olney, "The Founding Fathers—Frederick Douglass and Booker T. Washington," in McDowell and Rampersad 1–24; and Baker. Gordon also touches on the problems of the slave narrative as form; see 144–46. And the argument persists in the wake of the U.S. Supreme Court's 5–4 decision (2003) to allow affirmative action to stand in the admissions process to law schools: see Milloy.

8. Gordon, perhaps responding to Morrison's modernist fragmentation of narrative, reconciles the plot of *Beloved* to historical sequence (139–41), then follows with a summary and acute textual analysis of the historical record on Margaret Garner, the slave mother whose killing of her baby rather than see her returned to slavery in 1856 is the origin of Morrison's novel.

9. This is the interpretation put upon *Beloved* by Oprah Winfrey in the film adaptation of the novel.

10. Two contesting and contrasting views are deliberately conflated in this sentence. "Sayable" hearkens to George P. Handley's theory of "the poetics of oblivion," which attempts to explain the impossibilities of representing an experience—New World slavery—for which there is "understated or erased" tangible evidence. The second quoted phrase is taken from Crouch's "Aunt Medea," and calls for confidence in the writer's ability to represent the record of slavery. For a more thorough discussion of Handley's "poetics of oblivion," see chapter 4.

2. Robert Penn Warren:
The Real Southerner and the "Hypothetical Negro"

1. Carter, *An Hour Before Daylight*; Morris; Moody.

2. Hobson also examines the conversion narratives of representative white southern women: Lillian Smith, Katharine Du Pre Lumpkin, and Sarah Patton Boyle. For another discussion of Lumpkin, see T. McPherson. McPherson makes explicit what Hobson strongly implies: for white southern women, supremacist racial mores and compulsory heterosexuality were inseparable—reject one, reject the other. Margaret Mitchell also belongs in this category.

3. And turn on the novel a generation after that—see Malcolm Gladwell, "The Courthouse Ring: Atticus Finch and the Limits of Southern Liberalism," *New Yorker*, 10, 17 August 2009: 26–32.

4. The literature of research on mind and memory is thick with such commentary. See Nobel Laureate Kandel: "In a larger sense memory provides our lives with continuity. It gives us a coherent picture of the past that puts current experience in perspective. The picture may not be rational or accurate, but it persists. Without the binding force of memory, experience would be splintered into as many fragments as there are moments in life. . . . We are who we are because of what we learn and what we remember" (8).

5. Warren tried to reconcile the two identities in Brooks, Lewis, and Warren, *American Literature*.

6. See also "Careers Open to College-Bred Negroes," in Du Bois, *Writings* 827–41.

7. Lest I give the impression that Washington had no followers after his death in 1903, see Woodson 14–15.

8. Nor is it unreasonable to think that Warren, writing "The Briar Patch" in 1929, did not remember the Fisk student revolt (supported by Du Bois) against the "Code of Discipline" enforced by (white) Fisk University president Fayette McKenzie and supported by Booker T. Washington's widow, who was a member of Fisk's board of trustees. The resistance mounted in 1924–25, Warren's senior year at Vanderbilt, culminating in the invasion of a Fisk men's dormitory by white Nashville police ostensibly enforcing President McKenzie's curfew rules. See Lewis, *Fight for Equality* 133–42.

9. Warren, *New and Selected Poems* 319–21. See also Szczesiul's excellent discussion of the poem, 8–25.

10. Blotner, *Robert Penn Warren* 105–06.

11. See J. McPherson, "Days of Wrath." McPherson inadvertently illustrates the intensity of feeling about the South and race that the figure of Brown can still conjure. McPherson apparently repeats an error of attribution in Merrill D. Peterson's book *John Brown* (118) by way of evidence that Warren's biography is "typical" of "the white South's image of Brown as a terrorist and murderer." McPherson also quotes Warren as describing Brown as "possessed to a considerable degree [of] that tight especial brand of New England romanticism which manifested itself in stealing Guinea niggers, making money, wrestling with conscience, hunting witches . . . or being an Abolitionist" (16). In fact, this is Warren's description of Frank B. Sanborn, one of Brown's promoters and early biographers (Warren, *John Brown* 226–27). Warren, of course, had equally withering things to say about Brown himself.

12. On this point, John Brown as harbinger and symbol of a capitalist-industrialist world order, Warren and Stephen Vincent Benét seem to agree. See Benét 373–77.

13. "Mr. Chamberlain": Amos Chamberlain, who bought a Brown homestead at a bankruptcy sale in 1841. "New England Woolen Mills": The New England Woolen Company advanced Brown $2,800 in 1840 to purchase wool in Ohio to be shipped to the mills in Connecticut; Brown instead bought land in Virginia. The "Canal Company": a land deal Brown entered into in northeast Ohio in 1837; he lost his investment in the general crash of that year.

14. See, in passing, Lewis, *W. E. B. Dubois: The Fight for Equality.*

15. See Warren, *Who Speaks for the Negro?* 10–12, for his recantation and self-examination. It might not be coincidental that one of Warren's closest friends among the African American writers of his lifetime was a man who had attended Tuskegee, Ralph Ellison. An archive of Warren's audio recordings is available at www.whospeaks.library.vanderbilt.edu. Kristina Morris Baumli has pointed out many of the refinements Warren exercised upon the raw tape recordings of his interviews. One in particular, presented at the American Literature Association meeting in 2005, was important in the early stages of this chapter.

16. "Men" because there is only one full-scale interview with an African American woman in the published book.

17. Hobson, in *But Now I See,* takes a similarly skeptical view of Warren's "memory" in this passage (80–82).

18. The film version of *Band of Angels* (1957) reinforces the echoes of *Gone With the Wind* because Clark Gable plays Hamish Bond, "owner" of the slave Rau-Ru (Sidney Poitier) and purchaser/lover of the mulatta Amantha Starr (Yvonne DeCarlo).

19. In *The Fire Next Time* (1963), Baldwin had taken a position in the complex field of cultural and racial identity that might not have comforted Warren. The epigraph to this chapter is indicative of Baldwin's stance.

20. Warren had also backed away from *John Brown* in *Who Speaks for the Negro?* (320–21).

21. Gilroy, in *The Black Atlantic,* uncovers the Du Bois who proved so indigestible to Warren. Gilroy's formulation is that Du Bois opted to be free and to be himself—not the Negro Warren and white America had imagined for him. After many "periods" in his life, Gilroy argues, Du Bois arrived at the conclusion that "other types of racial association, of a local, urban, or even international nature, can be shown to be more significant than the overdue chance to be an American" (122–23). Malcolm X was, eventually, struck from the same mold.

3. Arms and the Man:
Southern Honor and the Memory of Vietnam

I want to thank John Schafer, who spent four years in Vietnam with International Voluntary Services, for his help in sorting out the tangled threads of this chapter. The surviving knots are of my own making.

1. See Moore, *The Green Berets,* and the movie *The Green Berets* (Warner Bros., 1968). Not surprisingly, John Wayne's production enjoyed the cooperation of the U.S. Army—it was filmed in the South, at Fort Benning, Georgia, where the court-martial of Captain Medina took place.

2. Southern novelist William Styron exiled William Calley as far from honorable as possible: "Banal, stunted in mind and body, colorless, lacking even a native acumen, with an airless, dreary brain devoid of wit—he is not the first nobody whose brush with a large moment in history has personified that moment and helped to define it. One thinks of Eichmann" (Styron 219).

3. Hellmann, certainly not uniquely, sees Lincoln as a "visionary" president who, in the midst of civil war, "reinvigorated the American errand" (72).

4. *Flags in the Dust* (1974) is the original and uncut manuscript from which *Sartoris* (1929) was carved. The Vintage 1974 edition was edited by Douglas Day.

5. As is, for example, the film version of *Gods and Generals* (2003), based on the "prequel" to *The Killer Angels* written by Michael Shaara's son Jeff Shaara: *Gods and Generals* (1996).

6. See also Faust, and Ward, "Death's Army."

7. Dixon was the author of *The Clansman* (1905) and other historical romances glorifying the Ku Klux Klan. Griffith adapted Dixon's work for *The Birth of a Nation* (1915), the first movie screened in the White House.

8. For Hellmann, Kurtz "represents that mythic ideal [the grail of its lost sense of mission] and finally the horrific self-awareness of its hollowness" (190).

9. James (Jim) Webb is serving his first term as U.S. senator from Virginia. He is a decorated marine veteran of Vietnam, former secretary of the navy, and Emmy-winning journalist. For another reading of *Fields of Fire,* see Hellmann (102–103 and 106–19).

10. For an edgier digest of this plot, see Barbara Ehrenreich, "The Warrior Culture," in Bennis and Moushabeck 129–31.

11. It might be worth noting the coincidence that a central resource for Tony Horwitz's chronicle of Civil War reenactors in *Confederates in the Attic* (1998) carries a very similar name: Robert E. Lee (Rob) Hodge.

12. This John Wayne role bears a wide and heavy weight of significance. It has been claimed

by, among many others, former Speaker of the U.S. House of Representatives Newt Gingrich. See Wills 149.

13. The Dewey Canyon demonstrations of 1971, in which some veterans threw their medals onto the steps of the Capitol (see *Forrest Gump* below), were organized by Vietnam Veterans Against the War, in which future U.S. senator and presidential candidate John Kerry was prominent.

14. See such Reconstruction romances, reconciled in marriages, in DeForest, Dixon, and H. James. Marriages between lovers from the formerly warring sections conclude each novel; in *The Clansman,* as double insurance of reconciliation, brother and sister of a Rebel family marry brother and sister of a Union family.

15. The rewriting of this mistake is the applauded theme of Gen. David H. Petraeus in "Counterinsurgency Reader."

16. Tim O'Brien's *Going After Cacciato* (1979) is also built on the irreconcilability of facts and imagination. Paul Berlin, O'Brien's protagonist, deploys a similar, but less farcical, anti-realist strategy.

17. In an irony not infrequent in cultural history, Bly's rhetoric of weak and soft masculinity echoes in contrast to John F. Kennedy's rhetoric of "vigor" and the rhetoric of threatened national/male character in cold war U.S. policy. See Hellmann on JFK's fixation with Special Forces (112–15) and Dean, especially chap. 3: "Heroism, Bodies, and the Construction of Elite Masculinity," 37–62.

18. For a possible subtext to Bly's weak admiration, see Dean, chap. 4: "'Lavender Lads' and the Foreign Policy Establishment," 63–96.

19. Stonewall Jackson. He got this nickname, according to Foote, "because of the way his eyes would light up in battle" (Ward, *Civil War* 272).

20. Only to have their names immortalized as street names in the upscale subdivision adjacent to the Confederate cemetery in Franklin, Tennessee.

4. Haiti:
Phantom Southern Memory in Faulkner and Madison Smartt Bell

1. "I Won't Dance," music by Jerome Kern. Original lyrics by Oscar Hammerstein II and Otto Harbach (play, 1933). Revised lyrics by Dorothy Fields and Jimmy McHugh for *Roberta* (1935).

2. For a discussion of Paris and France in the American imaginary fostered by Hollywood film, see D. Smith.

3. J. Michael Dash supplies a bridge from O'Brien's historical order to the symbolic order of cultural narrative. See Dash 11–15.

4. See Bové.

5. Michael O'Brien, quoted just above, documents a South that was much more closely tied, socially and economically, to the Caribbean in the eighteenth and early nineteenth centuries than it was to its continental North.

6. Glissant; Smith and Cohn; Ladd, *Nationalism and the Color Line* and *Resisting History.*

7. My questions echo those raised by Kutzinski 644–49. Specifically, Kutzinski warns, of work like *Look Away!* against "methodological and ideological biases . . . retain[ed] and implicitly map[ped] onto other geographies" (645). Less cautious is Benson 16–18. Benson credits the application of postcolonial theory with liberating the "long-segregated field of U.S. southern literature" (17).

8. Bell's advocacy of Haitian writers is not confined to fiction and biography, as his review of books by Haitian writers in the *New York Review of Books* attests. See "A Hidden Haitian World" 40–42. The biography is *Toussaint Louverture: A Biography* (2007).

9. The prime example is Woodward, *Burden*. Woodward, a historian, privileged southern writers like Faulkner and Warren on the level of his other sources.

10. Bell's parents, Judge Henry Denmark Bell and Allen Bell, were members of the Nashville social circle that included the generation of Agrarian protégés such as Walter Sullivan and Madison Jones. Allen Tate, who died in Nashville in 1979, had lived in Sewanee, Tennessee, and Nashville since 1967.

11. Nomenclature choices shape the discussion: "U.S. South" or "American South"? I take the former term to be weighted with political and nationalistic policy and force, and the latter with cultural myth, and use them therefore in different contexts. "Caribbean" and "the islands" present another either/or. I try to use the former to represent the geographical and political entity, the latter to signify the cultural entity.

12. William Luis also uses the trope of dancing in his study of crosscultural dialogue *Dance Between Two Cultures*. More recently, see *PMLA* 124 (2009): Yaeger 11–24, and the articles in the special section "Theories and Methodologies: The Neobaroque and the Americas," 127–88.

13. Simpich's metaphor comes in a scene where the *National Geographic* plane buzzes a wetland area to scare up a flight of flamingos, some of which are so startled they drop back into the water "in sheer fright" (20).

14. Another example, more contemporary to Bell's trilogy but too complicated to be fleshed out here, is in the genealogy that connects Wade Davis's novel of Haiti and zombification, *The Serpent and the Rainbow* (1985), his more scholarly ethnographic work on the same material, *Passage of Darkness: The Ethnobiology of the Haitian Zombie* (1988), and the film of *The Serpent and the Rainbow* made by Wes Craven and released in 1988. Those who watch Craven's film will have to suspend a small mountain of disbelief, but even so will find wicked parallels with Bell's trilogy—suggesting that the story of Haiti surreptitiously takes over our attempts to tell it.

15. Dash likewise traces the feminization of Haiti/Caribbean. He goes further than Benitez-Rojo in suggesting that the imaginary embodiment of the place devolves to disease and corruption in/of that body (ix–x).

16. See Graham Greene's *The Comedians* (1966) for an example of the dystopic end of the Columbus myth set in Duvalier's Haiti. The narrator and his mistress have their assignations in her Peugeot parked next to the Columbus memorial in Port-au-Prince. Coincidentally, *The Comedians* "recalls" the U.S. South. An American couple visiting Haiti assume that their experience in the civil rights movement in the South will translate the situation under Duvalier. The British narrator pleads with them to abandon that assumption as dangerously naïve.

17. See James Michener's *Caribbean*, in which the story of Guadeloupe is told along the hackneyed lines of romantic melodrama: a handsome hero torn between two women, one blonde and blue-eyed, the other fiery and dark.

18. In Hollywood, the unfinished manuscript of *Absalom Absalom!* with him, Faulkner, Matthews tells us in his essay, worked on a screen adaptation of just such a swashbuckler: George S. King's *The Last Slaver* (1933). King's sea tale involves outlawed slave trade between Africa and Cuba. Jimmy Kane, the handsome American hero, unwillingly captains a slave ship between Congo and Cuba (before the Civil War) until he can overcome the sinister, New Orleans–born Captain LaRoche,

who spends most of each voyage drunk in his cabin. "The girl" is rescued by our hero from the wreckage of a ship destroyed in a fierce hurricane. She turns out to be the son of an English peer who is also a rich merchant, and she looks good in sailor's togs (199). Our hero eventually returns a cargo of slaves to the shores of Africa and even burns the barracoons in which they had been held for shipment. But he only trades one form of extractive colonial economy for another: into the hold empty of slaves he loads a cargo of ivory.

19. Bell, among others, makes a strong point that the "Kreyòl" among the languages of Haiti is of central importance in understanding the people and the place. See "A Hidden Haitian World" 40.

20. Melville 296.

21. See Renda, who suggests several popular conduits for the circulation of the image of Haiti in the American imagination. My interpretation of Edna Taft's *A Puritan in Voodoo-Land* is similar to Renda's.

22. See W. Davis, *Passage of Darkness*. In a chapter titled "The Historical and Cultural Setting," Davis begins a brief outline of the types of heterosexual partnering on the island with laconic understatement: "Sexual relations among the Haitian peasants do not follow European patterns" (41). More generally, the linking of colonial expansion with erotic subtext has not gone unnoticed; see Bernstein.

23. Joseph Blotner points out that one bright spot in Faulkner's otherwise dismal academic record as an undergraduate at Ole Miss was his affinity for French. See Blotner I, 260–75. Faulkner apparently decided to devote more time to extracurricular studies than to classwork; most of that was early poetry either in French or modeled on Villon, Verlaine, and other French poets.

24. John Houston Craige wrote two memoirs of his service with the occupation in Haiti; *Cannibal Cousins* (1934) is the second. For another angle on Craige and other occupation texts, see Dash 22–36.

25. *Gunga Din,* a film loosely "based" on Kipling's poem, was released in 1939. Joel Sayre, with whom Faulkner had worked in Hollywood earlier in the 1930s, cowrote the script. *King Solomon's Mines,* based on the H. Rider Haggard novel, was first adapted as a film in 1937; Paul Robeson played the generic role of loyal native "Number One Boy."

26. See Seabrook for the story of a white man who became "king, sultan and dictator" in Haiti. Mary Renda has an excellent analysis of Seabrook's story in *Taking Haiti* (246–55). The character of Yen Leabrook in Virgile Valcin's *La Blanche Négresse* (see n. 29) might be a jab at Seabrook. Leabrook is a visiting American who writes doggerel odes to Haitian rum and a very popular (in the States) book about vodou that is, according to Haitian characters, totally shallow.

27. Taft, too, feels the unrest of the killing grounds beneath her feet (299).

28. In fact, even a cursory reading of the history of Haiti suggests that violent unrest did not end with the establishment of independence by Dessalines in 1803.

29. See Valcin, *La Blanche Négresse* (1934). In this novel, the blonde heroine is denounced and eventually divorced by her American playboy husband when (at a party celebrating the end of Prohibition) a letter arrives disclosing that she is in fact *Africaine:* her grandmother had possessed some African DNA.

30. To further extend the reach of desire in this cultural matrix, see Taft's *A Puritan in Voodoo-Land.* At her first social occasion, a dance, the American puritan is first anxious about the possibility of, then attracted and finally almost erotically exhausted by, a series of dances with mixed-race Haitian men (chap. 2: "Attending a Dusky Dance").

31. Consider, for example, the succession of zombie films produced in the United States, beginning arbitrarily with *The White Zombie* (1932), starring Bela Lugosi. According to Hollywood legend, this film was completed in eleven days, and it shows. But its very superficiality is telling. The plot is an almost scene-for-scene importation of the typical Lugosi vampire plot; the setting is merely shifted to a Haitian sugar plantation. The lack of originality is in itself an indication of how U.S. publics, over time, come to know "Haiti." On one level, the argument goes: if you know the vampire story, you know "Haiti," for "Haiti" operates on the level of fable, not history. Renda, in *Taking Haiti*, discusses this film and the zombie genre (223–27). Refer also to the various works on Haiti by Wade Davis.

32. Toni Morrison, in *Beloved*, I argue in the first chapter, faced the same problem.

33. The particular legend of an eradicated original people who were highly cultured and pacific was exported to Louisiana with the Saint-Domingue émigrés. On the Continent, the corresponding noble indigenous people were the Natchez. See Chateaubriand.

34. For a view of Louverture that debates his status as indigenous revolutionary hero, see W. Davis, *Passage of Darkness* 15–29.

35. Michelet was swimming with the school. Raynal had concluded that black and native women of the islands are chaste unless "the vanity of being loved by white men makes them inconstant" (157).

36. See William Styron's *The Confessions of Nat Turner* (1968) for a similar use of jail-cell interviews interspersed between episodes of Turner's life up to and during the rebellion.

37. Many reviewers seem satisfied with Bell's attention to history. See a symposium on his trilogy in *Small Axe* 12.1 (2007).

38. The other "trilogy" mentioned in footnote 14 above—Wade Davis's novel, his ethnobiological report, and Wes Craven's film adaptation of the novel—is constructed on the same "folk knowledge meets laboratory science" armature. Indeed, Craven's film, *The Serpent and the Rainbow,* bears a discomforting (even if shallow) resemblance to the general plotline of Bell's novel—suggesting the power of Haiti-as-text to infiltrate all attempts to imagine it "otherwise."

39. Rodgers and Hammerstein's musical *South Pacific* opened on Broadway in 1949. It is based on James Michener's *Tales of the South Pacific* (1947), winner of the Pulitzer Prize for fiction in 1948.

40. Graham Greene, mentioned in an earlier footnote, is the source for a notable example of whiskey-priest in *The Power and the Glory* (1940).

41. A similarly staged uprising, based on the race riot in Wilmington, North Carolina, in 1898, goes violently awry in Charles Chesnutt's *The Marrow of Tradition* (1901).

42. Fear, thrill, and passion permeate the image of "Haiti" in white imagination. Edna Taft, knowing that certain dances end in "consummate phallic rites" in the brush outside the firelit circle of the dance, nevertheless cannot resist the thrill of creeping close to watch, and is moved by the drums to the brink of leaping into the dance herself (248, 212).

5. Parody, Memory, and Copyright:
The Southern Memory Market

1. The phrase is borrowed from Joan Didion's *The Year of Magical Thinking* (2005). Didion's book is not about terrorist attacks but rather a memoir of the death of her husband, John Gregory Dunne. Still, her immersion in memory triggered by trauma is relevant.

2. The issue of the *New Yorker* that carries Gopnik's comment, 9 April 2001, is illustrated with a small sketch of a southern belle in blackface, a peacock and Taralike mansion in the background. The black-faced belle suggests an earlier parody of *Gone With the Wind,* by The Lady Chablis, who bills herself in the preface to her autobiography as the "Negro Scarlett O'Hara." See The Lady Chablis, *Hiding My Candy,* and Talley and Lagerfeld, "Scarlett 'n the Hood." The peacock apparently wandered into the *New Yorker* from Andalusia, Flannery O'Connor's home. See also Pyron 330–38.

3. See Romine's navigation of the field of *GWTW* simulacra in *The Real South* 27–59.

4. See *Metro-Goldwyn-Mayer v. Showcase Atlanta Cooperative Productions.* In April 2008, a musical based on *GWTW* opened in London, directed by the Royal Shakespeare Company's Trevor Nunn. Critical reception was cool.

5. *Gone With the Wind* still sells about one-half million copies annually. A new paperback edition was published by Scribner in 2007 (retailing in the United States for $17.00). Macmillan, the original publisher, merged with Charles Scribner's Sons in 1984, and the merged houses were bought by Simon & Schuster in 1994. The Trusts had already licensed one sequel, *Scarlett,* by Alexandra Ripley (1991), one year ahead of the expiration of the second and last twenty-eight-year period of original copyright protection which attached to the first publication. A second "derivative," *Rhett Butler's People,* was published in 2007.

6. The text of the opinion can be found at www.altlaw.org/v1/cases/173243.

7. 1:01 CV-701-CAP. Affidavit of Kevin J. Anderson, p. 3. Unless otherwise noted, all legal documents relating to this case, with the exception of 1:01 CV-701-CAP itself, can be found at www .thewinddonegone.com. Italics added.

8. *SunTrust v. Houghton Mifflin,* fn. 7, p. 18: "Parody or satire is 'when one artist, for comic effect or social commentary, closely imitates the style of another artist and in so doing creates a new art work that makes ridiculous the style and expression of the original.'"

9. *The Carol Burnett Show,* episode 238, originally broadcast 13 November 1976. This two-part sketch has been ranked among the funniest television comedy sketches of all time in *TV Guide's 50 Funniest Moments* special issues.

10. www.law.cornell.edu/supct/html/92-1292.ZS.html. The text of the decision on this site is not paged.

11. This and similar language appears on the cover of the Avon paperback. The Scribner trade paperback (2007) modifies the "love story" theme and suggests that *Gone With the Wind* is also (or rather) an "epic novel of love and war," and a "timeless story of survival under the harshest of circumstances." The back-cover blurb concludes, though, by ranking Rhett and Scarlett as "two of the most famous lovers in the English-speaking world since Romeo and Juliet."

12. See Eric Sundquist's discussion of the cake walk in part 2, section 4, of *To Wake the Nations.*

13. Pyron 56–57. Mr. Mitchell's lecture must have had only limited results. The yellow sash Scarlett gives to Ashley when he returns to the field from leave in Atlanta closely resembles the one Marion Lenoir, the *ingénue* of *The Clansman,* gives to the hero Ben Cameron when he goes off to war. Marion also makes do after the war with dresses made from window treatments.

14. If this scene is loosely echoed in *Gone With the Wind,* it is much more exactly present in *Rhett Butler's People.* There Rhett's sister Rosemary is ordered by her Klansman husband to make a set of robes for another member of the Klan. She protests, against the Klan vociferously, if not against the sexist arrogance of her Confederate-veteran husband (McCaig, 345).

15. "The slap" is remembered as occurring once because in the film only one of the several blows

Scarlett inflicts on Prissy is included in the script. This total does not include the verbal abuse Scarlett lavishes on her maid.

16. This legal life span is indeed fixed. The Copyright Act of 1909 decreed a period of copyright protection of the life of the author plus twenty-eight years, with one additional period of twenty-eight years. The 1976 act extended this period of protection (for works published after enactment) to the author's life plus fifty years. An extension in 1998 prolonged the life span of copyright to life plus seventy years, or plus ninety-five years from the date of publication for "works for hire," a category that covers sequels legally commissioned by the copyright holder and for which the original owner retains copyright.

17. See Williamson 87–107.

18. Rhett is presumed dead yet returns at least twice more in the novel, giving him a supernatural aura.

19. The mob's desecration of Bonneau's body, culminating in hoisting its charred remains into a tree on the courthouse lawn, is rendered in images reminiscent of those of U.S. private security contractors killed in Iraq (McCaig 277).

20. See Romine 21–22 for a discussion of the novel.

6. Nostalgia, Alternate History, and the Future of Southern Memory

1. Or not. See Faust. Faust analyzes the balance between the calculable facts of maiming and death and the rhetorics by which the surviving public, then and still, copes with those facts.

2. See Dickey. Dickey found disturbing confirmations of this latent racism among southerners during the Obama presidential campaign.

3. See Jencks, *The New Paradigm in Architecture*. The first edition of this book was published as *The Language of Postmodernism* in 1977.

4. Dr. Samuel Adolphus Cartwright (1793–1863) was real, but the institute bearing his name is invented. Cartwright apprenticed to Dr. Benjamin Rush at the University of Pennsylvania Medical School and performed important work in improving sanitary conditions in Confederate army camps and in Vicksburg during the siege in 1863. He is also responsible for the "science" on slave physiology and psychology for which Willmott skewers him.

5. Perhaps not strangely, "Betty Crocker," who began her brand life as the image of the Caucasian housewife, is now edging into panethnic identity. The current Aunt Jemima is less "mammy." Uncle Ben is a different case. The Internet is replete with virtual renditions of the icons. See particularly YouTube.

6. Willmott's film was released into a marketplace replete with similar opportunities for revisiting the U.S. fixation with race, sex, and presidential politics, many of which swirled around Thomas Jefferson's relationship with his slave Sally Hemings. See Gordon-Reed, *Thomas Jefferson and Sally Hemings* and *The Hemingses of Monticello; Sally Hemings: An American Scandal* (2000), CBS Productions; Chase-Riboud, *Sally Hemings*.

7. The rhythm of history/alternate history is ongoing. See Keith, *The Colfax Massacre: The Untold Story of Black Power, White Terror, and the Death of Reconstruction*. Keith might have, alternatively, used the word *Unremembered* for *Untold* in her title.

8. Mourning her passing is a little difficult; Mrs. Lee was one of her husband's most caustic critics when he described his plan to bring the slaves of the South to citizenship (379).

9. Brinkmeyer, in *The Fourth Ghost,* writes extensively about the grip with which Hitler and Fascism seized the imaginations of many white southern writers in midcentury.

10. Willmott had imagined a similar episode in *C.S.A.*

11. See Cable, *The Grandissimes.* See also Wagner, "Disarmed and Dangerous."

12. The name "Manderlay" is rich with suggestion. Manderley is the name of house and estate in Daphne du Maurier's *Rebecca,* a novel-film coupling (1938/1940) with abundant allusions to sexual impropriety and repression. It is also a more remote echo of another novel-film for which the word "coupling" is luridly apt: Kyle Onstott's novel *Mandingo* (1957) and the film of the same name released in 1975.

13. My allusion here is to Simpson, *The Brazen Face of History.*

WORKS CITED

PRINTED SOURCES

Andrews, Eliza Frances. *The War-Time Journal of a Georgia Girl, 1864–1865*. 1908. Lincoln: U of Nebraska P, 1997.

Andrews, William L., Minrose C. Gwin, Trudier Harris, and Fred Hobson, eds. *The Literature of the American South: A Norton Anthology*. New York: Norton, 1998.

Avary, Myrta Lockett. *Dixie After the War: An Exposition of Social Conditions Existing in the South, During the Twelve Years Succeeding the Fall of Richmond*. 1906. New York: Negro Universities Press, 1969.

Bacevich, Andrew J. *The New American Militarism: How Americans Are Seduced by War*. New York: Oxford UP, 2005.

Baker, Houston A., Jr. *Turning South Again*. Durham: Duke UP, 2000.

Baldwin, James. *The Fire Next Time*. 1963. New York: Vintage, 1991.

Beidler, Philip D. *Re-Writing America: Vietnam Authors in Their Generation*. Athens: U of Georgia P, 1991.

Bell, Madison Smartt. *All Souls' Rising*. New York: Penguin, 1995.

———. *Master of the Crossroads*. New York: Penguin, 2000.

———. "Engaging the Past." In Carnes 197–208.

———. *The Stone That the Builder Refused*. New York: Vintage, 2004.

———. "A Hidden Haitian World." *New York Review of Books* 17 July 2008: 40–42.

Benét, Stephen Vincent. *John Brown's Body*. Garden City, NY: Country Life P, 1928.

Benitez-Rojo, Antonio. *The Repeating Island: The Caribbean and the Postmodern Perspective*. 2nd ed. Trans. James E. Maraniss. Durham: Duke UP, 1996.

Bennis, Phyllis, and Michel Moushabeck, eds. *Beyond the Storm: A Gulf Crisis Reader*. New York: Olive Branch P, 1991.

Benson, Melanie R. *Disturbing Calculations: The Economics of Identity in Postcolonial Southern Literature, 1912–2002*. Durham: Duke UP, 2008.

Bernstein, Richard. *The East, the West, and Sex: A History of Erotic Encounters*. New York: Knopf, 2009.

Blotner, Joseph. *Faulkner: A Biography. Volume I*. New York: Random House, 1974.

———. *Faulkner: A Biography. Volume II*. New York: Random House, 1974.

———. *Robert Penn Warren: A Biography*. New York: Random House, 1997.

Bly, Robert. *Iron John: A Book About Men.* Reading, MA: Addison-Wesley, 1990.

Bogue, Barbara. *James Lee Burke and the Soul of Dave Robicheaux: A Critical Study of the Crime Fiction Series.* Jefferson, NC: McFarland, 2006.

Bone, Martyn. *The Postsouthern Sense of Place in Contemporary Fiction.* Baton Rouge: Louisiana State UP, 2005.

Bontemps, Arna. *Drums at Dusk.* New York: Macmillan, 1939.

Bové, Paul. "Agriculture and Academe: America's Southern Question." *boundary 2* 14.3 (1986): 169–96.

Brinkley, Douglas. *The Unfinished Presidency: Jimmy Carter's Journey Beyond the White House.* New York: Viking, 1998.

———. *Gerald R. Ford.* New York: Times Books, 2007.

Brinkmeyer, Robert H., Jr. *The Fourth Ghost: White Southern Writers and European Fascism, 1930–1950.* Baton Rouge: Louisiana State UP, 2009.

Brooks, Cleanth, R. W. B. Lewis, and Robert Penn Warren, eds. *American Literature: The Makers and the Making.* 2 vols. New York: St. Martin's, 1973.

Brown v. Board of Education. 347 U.S. 483 (1954).

Bryan, C. D. B. *Friendly Fire.* New York: Putnam, 1976.

Buckley, Christopher. "Viet Guilt." *Esquire* 100.3 (1983): 68–72.

Burt, John. *Robert Penn Warren and American Idealism.* New Haven: Yale UP, 1988.

Butler, Octavia. *Kindred.* Garden City, NY: Doubleday, 1979.

Cable, George Washington. *The Grandissimes: A Story of Creole Life.* New York: Scribner's, 1880.

Campbell v. Acuff-Rose Music, Inc. 510 U.S. 569. 1993.

Cannon, Lou. *Reagan.* New York: Putnam, 1982.

Carby, Hazel V. "Ideologies of Black Folk: The Historical Novel of Slavery." In *Slavery and the Literary Imagination.* Ed. Deborah E. McDowell and Arnold Rampersad. Baltimore: Johns Hopkins UP, 1989. 125–43.

Carnes, Mark C., ed. *Novel History: Historians and Novelists Confront America's Past (and Each Other).* New York: Simon & Schuster, 2001.

Carter, Jimmy. *Keeping Faith: Memoirs of a President.* New York: Bantam, 1982.

———. *An Hour Before Daylight: Memories of a Rural Boyhood.* New York: Simon & Schuster, 2001.

Cash, W. J. *The Mind of the South.* 1941. New York: Knopf, n.d.

Chase-Riboud, Barbara. *Sally Hemings: A Novel.* New York: St. Martin's, 2000.

Chateaubriand. *Les Natchez.* 1827. In *Oeuvres Complètes, Tome III.* Paris: Librairie Garnier Frères, 1861. 184–526.

Chesnutt, Charles. *The Marrow of Tradition.* 1901. New York: Penguin, 1993.

"Cincinnatus." *Self-Destruction: The Disintegration and Decay of the United States Army during the Vietnam Era.* New York: Norton, 1981.

Clay-Clopton, Virginia. *A Belle of the Fifties: Memoirs of Mrs. Clay, of Alabama, Covering Social and Political Life in Washington and the South, 1853–66. Put into Narrative Form by Ada Sterling.* New York: Doubleday, 1904.

Coser, Lewis A., ed. *Maurice Halbwachs on Collective Memory.* Chicago: U of Chicago P, 1992.

Craige, John H. *Black Bagdad.* New York: Minton, Balch, 1933.

Crouch, Stanley. "Aunt Medea." *New Republic* 19 October 1987: 38–43.

Cuddon, J. A. *A Dictionary of Literary Terms.* New York: Penguin, 1982.

Dash, J. Michael. *Haiti and the United States: National Stereotypes and the Literary Imagination.* 2nd ed. New York: St. Martin's, 1997.

Davis, Natalie Zemon, and Randolph Starn. Introduction to *Memory and Counter-Memory.* Spec. issue of *Representations* 26 (Spring 1989): 1–6.

Davis, Wade. *The Serpent and the Rainbow.* New York: Farrar, 1985.

———. *Passage of Darkness: The Ethnobiology of the Haitian Zombie.* Chapel Hill: U of North Carolina P, 1988.

Dayan, Joan. *Haiti, History, and the Gods.* Berkeley: U of California P, 1995.

Dean, Robert D. *Imperial Brotherhood: Gender and the Making of Cold War Foreign Policy.* Amherst: U of Massachusetts P, 2001.

DeForest, John William. *Miss Ravenel's Conversion from Secession to Loyalty* (New York: Harper & Brothers, 1867.

Dickey, Christopher. "Southern Discomfort: A Journey Through a Troubled Region." *Newsweek* 11 August 2008. www.newsweek.com/id/150576.

Didion, Joan. *The Year of Magical Thinking.* New York: Knopf, 2005.

Dixon, Thomas W. *The Clansman.* New York: Doubleday, 1905.

Donaldson, Susan V., and Anne Goodwyn Jones, eds. *Haunted Bodies: Gender and Southern Texts.* Charlottesville: UP of Virginia, 1997.

Drew, Elizabeth. *Portrait of an Election: The 1980 Presidential Campaign.* New York: Simon & Schuster, 1981.

Du Bois, W. E. B. *The Souls of Black Folk: Essays and Sketches.* Chicago: A. C. McClurg, 1903.

———. *John Brown.* 1909, rev. ed. 1962. Millwood, NY: Kraus-Thompson, 1973.

———. *Writings.* New York: Library of America, 1986.

Duck, Leigh Anne. *The Nation's Region: Southern Modernism, Segregation, and U.S. Nationalism.* Athens: U of Georgia P, 2006.

Egginton, William. "The Baroque as a Problem of Thought." *PMLA* 124 (2009): 143–49.

Elkins, Stanley M. *Slavery: A Problem in American Institutional and Intellectual Life.* 1959. 3rd ed. Chicago: U of Chicago P, 1976.

Farmer, Paul. *The Uses of Haiti..* 1994. Monroe, ME: Common Courage P, 2003.

Faulkner, William. *Sartoris.* New York, 1929.

———. *Absalom, Absalom! The Corrected Text.* 1936. New York: Vintage, 1986.

———. *Flags in the Dust.* New York: Vintage, 1974.

Faust, Drew Gilpin. *This Republic of Suffering: Death and the American Civil War.* New York: Knopf, 2008.

Felman, Shoshana, and Dori Laub. *Testimony: Crises of Witnessing in Literature, Psychoanalysis, and History.* New York: Routledge, 1992.

Ford, Gerald R. "The Ford Presidency: What It Looks Like Twelve Years Later." In *Gerald R. Ford and the Politics of Post-Watergate America*. Ed. Bernard J. Firestone and Alexej Ugrinsky. Westport, CT: Greenwood, 1993.

Froude, James Anthony. *The English in the West Indies; or, The Bow of Ulysses*. London: Longmans, 1888.

Fussell, Paul. *The Great War and Modern Memory*. New York: Oxford UP, 1975.

Gay, Mary A. H. *Life in Dixie during the War*. Atlanta: Foote and Davies, 1894.

Genette, Gérard. *Palimpsests: Literature in the Second Degree*. Trans. Channa Newman and Claude Doubinsky. Lincoln: U of Nebraska P, 1997.

Gilman, Owen W. *Vietnam and the Southern Imagination*. Jackson: UP of Mississippi, 1992.

Gilroy, Paul. *The Black Atlantic: Modernity and Double Consciousness*. Cambridge: Harvard UP, 1993.

Gladwell, Malcolm. "The Courthouse Ring: Atticus Finch and the Limits of Southern Liberalism." *New Yorker* 17 August 2009: 26–32.

Glissant, Edouard. *Faulkner, Mississippi*. Trans. Barbara Lewis and Thomas C. Spear. New York: Farrar, 1999.

Godden, Richard. *Fictions of Labor: William Faulkner and the South's Long Revolution*. Cambridge: Cambridge UP, 1997.

Goodheart, Adam. "The Bonds of History." *Preservation* (September–October, 2001): 36–43, 94.

Gopnik, Adam. "Talk of the Town." *New Yorker* 9 April 2001: 37–38.

Gordon, Avery F. *Ghostly Matters: Haunting and the Sociological Imagination*. Minneapolis: U of Minnesota P, 1997.

Gordon-Reed, Annette. *Thomas Jefferson and Sally Hemings: An American Controversy*. Charlottesville: U of Virginia P, 1998.

———. *The Hemingses of Monticello: An American Family*. New York: Norton, 2008.

Gray, Richard. *The Literature of Memory: Modern Writers of the American South*. Baltimore: Johns Hopkins UP, 1977.

———. *A Web of Words: The Great Dialogue of Southern Literature*. Athens: U of Georgia P, 2007.

Gray, Richard, and Waldemar Zacharasiewicz, eds. *Transatlantic Exchanges: The American South in Europe—Europe in the American South*. Vienna: Verlag de Osterreichischen Akademie der Wissenschaften, 2007.

Greene, Graham. *The Comedians*. New York: Viking, 1966.

Greene, Roland. "Baroque and Neobaroque: Making Thistory." *PMLA* 124 (2009): 150–55.

Grier, William H., and Price M. Cobbs. *Black Rage*. New York: Basic, 1968.

Groom, Winston. *Better Times Than These*. New York: Summit, 1978.

———. *Forrest Gump*. New York: Pocket, 1986.

Halbwachs, Maurice. *The Collective Memory*. 1950. New York: Harper, 1980.

Handley, George P. "A New World Poetics of Oblivion." In Smith and Cohn, 24–51.

Hannah, Barry. *Airships*. New York: Delta, 1979.

Harwell, Richard, ed. *Margaret Mitchell's "Gone With the Wind" Letters, 1936–1949*. New York: Macmillan, 1976.

Hellmann, John. *American Myth and the Legacy of Vietnam*. New York: Columbia UP, 1986.

Herr, Michael. *Dispatches*. New York: Knopf, 1977.

Hobson, Fred. *The Southern Writer in the Postmodern World*. Athens: U of Georgia P, 1991.

———. *But Now I See: The White Southern Racial Conversion Narrative*. Baton Rouge: Louisiana State UP, 1999.

Hoffman, Eva. *Complex Histories, Contested Memories: Some Reflections on Remembering Difficult Pasts*. Berkeley: U of California P, 2000.

Horwitz, Tony. *Confederates in the Attic: Dispatches from the Unfinished Civil War*. New York: Random House, 1998.

Hunt, Alfred N. *Haiti's Influence on Antebellum America: Slumbering Volcano in the Caribbean*. Baton Rouge: Louisiana State UP, 1988.

Hutcheon, Linda. *A Theory of Parody: The Teachings of Twentieth-Century Art Forms*. Urbana: U of Illinois P, 1985.

"In Bush's Words: Resist the 'Allure of Defeat.'" *New York Times,* 23 August 2007: 8A.

Irwin-Zarecka, Iwona. *Frames of Remembrance: The Dynamics of Collective Memory*. New Brunswick: Transaction, 1994.

James, C. L. R. "The Black Jacobins." 1936. In *The C. L. R. James Reader*. Ed. Anna Grimshaw. Oxford: Blackwell, 1992. [67]–111.

———. *The Black Jacobins: Toussaint L'Ouverture and the San Domingo Revolution*. 2nd ed., rev. New York: Vintage, 1963.

James, Henry. *The Bostonians*. New York: Macmillan, 1886.

Jefferson, Thomas. *Notes on the State of Virginia*. Ed. William Peden. New York: Norton, 1972.

Jencks, Charles. *The New Paradigm in Architecture: The Language of Postmodernism*. 7th ed. New Haven: Yale UP, 2002.

Johnson, Charles. *Middle Passage*. New York: Atheneum, 1990.

Johnson, Karen Ramsay. "'Voices in My Own Blood': The Dialogic Impulse in Warren's Non-fiction Writings about Race." *Mississippi Quarterly* 52.1 (1998–99): 33–45.

Johnston, Donald F. *Copyright Handbook*. 2nd ed. New York: Bowker, 1982.

Jones, Anne Goodwyn. *Tomorrow Is Another Day: The Woman Writer in the South, 1859–1936*. Baton Rouge: Louisiana State UP, 1981.

Jones, James. *From Here to Eternity*. New York: Scribner's, 1952.

Judt, Tony. *Postwar: A History of Europe Since 1945*. New York: Penguin, 2005.

Kandel, Eric R. *In Search of Memory: The Emergence of a New Science of Mind*. New York: Norton, 2006.

Kaup, Monica. "'!Viva Papaya!': Cuban Baroque and Visual Culture in Alejo Carpentier, Ricardo Porro, and Ramon Alejandro." *PMLA* 124 (2009): 156–71.

Kazdin, Alan F., ed. *Encyclopedia of Psychology.* Vol. 5. New York: Oxford UP, 2000.

Keith, LeeAnna. *The Colfax Massacre: The Untold Story of Black Power, White Terror, and the Death of Reconstruction.* New York: Oxford UP, 2008.

King, George S. *The Last Slaver.* New York: Putnam, 1933.

King, Richard H. *A Southern Renaissance: The Cultural Awakening of the American South, 1930–1955.* New York: Oxford UP, 1980.

Komunyakaa, Yusef. *Neon Vernacular: New and Selected Poems.* Hanover: Wesleyan UP/ UP of New England, 1993.

Kreyling, Michael. "Southern Literature: Consensus or Dissensus?" *American Literature* 60 (March 1988): 83–95.

———. *Inventing Southern Literature.* Jackson: UP of Mississippi, 1998.

Kutzinski, Vera. "A Symposium: The U.S. South, the Caribbean, and Latin America." *Mississippi Quarterly* 53 (Summer 2006): 644–49.

Ladd, Barbara. *Nationalism and the Color Line in George W. Cable, Mark Twain, and William Faulkner.* Baton Rouge: Louisiana State UP, 1996.

———. "Literary Studies: The Southern United States, 2005." *PMLA* 120 (2005): 1628–39.

———. "Forum." *PMLA* 121 (2006): 550–52.

———. *Resisting History: Gender, Modernity, and Authorship in William Faulkner, Zora Neale Hurston, and Eudora Welty.* Baton Rouge: Louisiana State UP, 2007.

The Lady Chablis, with Theodore Bouloukos. *Hiding My Candy: The Autobiography of the Grand Empress of Savannah.* New York: Pocket Books, 1996.

Lee, Harper. *To Kill a Mockingbird.* 1960. New York: Warner, 1982.

Lewis, David Levering. *W. E. B. Du Bois: Biography of a Race, 1868–1919.* New York: Henry Holt, 1993.

———. *W. E .B. Du Bois: The Fight for Equality and the American Century, 1919–1963.* New York: Holt, 2000.

Luis, William. *Dance Between Two Cultures: Latino Caribbean Literature Written in the United States.* Nashville: Vanderbilt UP, 1997.

Lytle, Andrew Nelson. *Bedford Forrest and His Critter Company.* New York: Minton, Balch, 1931.

Mason, Bobbie Ann. *In Country.* New York: Harper & Row, 1985.

Matthews, John T. "Recalling the West Indies: From Yoknapatawpha to Haiti and Back." *American Literary History* 16.2 (2004): 238–56.

McCaig, Donald. *Rhett Butler's People.* New York: St. Martin's, 2007.

McCarthy, Mary. *Medina.* New York: Harcourt Brace Jovanovich, 1972.

McDowell, Deborah E., and Arnold Rampersad. *Slavery and the Literary Imagination.* Baltimore: Johns Hopkins University Press, 1989.

McPherson, James M. Rev. of *John Brown, Abolitionist: The Man Who Killed Slavery, Sparked the Civil War, and Seeded Civil Rights,* by David Reynolds; *John Brown: The Legend Revisited,* by Merrill D. Peterson; *Terrible Swift Sword: The Legacy of John Brown,* edited by Peggy A. Russo and Paul Finkleman. *New York Review of Books* 12 May 2005: 14–17.

McPherson, Tara. *Reconstructing Dixie: Race, Gender, and Nostalgia in the Imagined South.* Durham: Duke UP, 2003.

Melville, Herman. "Benito Cereno." In *The Complete Stories of Herman Melville.* Ed. Jay Leyda. New York: Random House, 1949. 255–354.

Metro-Goldwyn-Mayer, Inc. v. Showcase Atlanta Cooperative Productions, Inc. 479 F. Supp. 351.

Michener, James. *Tales of the South Pacific.* New York: Macmillan, 1947.

———. *Caribbean.* New York: Random House, 1989.

Middleton, Peter, and Tim Woods. *Literatures of Memory: History, Time, and Space in Postwar Writing.* Manchester, UK: Manchester UP, 2000.

Milloy, Courtland. "Twisting Words in an Effort to Rewrite History." *Washington Post* 29 June 2003, C-1.

Mitchell, Margaret. *Gone With the Wind.* New York: Macmillan, 1936.

Moody, Anne. *Coming of Age in Mississippi.* New York: Dial, 1968.

Moore, Robin. *The Green Berets.* New York: Crown, 1965.

Moreau de Saint-Méry, M. L. E. *Description topographique, physique, civile, politique et historique de la partie française de l'Isle Saint Domingue.* Philadelphia, 1797.

Morris, Willie. *North Toward Home.* Boston: Houghton Mifflin, 1967.

Morrison, Toni. *Beloved.* 1987. New York: Penguin, 1988.

Munro, Martin. "Haitian Novels and Novels of Haiti: History, Haitian Writing, and Madison Smartt Bell's Trilogy." *Small Axe* 12.1 (2007): 163–76.

Nabokov, Vladimir. *Speak, Memory: An Autobiography Revisited.* Rev. ed. New York: Putnam, 1966.

Nora, Pierre. "Between Memory and History: *Les Lieux de Mémoire.*" *Representations* 26 (Spring 1989): 7–25.

Novick, David. *The Holocaust in American Life.* Boston: Houghton Mifflin, 1999.

Nzengou-Tayo, Marie-José. "Haitian Gothic and History: Madison Smartt Bell's Trilogy on Toussaint Louverture and the Haitian Revolution." *Small Axe* 12.1 (2007): 184–93.

O'Brien, Michael. *Conjectures of Order: Intellectual Life and the American South, 1810–1860.* 2 vols. Chapel Hill: U of North Carolina P, 2004.

O'Brien, Tim. *Going After Cacciato.* New York: Delacorte, 1979.

Oliver, Kendrick. *The My Lai Massacre in American History and Memory.* Manchester, UK: Manchester UP, 2006.

Onstott, Kyle. *Mandingo.* Richmond: Denlinger, 1957.

Oropesa, Salvador A. "*Obscuritas* and the Closet: Queer Neobaroque in Mexico." *PMLA* 124 (2009): 172–79.

O'Toole, James M. *Passing for White: Race, Religion, and the Healy Family, 1820–1920.* Amherst: U of Massachusetts P, 2002.

Patterson, Orlando. *Slavery and Social Death: A Comparative Study.* Cambridge: Harvard UP, 1982.

Percy, Walker. *The Last Gentleman.* New York: Farrar, 1966.

Perkins, James A. "Racism and the Personal Past in Robert Penn Warren." *Mississippi Quarterly* 48.1 (1994): 73–83.

Petraeus, Gen. David H. "Counterinsurgency Reader." In *Military Review: Special Edition* (Fort Leavenworth, KS: Combined Arms Center, 2006).

Phillips, Jayne Anne. *Machine Dreams.* New York: Washington Square P, 1984.

Pyron, Darden Asbury. *Southern Daughter: The Life of Margaret Mitchell.* New York: Oxford UP, 1991.

Raimon, Eve Allegra. *The "Tragic Mulatta" Revisited: Race and Nationalism in Nineteenth-Century Antislavery Fiction.* New Brunswick: Rutgers UP, 2004.

Rampersad, Arnold. *Ralph Ellison: A Biography.* New York: Knopf, 2007.

Randall, Alice. *The Wind Done Gone.* Boston: Houghton Mifflin, 2001.

Raynal, Abbé. *A History of the Two Indies: A Translated Selection of Writings from Raynal's "Histoire philosophique et politique des établissements des Européens dans les Deux Indes."* Ed. Peter Jimack. Hampshire, UK: Ashgate, 2006.

Renda, Mary. *Taking Haiti: Military Occupation and the Culture of U.S. Imperialism, 1915–1940.* Chapel Hill: U of North Carolina P, 2001.

Ripley, Alexandra. *Scarlett.* New York: Warner, 1991.

Robinson, Forrest G. "A Combat with the Past: Robert Penn Warren on Race and Slavery." *American Literature* 67.3 (1995): 511–30.

Romine, Scott. *The Real South: Southern Narrative in the Age of Cultural Reproduction.* Baton Rouge: Louisiana State UP, 2008.

Rubin, Louis D., Jr., et al. *The History of Southern Literature.* Baton Rouge: Louisiana State UP, 1985.

Ruppersburg, Hugh. *Robert Penn Warren and the American Imagination.* Athens: U of Georgia P, 1990.

Schell, Jonathan. *The Jonathan Schell Reader.* New York: Nation, 2004.

Schmidt, Hans. *The United States Occupation of Haiti, 1915–1934.* 1971. New Brunswick: Rutgers UP, 1995.

Seabrook, William B. *The Magic Island.* New York: Harcourt Brace, 1929.

Sedgwick, Eve Kosofsky. *Between Men: English Literature and Male Homosocial Desire.* New York: Columbia, 1985.

Shaara, Jeff. *Gods and Generals.* New York: Ballantine, 1996.

Shaara, Michael. *The Killer Angels.* 1974. New York: Ballantine, 1975.

Sheehan, Neil. *A Bright and Shining Lie: John Paul Vann and America in Vietnam.* New York: Random House, 1988.

Simpich, Frederick. "Skypaths Through Latin America." *National Geographic* 54.1 (1931): 1–79.

Simpson, Lewis P. *The Brazen Face of History: Studies in the Literary Consciousness in America.* Baton Rouge: Louisiana State UP, 1980.

Smith, Dina M. "Global Cinderella: *Sabrina* (1954), Hollywood, and Postwar Internationalism." *Cinema Journal 41* 4 (Summer 2002): 27–51.

Smith, Jon. "Forum." *PMLA* 121 (2006): 549–50.

Smith, Jon, and Deborah Cohn, eds. *Look Away! The U.S. South in New World Studies.* Durham: Duke UP, 2004.

Smith, Jon, Kathryn McKee, and Scott Romine, eds. "Postcolonial Theory, the U.S. South, and New World Studies: Part I." *Mississippi Quarterly* 56.4. "Part II," 57.1.

Spillers, Hortense J. "Changing the Letter: The Yoke, the Jokes of Discourse, or, Mrs. Stowe and Mr. Reed." In McDowell and Rampersad 25–61.

Styron, William. *The Confessions of Nat Turner.* New York: Random House, 1968

———. "Calley." 1971. Rpr. in *This Quiet Dust and Other Writings.* New York: Random House, 1982.

Sundquist, Eric. *To Wake the Nations: Race in the Making of American Literature.* Cambridge: Belknap P of Harvard UP, 1993.

SunTrust Bank v. Houghton Mifflin Company. 1:01-CV-701-CAP. U.S. District Court, Northern District of Georgia, Atlanta Division, 2001.

Szabo, Julia. "Kara Walker's Shock Art." *New York Times Magazine* 23 March 1997: 48–50.

Szczesiul, Anthony. *Racial Politics and Robert Penn Warren's Poetry.* Gainesville: UP of Florida, 2002.

Taft, Edna. *A Puritan in Voodoo-Land.* Philadelphia: Penn, 1938.

Talley, André Leon, and Karl Lagerfeld. "Scarlett 'n the Hood." *Vanity Fair* (May 1996): 182–91.

Tate, Allen. *Stonewall Jackson: The Good Soldier.* New York: Minton, Balch, 1928.

———. *Jefferson Davis: His Rise and Fall. A Biographical Narrative.* New York: Minton, Balch, 1929.

Thomas, Lowell. *Old Gimlet Eye: The Adventures of Smedley D. Butler.* New York: Farrar & Rinehart, 1933.

Thrall, William Flint, and Addison Hibbard. *A Handbook to Literature.* 1936. Rev. and enlarged by C. Hugh Holman. New York: Odyssey, 1960.

"Transcript of Bush's Inaugural Address: 'Nation Stands Ready to Push On.'" *New York Times* 21 January 1989: 10.

Trouillot, Michel-Rolph. "Bodies and Souls: The Haitian Revolution and Madison Smartt Bell's *All Souls' Rising.*" In Carnes 184–97.

Turner, Fred. *Echoes of Combat: The Vietnam War in American Memory.* New York: Anchor, 1996.

Turtledove, Harry. *The Guns of the South: A Novel of the Civil War.* New York: Ballantine, 1992.

Twelve Southerners. *I'll Take My Stand: The South and the Agrarian Tradition.* 1930. Baton Rouge: Louisiana State UP, 1977.

Valcin, Virgile. *La Blanche Négresse.* Port-au-Prince: V. Valcin, 1934.

Villard, Oswald Garrison. *John Brown, 1800–1859: A Biography Fifty Years After.* Boston: Houghton Mifflin, 1910.

Wagner, Bryan. "Disarmed and Dangerous: The Strange Career of Bras-Coupé." *Representations* 92 (Fall 2005): 117–51.

Ward, Geoffrey C. *The Civil War: An Illustrated History.* New York: Knopf, 1990. Based on a documentary filmscript by Geoffrey C. Ward, Ric Burns, and Ken Burns.

———. "Death's Army." Rev. of *This Republic of Suffering,* by Drew Faust. *New York Times Book Review* 27 January 2008.

Warren, Robert Penn. *John Brown: The Making of a Martyr.* New York: Payson & Clarke, 1929.

———. *Band of Angels.* New York: Random House, 1955.

———. *Segregation: The Inner Conflict of the South.* New York: Random House, 1956.

———. *Who Speaks for the Negro?* New York: Random House, 1965.

———. *New and Selected Poems, 1923–1985.* New York: Random House, 1985.

"'We Love You': New View of the Viet Nam Vet." *Time* 11 June 1979: 21.

Webb, James. *Fields of Fire.* Englewood Cliffs, NJ: Prentice-Hall, 1978.

Westmoreland, Gen. William C. *A Soldier Reports.* Garden City, NY: Doubleday, 1976.

Whitman, Walt. *Specimen Days.* In *Leaves of Grass and Selected Prose.* Ed. Lawrence Buell. New York: Modern Library, 1981. 553–754.

Williamson, Joel. "How Black Was Rhett Butler?" In *The Evolution of Southern Culture.* Ed. Numan V. Bartley. Athens: U of Georgia P, 1988. 87–107.

Wills, Garry. *John Wayne's America: The Politics of Celebrity.* New York: Simon & Schuster, 1997.

Wolfe, Tom. *A Man in Full.* New York: Farrar, Straus and Giroux, 1998.

Woodson, Carter Godwin. *The Mis-Education of the American Negro.* Washington, D.C.: Associated Publishers, 1933.

Woodward, C. Vann. *The Burden of Southern History.* Rev. ed. Baton Rouge: Louisiana State UP, 1968.

Wyatt-Brown, Bertram. *Southern Honor: Ethics and Behavior in the Old South.* New York: Oxford UP, 1982.

Yaeger, Patricia. *Dirt and Desire: Reconstructing Southern Women's Writing, 1930–1999.* Chicago: U of Chicago P, 2000.

———. "Editor's Column: 'Black Men Dressed in Gold'—Eudora Welty, Empty Objects, and the Neobaroque." *PMLA* 124 (2009): 11–24.

Yoder, J. Wes. "Shack Up Here." *Garden & Gun* June–July 2009, 89–91.

Young, Elizabeth. *Disarming the Nation: Women's Writing and the American Civil War.* Chicago: U of Chicago P, 1999.

Zamora, Lois Parkinson. "New World Baroque, Neobaroque, Brut Barroco: Latin American Postcolonialisms." *PMLA* 124 (2009): 127–42.

FILM

Apocalypse Now. Dir. Francis Ford Coppola. Perf. Martin Sheen and Marlon Brando. United Artists, 1979.

Band of Angels. Dir. Raoul Walsh. Perf. Clark Gable, Sidney Poitier, and Yvonne De-Carlo. Warner Bros., 1957.

Beloved. Dir. Jonathan Demme. Prod. Jonathan Demme and Oprah Winfrey. Perf. Oprah Winfrey and Danny Glover. Touchstone Pictures, 1998.

The Best Years of Our Lives. Dir. William Wyler. Perf. Fredric March, Myrna Loy, Dana Andrews, and Theresa Wright. RKO, 1946.

Coming Home. Dir. Hal Ashby. Perf. Jon Voight, Jane Fonda, and Bruce Dern. United Artists, 1978.

C.S.A.: The Confederate States of America. Writ. and dir. Kevin Willmott. IFC Films, 2005.

The Deer Hunter. Dir. Michael Cimino. Perf. Robert De Niro, Christopher Walken, and Meryl Streep. Universal, 1978.

First Blood. Dir. Ted Kotcheff. Perf. Sylvester Stallone and Richard Crenna. Orion Pictures, 1982.

Flags of Our Fathers. Dir. Clint Eastwood. Perf. Ryan Phillippe, Jesse Bradford, and Adam Beach. Warner Bros., 2006.

Forrest Gump. Dir. Robert Zemeckis. Perf. Tom Hanks, Robin Wright, and Gary Sinise. Paramount, 1994.

Friendly Fire. Dir. David Greene. Perf. Carol Burnett, Ned Beatty. Fox Home Entertainment, 1979.

Full Metal Jacket. Dir. Stanley Kubrick. Perf. Matthew Modine, Lee Ermey, and Vincent Dinofrio. Warner Bros., 1987.

Gettysburg. Dir. Ronald Maxwell. Perf. Martin Sheen, Tom Berenger, and Jeff Daniels. New Line Cinema, 1993.

Gods and Generals. Dir. Ronald Maxwell. Perf. Jeff Daniels, Robert Duval, and Stephen Lang. Warner Bros., 2003.

Gone With the Wind. Dir. Victor Fleming. Prod. David O. Selznick. Perf. Clark Gable, Vivien Leigh, Hattie McDaniel, Leslie Howard, Olivia de Havilland. Selznick, 1939.

The Green Berets. Dir. Roy Kellogg and John Wayne. Perf. John Wayne. Warner Bros., 1968.

Gunga Din. Dir. George Stevens. Perf. Cary Grant, Victor McLaglen, Douglas Fairbanks, Jr. RKO,1939.

King Solomon's Mines. Dir. Robert Stevenson. Perf. Paul Robeson, Cedric Hardwicke. Gaumont, 1937.

Lethal Weapon. Dir. Richard Donner. Perf. Mel Gibson and Danny Glover. Warner Bros., 1987.

Letters from Iwo Jima. Dir. Clint Eastwood. Perf. Ken Watanabe and Kazunara Ninomiya. Warner Bros., 2007.

Manderlay. Writ. and dir. Lars Von Trier. Perf. Bryce Dallas Howard, Danny Glover, and Willem Dafoe. IFC Films, 2005.

Mandingo. Dir. Richard Fleischer. Perf. James Mason, Susan George. Paramount, 1975.

The Matrix. Dir. Larry Wachowski. Perf. Keanu Reeves, Laurence Fishburne, Carrie-Anne Moss. Warner, 1999.

Platoon. Dir. Oliver Stone. Perf. Charlie Sheen, Willem Dafoe, and Tom Berenger. Orion Pictures, 1986.

Roberta. Dir. William A. Seiter. Perf. Fred Astaire, Ginger Rogers, Irene Dunne, and Randolph Scott. RKO, 1935.

Sally Hemings: An American Scandal. Writ. Tina Andrews. Dir. Charles Haid. Perf. Sam Neill and Carmen Ejogo. CBS Productions, 2000.

The Sands of Iwo Jima. Dir. Allan Dwan. Perf. John Wayne, John Agar, and Forrest Tucker. Republic, 1949.

The Serpent and the Rainbow. Dir. Wes Craven. Perf. Bill Pullman. Universal, 1988.

Sherman's March. Writ. and dir. by Ross McElwee. First Run Features, 1986.

Taxi Driver. Dir. Martin Scorcese. Perf. Robert De Niro and Jodie Foster. Columbia, 1976.

Tracks. Dir. Henry Jaglom. Perf. Dennis Hopper and Dean Stockwell. Rainbow Pictures, 1976.

The White Zombie. Dir. Victor Halperin. Perf. Bela Lugosi. United Artists, 1932.

ONLINE SOURCES

www.gwtwthemusical.com

www.law.cornell.edu/supct/html/92-1292.ZS.html

www.mpg.de

www.newsweek.com/id/150576

INDEX